# Teaching and learning at university

## Second edition

LEARNING & TEACHING CENTRE
UNIVERSITY OF VICTORIA
PO BOX 1700 STN CSC
VICTORIA BC  V8W 2Y2
CANADA

LEARNING & TEACHING CENTRE
UNIVERSITY OF VICTORIA
PO BOX 1700 STN CSC
VICTORIA BC  V8W 2Y2
CANADA

*SRHE and Open University Press Imprint*
*General Editor*: Heather Eggins

# Teaching for quality learning at university

What the student does

Second edition

# John Biggs

The Society for Research into Higher Education
& Open University Press

Open University Press
McGraw-Hill Education
McGraw-Hill House
Shoppenhangers Road
Maidenhead
Berkshire
SL6 2QL
United Kingdom

Email: enquiries@openup.co.uk
World wide web: www.openup.co.uk

and

Two Penn Plaza
New York, NY 10121-2289, USA

First published 2003
Reprinted 2001, 2003 (twice), 2004 & 2005

Copyright © John Biggs 2003

All rights reserved. Except for the quotation of short passages for the purpose of criticism and review, no part of this publication may be reproduced, stored in a retrieval system, or transmitted, in any form or by any means, electronic, mechanical, photocopying, recording or otherwise, without the prior written permission of the publisher or a licence from the Copyright Licensing Agency Limited. Details of such licences (for reprographic reproduction) may be obtained from the Copyright Licensing Agency Ltd of 90 Tottenham Court Road, London, W1P 0LP.

A catalogue record for this book is available from the British Library

ISBN 0 335 21168 2 (pb)     0 335 21169 0 (hb)

*Library of Congress Cataloging-in-Publication Data*
Biggs, John B. (John Burville)
    Teaching for quality learning at university : what the student does / John
    Biggs.—2nd ed.
        p. cm.
    Includes bibliographical references (p. ) and index.
    ISBN 0-335-21169-0 — ISBN 0-335-21168-2 (pbk.)
    1. College students.   2. Learning.   3. College students—Rating of.
    I. Title.
    LB2331 .B526 2003
    378.1'25—dc21

2002074964

Typeset by Graphicraft Limited, Hong Kong
Printed in Great Britain by The Cromwell Press,
Trowbridge, Wiltshire.

Learning takes place through the active behavior of the student: it is what *he* does that he learns, not what the teacher does.

Ralph W. Tyler (1949)

If students are to learn desired outcomes in a reasonably effective manner, then the teacher's fundamental task is to get students to engage in learning activities that are likely to result in their achieving those outcomes . . . It is helpful to remember that what the student does is actually more important in determining what is learned than what the teacher does.

Thomas J. Shuell (1986)

# Contents

# Foreword to first edition

This book is an exceptional introduction to some difficult ideas. It is full of downright good advice for every academic who wants to do something practical to improve his or her students' learning. So much of what we read on this subject is either a recycling of sensible advice topped by a thin layer of second-hand theory, or a dense treatise suitable for graduate students with a taste for the tougher courses. Not many writers are able to take the reader along the middle road, where theory applied with a delicate touch enables us to transform our practice. What is unique about Biggs is his way with words, his outspoken fluency, his precision, his depth of knowledge, his inventiveness – or rather, how he blends these things together. Like all good teachers, he engages us from the start, and he never talks down to us. He achieves unity between his objectives, his teaching methods and his assessment; and thus, to adapt his own phrase, he entraps the reader in a web of consistency that optimizes his or her learning.

Perhaps not everyone will agree with Biggs's treatment of the academic differences between phenomenography and constructivism. I'm not sure I do myself. But does it matter? The author himself takes a pragmatic approach. In the daunting task that faces lecturers in responding to the pressures of mass higher education, reduced public funding and students who are paying more for their education, the bottom line of engineering better learning outcomes matters more than nice theoretical distinctions.

Readers of the present book will especially enjoy its marvellous treatment of issues of student assessment (particularly Chapters 3, 8 and 9). Biggs's most outstanding single contribution to education has been the creation of the Structure of Observed Learning Outcome (SOLO) taxonomy. Rather than read about the extraordinary practical utility of this device in secondary sources, get it from the original here. From assessing clinical decision-making by medical students to classifying the outcomes of essays in history, SOLO remains the assessment apparatus of choice.

There are very few writers on the subject of university teaching who can engage a reader so personally, express things so clearly, relate research findings so eloquently to personal experience and open our eyes to the wonder around us. John Biggs is a rare thing: an author who has the humility born of generosity and intelligence to show us how he is still learning himself.

Paul Ramsden
Brisbane

# Preface to second edition

I have been very gratified by the reception of the first edition of this book, particularly that the concept of constructive alignment has become part of the working theory of many teachers, course designers, researchers and teaching developers. However, there have also been some criticisms, thankfully more about what I didn't say than what I did. These criticisms have become increasingly cogent with time, as so much has happened to the tertiary sector since the first edition was published in 1999.

*Educational technology* (ET) is no longer a 'gee-whiz' toy for the geek. It has established a place in the normal delivery system of most universities, whether on or off campus. Teachers will increasingly be expected to use it. I would have preferred to have contextualized references to ET in the other chapters, but ET raises specific issues, sounds its own warnings and has some unique uses. In giving ET a separate chapter, however, I am not implying that ET is anything other than another medium for teaching and assessing, and the same rules apply.

*Quality assurance* (QA) and *quality enhancement* (QE) procedures are now required at the institutional level. QA procedures, like ET, have their upside and their downside. I am concerned that they should be used positively to improve teaching within institutions, and not become just another bureaucratic exercise, taking valuable time from teaching and research. The concept of constructive alignment is equally applicable at the level of the institution as it is to the individual teacher, so there is a new chapter on 'the reflective institution', where the principles discussed in this book become a powerful underpinning to quality enhancement procedures.

On the personal side, I had two experiences since writing the last edition that interacted with these developments. I was Advisory Professor for three years at the Hong Kong Institute of Education (HKIEd), which comprises a consortium of teachers' colleges now working towards university status as a single institution. In my occasional visits to that magnificent campus at the foot of the Pat Sing Leng Range, I was able to see how the 'old culture' of the colleges attempted to come to terms with the new. This prompted the thought, very pertinent to the QA/QE debate, that good teaching is more than individual teachers reflecting on their practice. Teachers operate within a whole institution, which has itself developed a culture that may facilitate or impede good teaching.

Then, in 1999, an unavoidable staffing crisis in the Psychology Department at the University of Hong Kong created a sudden and temporary hole that matched my educational psychological shape. Would I be interested in a year's contract? I most certainly would, so I came out of semi-retirement to become an Associate Professor of Psychology teaching my original content discipline. Here was an opportunity to do a bit more reflective practice of my own, to be stimulated with the ideas generated by my new colleagues, and to experience teaching those wonderful students again.

The University of Hong Kong is amongst the world's best 30 universities. Many departments, including mine for a year, are innovative and highly supportive of their students. But it is an old and conservative institution, with some regulations, particularly on the issue of final examinations, that require ingenuity to circumvent, a challenge that has improved the chapters on assessment.

So, with the university world moving faster than anticipated since the first edition, and my own intervening experience fleshing out some details, I thought the time was ripe for a second edition. I was very pleased that my then editor, John Skelton, thought so too.

# Acknowledgements

As I said in my Acknowledgements in the first edition, there are many ideas in this book that came about through interacting with friends and colleagues over the years. I will not repeat them here.

For this edition, I must mention my ex-colleagues in the Psychology Department at the University of Hong Kong: John Spinks and Faradeh Salili for inviting me to teach there, C.Y. Chiu for the genial but professional climate he generated, and Harry Hui for showing me how he wove ET into his in-class teaching. I am also grateful to Phil Moore for hosting most of my visits to the Hong Kong Institute for Education, and to Stuart Tyler, Matthew Nicholson and Bob Stewart for so nicely demonstrating how the alignment model fits with ET.

I am grateful to Denise Chalmers for her critical comments on earlier drafts of the two new chapters on ET and QE; to David Johnston for permission to use his material on PBL; and to Norman Jackson, Sue Johnston and David Woodhouse for providing me with information on current quality enhancement procedures. Anything I have not got right in these pages, however, is my fault alone, not that of anyone else.

My Hong Kong experiences prompted me to write an article that appeared in *Higher Education*, 14(2001): 221–38, under the title 'The reflective institution: assuring and enhancing the quality of teaching and learning', which forms the basis for much of Chapter 13. I am grateful to Kluwer Academic Publishers for kind permission to use this material here.

My special thanks to Catherine Tang for her support and continuing inspiration, which are evident throughout these pages.

Finally, I must thank the prompt and courteous John Skelton and his successor, Shona Mullen and their team who have seen me through both editions, patiently and helpfully.

John Biggs
Hobart
April 2002

# 1

# Changing university teaching

In the days when university classes contained highly
selected students, enrolled in their faculty of choice,
the traditional lecture and tutorial seemed to work
well enough. However, the expansion, restructuring
and refinancing of the tertiary sector that began in
the 1990s has meant that classes are not only larger
but quite diversified in terms of student ability,
motivation and cultural background. Teachers have
difficulty in just coping, let alone in maintaining
standards, and are stressed. However, if we regard
good teaching as encouraging students to use the
higher-order learning processes that 'academic'
students use spontaneously, standards need not
decline. This is not a matter of acquiring new
teaching techniques so much as tapping the large,
research derived, knowledge base on teaching and
learning that already exists. Through reflective
practice, teachers can then create an improved
teaching environment suited to their own context.

## The nature of the change

The past ten and more years have seen an extraordinary and worldwide
change in the structure, function, and financing of.the university system.
Teaching and decision-making generally are more centrally controlled,
and are much more subject to economic and managerial considerations
than used to be the case. Undergraduate courses, increasingly financed by
student fees, tend to follow the market, with international students a particularly rich source of funds. Academic staff tend to fall into two groups,
the older now working in a different *kind* of institution from the one they
have been used to, whereas younger staff tend increasingly to be on short-
term contracts and feel under pressure not to step out of line. Amongst
students, the following changes are particularly salient:

1 A greater proportion of school leavers are now in higher education. In the early 1990s the proportion was around 15 per cent; now it is over 40 per cent in many areas. The brightest and most committed students will still be there, as they have been in the past, but they will sit alongside students of rather different academic bent. The *range* of ability within classes is now considerable.

2 Most students are paying increasingly more for their education. They will be demanding value for money.

3 Students are more diverse in other ways: in age and experience, in socio-economic status and in cultural background.

4 Classes have increased in size as well as in diversity. Fewer staff are teaching more students.

5 More courses are vocationally oriented than used to be the case.

Many of these factors – class size, increased student intake, fewer staff, new courses, re-skilling of teachers – demand more in terms of teaching skill. Additional pressures come from the student-as-paying-client on the one hand, and from department heads to maintain research funding and publications on the other. All factors seem inexorably to suggest lower standards of teaching, and therefore of learning. This book has been written to suggest how teaching standards can not only be maintained, but positively improved.

When university classes contained highly selected students, the traditional methods of teaching – lecture followed by a tutorial – gave the appearance of working well. Today, with a much more diversified student population, these methods no longer seem to be working. To some, this suggests that many students who are at university should not be. But they are, and in numbers that seem to preclude any but the same methods of teaching and assessing that aren't working. With several hundred in a class, what can you reasonably do but teach by mass-lecture, and assess by multiple-choice and machine-marking?

The answer given here is to take a fresh look at what we mean by teaching. It is not just a matter of finding better techniques than lecturing. There is no single, all-purpose best method of teaching. Teaching is an individual matter. What works best is a complex resolution between us and the system that operates in the particular institution in which we are working. We have to adjust our teaching decisions to suit our subject matter, available resourcing, our students, and our own individual strengths and weaknesses as a teacher. It depends on how we *conceive* the process of teaching, and through reflection come to some conclusion about how we may do our job better.

This book invites you to begin this process of reflection and provides the tools for doing so. This chapter analyses the nature of good teaching and introduces the idea of teaching reflectively. Chapter 2 develops a framework for reflection, and each subsequent chapter develops an aspect of this framework. The final two chapters return to the idea of reflection: first, as it applies to you as an individual teacher, and then as it applies to the institution as a whole.

### Student ability and teaching method: the pay-off

Let us look at two students attending a lecture. Susan is academically committed; she is bright, interested in her studies and wants to do well. She has clear academic or career plans, and what she learns is important to her. So when she learns she goes about it in an 'academic' way. She comes to the lecture with sound, relevant background knowledge and possibly some question she wants answering. In the lecture she finds an answer to her pre-formed question; it forms the keystone for a particular arch of knowledge she is constructing. Or it may not be the answer she is looking for, and she speculates, wondering why it isn't. In either event, she reflects on the personal significance of what she is learning. Students like Susan (see Figure 1.1) virtually teach themselves, with little help from us.

Now take Robert. He is at university not out of a driving curiosity about a particular subject or a burning ambition to excel in a particular profession, but to obtain a qualification for a decent job. He is not studying in the area of his first choice. He is less committed than Susan, possibly not as bright, academically speaking, and has a less developed background of relevant knowledge; he comes to the lecture with few questions. He wants only to put in sufficient effort to pass. Robert hears the lecturer say the same words as Susan heard, but he doesn't see a keystone, just another brick to be recorded in his lecture notes. He believes that if he can record enough of these bricks, and can remember them on cue, he'll keep out of trouble come exam time.

Students like Robert (see Figure 1.1) are in higher proportions in today's classes than was the case 20, even 10, years ago. They will need help if they are to achieve the same levels of understanding that their more committed colleagues achieve spontaneously. To say that Robert is unmotivated may be true, but unhelpful. All that means is that he is not responding to the methods that work for Susan, the likes of whom were sufficiently visible in most classes in the good old days to satisfy us that our teaching *did* work. But of course it was the students who were doing the work and getting the results, not our teaching.

The challenge we face as teachers is to teach so that Robert learns more in the manner of Susan. Figure 1.1 suggests that the present differences

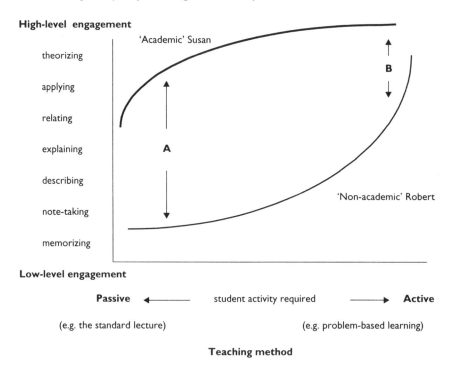

**Figure 1.1:**   Student orientation, teaching method and level of engagement

between Robert and Susan (point A) may be lessened by appropriate teaching (point B). There are three factors interacting here:

1 The students' levels of engagement.
2 The degree of learning-related activity that a teaching method is likely to stimulate.
3 The academic orientation of the students.

Point A in Figure 1.1 is towards the passive end of the teaching method continuum, where there is a large gap between Susan's and Robert's levels of engagement. A lecture would be an example of such passive teaching, and we get the picture just described: Susan working at a high level of engagement, Robert at a minimal level. Susan is relating, applying, possibly theorizing, while Robert is taking notes and memorizing.

At point B, towards the active end of the teaching method continuum, the gap between Susan and Robert is not so wide. Problem-based learning would be an example of an active method, because it *requires* students to question, to speculate, to generate solutions, so that Robert is now using the higher-order cognitive activities that Susan uses spontaneously. The teaching has narrowed the gap between their levels of active engagement in learning.

⟍ Of course, there are limits to what students can do that are beyond the teacher's control – a student's ability is one – but there are other things that *are* within our control, and capitalizing on them is what good teaching is all about. Although Figure 1.1 is a hypothetical graph, it helps us to define good teaching, as follows:

> *Good teaching is getting most students to use the higher cognitive level processes that the more academic students use spontaneously.*

Good teaching narrows the gap.

## Using the scholarship of teaching

Improving teaching on this scale – so that the Roberts who enter our classes emerge more like the Susans – requires a great deal of professional development as a teacher. It is therefore important that universities maintain teaching development centres or units to provide this help, yet many universities have downsized or closed such centres in a short-sighted attempt to save costs. To do so is rather like lightening an aircraft by throwing the doctors overboard when the pilot is having a heart attack. To 'save' on teaching development in the present teaching crisis is just as short-sighted.

This book is addressed to teachers, to teaching or staff developers and to administrators. Individual teachers experience the problems, and will need, with help, to generate the solutions. Those solutions will not be found in learning a whole new bag of teaching tricks, any one of which may or may not be useful for your particular circumstances, but in reflecting on your teaching problems, and deriving your own ways of handling them within your departmental context (see Chapter 12).

Staff (teaching) developers, for their part, need to continue to consult with individuals, but also with departments on their teaching programmes, and with administration to get the institutional policies and procedures right on teaching-related matters. If this book is to address quality teaching, we need to go beyond the individual and examine the institution. How the institution may be reflective is addressed in Chapter 13 together with the closely related theme of quality enhancement.

All three groups – teachers, teaching developers and administrators – need to immerse themselves in the 'scholarship of teaching' (Boyer 1990). Academics have always been teachers, but the first priority of the majority is to keep up with developments in their content discipline, and to contribute to them through research. Developing teaching expertise usually takes second place: a set of priorities dictated as much by institutional structures and reward systems as by individual choice. But there is another body of knowledge, apart from their content areas, that academics also have a responsibility to address. This is the body of knowledge that underwrites good teaching:

> The professional authority of the academic-as-scholar rests on a body of knowledge; the professional authority of the academic-as-teacher should rest on a body of didactic knowledge. This comprises knowledge of how the subject he or she professes is best learned and taught.
>
> (Ramsden 1992: 9)

There are two aspects to this didactic knowledge. The first arises from formally conducted research. There is a large research based literature on teaching and learning, much of it addressed in this book, forming the accepted theories of teaching. The second arises from your own personal experience as a teacher, out of which you have formed your personal implicit theory of teaching (Marland 1997). The point is that by combining these two domains of knowledge, the public and the personal, you as a teacher become able to derive useful ways of improving your own teaching by using the thinking and the concepts of accepted theories. This is where the untapped potential for improvement in teaching lies: each of you can tap that knowledge of learning and teaching to improve your own personal practice.

**Reflective teaching**

Wise and effective teaching is not, however, simply a matter of applying general principles of teaching according to rule; those principles need adapting to your own personal strengths and to your teaching context. A characteristic of award-winning university teachers is their willingness to collect student feedback on their teaching in order to see where their teaching might be improved (Dunkin and Precians 1992). Expert teachers continually reflect on how they might teach even better.

Now let us go back to Susan and Robert. They are older now, having both graduated 20 years ago, and they have become teachers. Susan is a teacher with 20 years' experience; Robert is a teacher with 1 year's experience repeated 19 times. Susan is a reflective teacher: each significant experience, particularly of failure, has been a learning experience, so she gets better and better. Robert is a reactive teacher. He goes through the same motions year after year, and when things go wrong he tends to blame the students, or the administration, or government intervention. If it worked last year, but didn't work this year, how can it be his teaching that is the problem?

The kind of thinking displayed here by Susan, but not by Robert, is known as reflective practice. Schon (1983) coined the term 'the reflective practitioner', pointing out that effective professionals, such as architects, or medicos, need to reflect when faced with new problems or difficulties for which they have not been specifically trained. It is the same with university teachers (Brockbank and McGill 1998). A particularly inspiring and personal account of reflective practice in university teaching is given by Cowan (1998).

Reflective practice can be formally encouraged and directed as 'action research' (Elliott 1991) or 'action learning' (Kember and Kelly 1993). In essence, action research is being systematic about changing your teaching, and making sure the changes are in the right direction; that your students are now learning better than they used to. The target of action learning is the teaching of the individual teacher herself or himself. The 'learning' in action learning refers not only to student learning, or even to learning about teaching, but to learning about *oneself as a teacher*, and learning how to use reflection to become a better teacher. Learning new techniques for teaching is like the fish that provides a meal today; reflective practice is the net that provides meals for the rest of your life.

'Reflection' is, however, a misleading word. When you stand in front of a mirror what you see is your reflection, what you *are*. 'Reflection', as we are using it here, is rather like the mirror in *Snow White*: it tells you what you *might be*. This mirror uses theory to enable the transformation from the unsatisfactory what-is to the more effective what-might-be.

Theory makes you aware that there is a problem, and it helps to generate a solution to it. This is where many tertiary teachers are lacking; not in theories relating to their content discipline, but in well-structured theories relating to *teaching* their discipline. Reflecting on your teaching, and seeing what is wrong and how it may be improved, requires you to have an explicit theory of teaching. We return to this issue of reflective practice in Chapter 12, when your theory of teaching will have been elaborated with the contents of this book.

As noted above, all teachers have some kind of implicit theory of teaching, but we need something more up-front, a consciously worked out theory that generates answers to teaching problems. The initial jolt that says 'there's a problem here' has to be defined in such a way that it becomes soluble. 'My stuff isn't getting across' doesn't define a soluble problem. 'The students are only giving me back what is in my lectures' does. The last statement is based on a theory: when students give back only what is in the lectures, something is wrong. A good theory would suggest that the something resides in the teaching, rather than as some defect inherent in the students. It might be that the assessment procedures are letting students get away with repeating the lectures. So we need to present them with assessment tasks where this will not work.

To recognize and then to solve problems in teaching involves reflecting on what is happening, using a framework that gives you an angle on what is going on in your teaching. In the next chapter we develop such a framework, based on what we know about student learning, which you can use to reflect on your teaching.

Finally, complete Task 1.1. The idea is to formulate problems that are currently in your teaching, and would like to solve.

---

**Task 1.1: What are the major problems in your own teaching that you would like to solve?**

Take a semester or year-length unit that you are currently teaching and that presents you with particular difficulties that you want to solve (e.g. teaching large classes, motivating students, lecturing successfully, dissatisfied with current assessment methods, covering the syllabus, getting students to understand, and so on). What are the *three most worrying* problems in teaching that unit, and that you would realistically hope to minimize by reading this book?

1 _____

_____

_____

2 _____

_____

_____

3 _____

_____

_____

Comment _____

_____

_____

In the following chapters, bear this unit in mind, even if the material being addressed is not particularly problematical. At the end, you have the chance to revisit these problems.

---

Task 1.1 is the first of several reflective tasks: I have included one or two such tasks in each chapter. They are intended to help with your self-questioning, reflecting and in your decisions about alternative ways to go. Teaching developers might find these tasks useful, in conjunction with their own, in conducting workshops or consultations with individual teachers or with departments.

## Summary and conclusions

### The nature of the change

With the expansion and restructuring of the tertiary sector in the 1990s, university teachers today face unprecedented problems of adjustment: to larger classes containing a greater spread of student ability and motivation, to under-resourcing, and to market-driven courses. This seems like a recipe for declining standards. This need not necessarily be so, if we take a fresh look at the *teaching* problem this poses. Good teaching is getting all students to use the higher cognitive level processes that academic students use spontaneously. The challenge is to achieve this in the face of the conditions now imposed on the tertiary sector.

### Student ability and teaching method: the pay-off

Teaching 'works' by getting students to engage in learning-related activities that help them attain the particular objectives set for the unit or course, such as theorizing, generating new ideas, reflecting, applying and problem-solving. Academically oriented students spontaneously carry out the higher levels of these activities more or less independently of the teaching; for them, lecturing can 'work'. The majority of students, however, need more support in order to carry out these higher-level activities; teaching is precisely to provide that support. If we do so appropriately, we shall be getting ordinary students to do the sorts of thing that only 'better' students used to do under thin methods such as lecturing.

### Using the scholarship of teaching

Improving teaching under these conditions is not a matter of simply learning a swag of teaching competencies. Teaching is personal, and the context in which each teacher works is different. What is effective for this teacher, for that subject, at this level, for those students, may not apply to other teachers, working under their own conditions. Individuals have to work out their own solutions. This requires *reflection*, a theory of teaching to reflect with, and a context of experiences as the object of reflection.

This process may be structured in action research, in which possible solutions are carefully monitored to gauge their success.

## Further reading

### On trends in higher education

Bourner, T. and Flowers, S. (1997) Teaching and learning methods in higher education: a glimpse of the future, *Reflections on Higher Education*, 9: 77–102.

Coady, T. (ed.) (2000) *Why Universities Matter*. Sydney: Allen & Unwin.

Dearing, R. (1997) *Higher Education in the Learning Society*, Report of the National Committee of Inquiry into Higher Education (Dearing Report). Norwich: HMSO.

Ramsden, P. (1998) *Learning to Lead in Higher Education*. London: Routledge.

West, R. (1998) *Learning for Life*. Canberra: Australian Government Publishing Service.

Dearing and West are the official blueprints for the futures of higher education in England and Australia, respectively. What they spell out, under the rhetoric, is very much what has been outlined in the introduction to this chapter: larger classes, an increasingly diverse student population, market-force provision, and big challenges to teachers. Both raise highly charged political issues, especially West.

Coady's book – which was peremptorily dropped by the University of Melbourne Press – is a collection of essays by prominent academics concerned about what has been happening to Australian universities after years of government 'initiatives'. Bourner and Flowers give their estimation of the seriousness of the situation, and their strategic solution, which is a highly diversified, largely off-campus environment, action learning for students, and lots of high tech. The present book nods in their direction (see Chapter 10) but takes a more conservative line, which is to assume on-campus teaching will continue as the major mode of delivery and will remain the main target for improving teaching.

Ramsden addresses academic managers and heads of departments, suggesting how appropriate leadership can increase all of research productivity, teaching and staff morale.

# 2

## Constructing learning by aligning teaching: constructive alignment

**The key to reflecting on the way we teach is to base our thinking on what we know about how students learn. Learning is constructed as a result of the learner's activities. Activities that are appropriate to achieving the curriculum objectives result in a deep approach to learning. Good teaching supports those appropriate activities, thereby encouraging students to adopt a deep approach. Poor teaching and assessment result in a surface approach, where students use inappropriate and low-order learning activities. A good teaching system aligns teaching method and assessment to the learning activities stated in the objectives, so that all aspects of this system act in accord to support appropriate learning. This system is called *constructive alignment*, based as it is on the twin principles of constructivism in learning and alignment in teaching.**

### Research into student learning

Learning has been the subject of research by psychologists for the whole of the last century, but remarkably little has directly resulted in improved teaching. The reason is that, until recently, psychologists were more concerned with developing the One Grand Theory of Learning than in studying the contexts in which people learned, such as schools and universities (Biggs 1993a). This focus has been rectified in the past 20 years or so, and there is now a great deal of research into the ways that students go about their learning. Appropriately, the field of study is now designated 'student learning' research.

Student learning research originated in Sweden, with Marton and Säljö's (1976a,b) studies of surface and deep approaches to learning. They gave students a text to read and told them they would be asked questions afterwards. Students responded in two different ways. The first group learned in anticipation of the questions, concentrating anxiously on the facts and details that might be asked. They 'skated along the surface of the text', as Marton and Säljö put it, using a *surface* approach to learning. What these students remembered was a list of disjointed facts; they did not comprehend the point the author was making. The second group, on the other hand, set out to understand the meaning of what the author was trying to say. They went below the surface of the text to interpret that meaning, using a *deep* approach. They saw the big picture and how the facts and details made the author's case.

Note that the terms 'deep' and 'surface' as used here describe ways of learning a particular task, they do *not* describe characteristics of students. We can say that Robert might typically use a surface approach, but the whole point of this book is to set up ways of getting him to go deep. We return to this important distinction shortly.

The Marton and Säljö studies struck a chord with ongoing work in other countries; in particular with that of Entwistle in the UK (e.g. Entwistle and Ramsden 1983), and that of Biggs in Australia (e.g. 1979, 1987a). The conceptual frameworks of these workers were originally quite different from that of the Swedish group, deriving in the first case largely from the psychology of individual differences, and in the second case from cognitive psychology, but the common focus was the study of learning in an institutional context. Some strong implications for teaching could be drawn.

### How do we learn?

Theories of teaching and learning focusing on student activity are based on two main theories: phenomenography and constructivism. 'Phenomeno-graphy' was a term coined by Marton (1981) to describe the theory that grew out of his original studies with Säljö, and has developed since then (Marton and Booth 1997). It is based on the idea that the learner's perspective defines what is learned, not what the teacher intends should be learned. Teaching is a matter of changing the learner's perspective, the way the learner sees the world.

Constructivism has a long history in cognitive psychology – Jean Piaget is a crucial figure (e.g Ginsberg and Opper 1987) – and today, it takes on several forms: individual, social, cognitive, postmodern (Steffe and Gale 1995). They have in common the idea that what the learner has to *do* to create knowledge is the important thing.

While there are differences between constructivist-driven and phenomeno-logically driven teaching (Trigwell and Prosser 1997; Prosser and Trigwell 1998), I assume that most teachers, including readers of this book, are not particularly interested in theories of learning so much as in improving their teaching. For that we need a framework to aid reflection: a theory of learning that is broad-based and empirically sound, and that easily translates into practice. To my mind that means constructivism, with its emphasis on what students have to do, rather than on how they represent knowledge. Both emphasize that the student creates knowledge – call it 'constructing knowledge' or 'constituting knowledge' as you will – so that knowledge is not imposed or transmitted by direct instruction.

Knowledge, then, is created by the student's *learning activities*, their 'approaches to learning' (see below). The low cognitive level of engagement deriving from the surface approach yields fragmented outcomes that do not convey the meaning of the encounter, whereas the deep approach yields the meaning at least as the student construes it. The surface approach is therefore to be discouraged, the deep approach encouraged – and that is the working definition of good teaching used in this book.

What people construct from a learning encounter depends on their motives and intentions, on what they know already, and on how they use their prior knowledge. Meaning is therefore personal. What else can it be? The alternative is that meaning is 'transmitted' from teacher to student, like dubbing an audio-tape, which is a common but untenable view.

Learning is thus a way of interacting with the world. As we learn, our conceptions of phenomena change, and we see the world differently. The acquisition of information in itself does not bring about such a change, but the way we structure that information and think with it does. Thus, education is about *conceptual change*, not just the acquisition of information.

Such educative conceptual change takes place when:

1 it is clear to students (and teachers) what is 'appropriate', what the objectives are, where all can see where they are supposed to be going;
2 students experience the felt need to get there. The art of good teaching is to communicate that need where it is initially lacking. 'Motivation' is a product of good teaching, not its prerequisite;
3 students feel free to focus on the task, not on watching their backs. Attempts to create a felt need to learn by the use of ill-conceived and urgent assessments are counterproductive. The game then becomes a matter of dealing with the test, not with engaging the task deeply;
4 students can work collaboratively and in dialogue with others, both peers and teachers. Good dialogue elicits those activities that shape, elaborate and deepen understanding.

These four points contain a wealth of implication for the design of teaching, and for personal reflection about what one is really trying to do. But first let us elaborate the fundamental concept of approach to learning.

## Surface and deep approaches to learning

The concepts of surface and deep approaches to learning are helpful in conceiving ways of improving teaching. Sometimes it is useful to refer to an 'achieving' approach (Biggs 1987a), or 'strategic approach' (Tait *et al.* 1998), which refer to how ambitious and how organized students are, whereas we are concerned here with how learning tasks are handled. The surface and deep approaches usefully describe how Robert and Susan typically go about their learning and studying – up to now. Remember that our aim is to teach so that Robert behaves more like Susan.

### The surface approach

The surface approach arises from an intention to get the task out of the way with minimum trouble while appearing to meet course requirements. Low-cognitive-level activities are used when higher-level activities are required to do the task properly. The concept of the surface approach may be applied to any area, not only to learning. The phrases 'cutting corners' and 'sweeping under the carpet' convey the idea: the job appears to have been done properly when it hasn't.

Applied to academic learning, examples include rote learning selected content instead of understanding it, padding an essay, listing points instead of addressing an argument, quoting secondary references as if they were primary ones. The list is very long. A common misconception is that memorization indicates a surface approach (e.g. Webb 1997). However, verbatim recall is sometimes entirely appropriate, such as learning lines for a play, acquiring vocabulary, learning formulae. Memorization becomes a surface approach when something more like understanding is required, and is used to give the impression of understanding. When Robert takes notes and selectively quotes them back, he is under-engaging in terms of what is properly required. That is a surface approach; and the problem is that it often works:

> I hate to say it, but what you have got to do is to have a list of 'facts';
> you write down ten important points and memorize those, then you'll
> do all right in the test . . . If you can give a bit of factual information
> – so and so did that, and concluded that – for two sides of writing,
> then you'll get a good mark.
>
> (Psychology undergraduate quoted in Ramsden 1984: 144)

Now, if the teacher of this student thought that an adequate understanding of psychology could be manifested by selectively memorizing, there would be no problem. But I rather doubt that the teacher did think that. I see this as a case where an inappropriate assessment task *allowed* the student to get a good mark on the basis of memorizing facts. As it happened, this particular student wrote essays in a highly appropriate way, and later graduated with first class honours. The problem is therefore not with the student but with the assessment task. This is an instance of unreflective practice by the teacher, highly reflective by the student.

Thus, do not think that Robert is irredeemably cursed with a surface approach. What we know is that *under current conditions of teaching*, he chooses to use a surface approach. Teaching and assessment methods often encourage a surface approach, because they are not aligned to the aims of teaching the subject, as in the case of the above psychology teacher. The presence of a surface approach is thus a signal that something is out of kilter in our teaching or in our assessment methods, and therefore is something we can hope to address. It might in the end turn out that Robert is a student who is hopelessly addicted to surface learning, but that conclusion is way down the track yet.

In using the surface approach, students focus on what Marton calls the 'signs' of learning; the words used, isolated facts, items treated independently of each other. This prevents them from seeing what the signs signify, the meaning and structure of what is taught. They cannot see the wood for the trees. Emotionally, learning becomes a drag, a task to be got out of the way. Hence the presence of negative feelings about the learning task: anxiety, cynicism, boredom. Exhilaration or enjoyment of the task is not part of the surface approach.

Factors that encourage students to adopt such an approach include:

*From the student's side*
- An intention only to achieve a minimal pass. Such may arise from a 'meal ticket' view of university, or from a requirement to take a subject irrelevant to the student's programme.
- Non-academic priorities exceeding academic ones.
- Insufficient time; too high a workload.
- Misunderstanding requirements, such as thinking that factual recall is adequate.
- A cynical view of education.
- High anxiety.
- A genuine inability to understand particular content at a deep level.

*From the teacher's side*
- Teaching piecemeal by bullet lists, not bringing out the intrinsic structure of the topic or subject.
- Assessing for independent facts, inevitably the case when using short-answer and multiple-choice tests.
- Teaching, and especially assessing, in a way that encourages cynicism: for example, 'I hate teaching this section, and you're going to hate learning it, but we've got to cover it.'

- Providing insufficient time to engage the tasks; emphasizing coverage at the expense of depth.
- Creating undue anxiety or low expectations of success: 'Anyone who can't understand this isn't fit to be at university.'

The two sides should not be seen as entirely separate. Most of the student-based factors are affected by teaching. Is insufficient time to engage properly a matter of poor student planning or poor teacher judgement? Much student cynicism is a reaction to the manner of teaching and assessment. Even the last student factor, inability to understand at a deep level, refers to the task at hand, and that may be a matter of poor teacher judgement concerning curriculum content as much as the student's abilities. But there are limits. Even under the best teaching some students will maintain a surface approach.

It is probably less likely that under poor teaching students will maintain a deep approach. Even Susan. Unfortunately, it is easier to create a surface approach than it is to support a deep approach (Trigwell and Prosser 1991).

*The first step in improving teaching, then, is to avoid those factors that encourage a surface approach.*

## The deep approach

The deep approach arises from a felt need to engage the task appropriately and meaningfully, so the student tries to use the most appropriate cognitive activities for handling it. Susan is interested in mathematics, is intrigued by mathematical structures and wants to get to the bottom of the subject; cutting corners is pointless.

When students feel this need to know, they automatically try to focus on underlying meaning, on main ideas, themes, principles or successful applications. This requires a sound foundation of relevant prior knowledge, so students needing to know will naturally try to learn the details, as well as make sure they understand the big picture. In fact, the big picture is not understandable without the details. When using the deep approach in handling a task, students have positive feelings: interest, a sense of importance, challenge, even of exhilaration. Learning is a pleasure. Students come with questions they want answered, and when the answers are unexpected, that is even better.

Factors that encourage students to adopt such an approach include:

*From the student's side*
- An intention to engage the task meaningfully and appropriately. Such an intention may arise from an intrinsic curiosity or from a determination to do well.
- Appropriate background knowledge.

- The ability to focus at a high conceptual level, working from first principles, which in turn requires a well-structured knowledge base.
- A genuine preference, and ability, for working conceptually rather than with unrelated detail.

*In the teaching environment*

- Teaching in such a way as to explicitly bring out the structure of the topic or subject.
- Teaching to *elicit* an active response from students, e.g. by questioning, presenting problems, rather than teaching to *expound* information.
- Teaching by building on what students already know.
- Confronting and eradicating students' misconceptions.
- Assessing for structure rather than for independent facts.
- Teaching and assessing in a way that encourages a positive working atmosphere, so students can make mistakes and learn from them.
- Emphasizing depth of learning, rather than breadth of coverage.
- In general, and most importantly, using teaching and assessment methods that support the explicit aims and objectives of the course. This is known as 'practising what you preach'.

Again, the student-based factors are not independent of teaching. Encouraging the need to know, instilling curiosity, building on students' prior knowledge are all things that teachers can attempt to do; and conversely, they are things that poor teaching can discourage. There are many things the teacher can do to encourage deep learning. Just what, will be a lot clearer by the end of this book.

To summarize, then, deep and surface approaches to learning describe the way students relate to a teaching/learning environment; they are not fixed characteristics of students, their 'academic personalities' so to speak.

## Learning approaches and learning styles

Some people speak of students' approaches to learning as if they were learning *styles* that apply whatever the task or the teaching (Schmeck 1988). At the other extreme, Marton and Säljö (1976a,b) speak of approaches as entirely determined by context, as if students walk into a learning situation without any preference for their way of going about learning.

The truth lies in the middle. Students do have predilections or preferences for this or that approach, but those predilections may or may not be realized in practice, depending on the teaching context. We are dealing with an *interaction* between the personal and the contextual, not unlike the interaction between heredity and environment. Both factors apply, but which predominates depends on particular situations. Turn back to Figure 1.1. At point A, under passive teaching, student factors make the difference, but at point B, active teaching predominates, lessening the differences between students. For an analysis of the differences between learning styles and learning approaches see Sternberg and Zhang (2001).

If you want to assess predilections for different approaches to learning, this can be done using questionnaires such as the Approaches and Study Skills Inventory for Students (ASSIST) (Tait *et al.* 1998), or the Study Process Questionnaire (SPQ) (Biggs 1987a). Responses to these questionnaires also tell us something about the quality of the teaching environment, because students' predilections tend to change when they are faced with a particular kind of teaching environment; they adapt to the expected requirements. Thus, questionnaires can be used to evaluate teaching environments (Biggs 1993a; Kember *et al.* 1998). For example, Eley (1992) found that students adapted their approaches to learning to their perception of what different units demanded; Meyer (1991) refers to this as 'study orchestration'. The practical details of using such questionnaires in research on teaching are given in Chapter 12.

### The 3P model of learning and teaching

Figure 2.1 puts all this together in the 3P model of teaching and learning, which elaborates Dunkin and Biddle's (1974) model of teaching to include approaches to learning.

The 3P model describes three points in time at which learning-related factors are placed:

1 presage, before learning takes place;
2 process, during learning;
3 product, the outcome of learning.

Presage factors are of two kinds:

1 *Student based* – the relevant prior knowledge the student has about the topic, interest in the topic, student ability, commitment to university, and so on.
2 *Teaching context based* – what is intended to be taught, how it will be taught and assessed, the expertise of the teacher, the 'climate' or ethos of the classroom and of the institution itself, and so on.

These factors interact at the process level to determine the student's immediate learning-related activities, as approaches to learning. Possible interactions here are manifold. A student with little prior knowledge of the topic will be unlikely to use a deep approach, even where the teaching is expert. Another student who already knows a great deal and is very interested in the topic is pre-set for a deep approach, but doesn't use it because of severe time pressures. Yet another, who typically picks out likely items for assessment and rote learns them, finds that approach won't work under portfolio assessment, so goes deep. You can

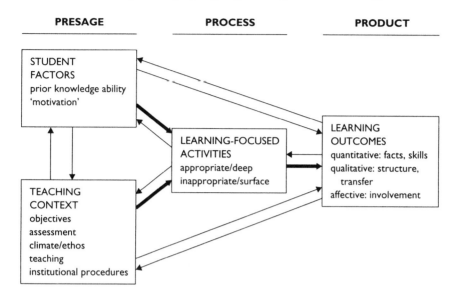

**Figure 2.1:** The 3P model of teaching and learning

see why it is inappropriate to write off particular students as surface learners.

The learning outcome is determined by many factors, acting in interaction with each other. The general direction of effects is marked by the heavy arrows: student and teaching presage factors jointly determine the approach a student uses for a given task, and that in turn determines the outcome. The light arrows connect everything to everything else, because all components form a *system* (Biggs 1993b).

A system is a set of components that interact to produce a common outcome, in service to a common goal (Romizowski 1981). Here the common goal is learning, and the immediate system comprises all things in and out of the classroom that might affect each other and thus the outcome. Systems are interactive, not linear, so that, for example, it is difficult to pin down *the* cause of good or poor learning. Students bring in their abilities, personalities and motives; teachers bring in theirs, and they make decisions about teaching and assessment. What works for one class does not work for another. Collectively, these background factors determine the cognitive processes the students are likely to use, which in turn determine the detail and structure inherent in the learning outcomes, and how the students feel about the outcome.

No two classes are ever the same. You may be the same, but the students are not, so you strike a different deal with each group of students each time; in a functional sense, it is not even true that you are the same. Likewise, you and a colleague teaching the same class create a different system, because one of the components is different, the teacher, and accordingly each individual achieves different results. Then there is the larger institutional system, of which the classroom is one component; that too strikes its own balance. This is important in quality assurance, as we see in the final chapter.

The 3P model contains within it various theories of teaching. Before examining these, let us see where you currently stand on your theory of teaching by completing Task 2.1.

## Levels of thinking about teaching

The 3P model draws attention to three sources that might affect the learning outcome: a direct effect from the student-based factors, another direct effect from the teaching-based factors, and an interactive effect from the system as a whole. Each of these ways of determining learning forms a theory of how teaching works:

1 Learning is a function of individual differences between students.
2 Learning is a function of teaching.
3 Learning is the result of students' learning-focused activities which are engaged by students as a result both of their own perceptions and inputs, and of the total teaching context.

These different 'theories' of teaching are in order of complexity and sophistication, and so we refer to them as 'levels'. They include what others call intentions or conceptions (Trigwell and Prosser 1996).

Teachers tend to hold these theories at different points in their teaching career, some progressing to level 3, others staying at levels 1 or 2 (Biggs 1996c). They describe a sequence in the development of teaching skill: a route map towards reflective teaching, if you like, where the level at which you operate depends on what you focus on as most important.

### Level 1. Focus: what the student is

Teachers at level 1 focus on the student presage factors. They are struck by student differences, as most beginning teachers are; there are good students, like Susan, and poor students, like Robert. As teachers, they see their responsibility to know the content well, and to expound it clearly. Thereafter, it's up to the student to attend lectures, to listen carefully, to take notes, to read the recommended readings, and to make sure the material is taken on board and unloaded on cue.

**Task 2.1:  What are your theories of teaching and learning?**

Learning is _____

_____

_____

_____

Teaching is _____

_____

_____

_____

When you have finished this chapter, come back to these statements and see how they check out against the transmission and student learning models, and the theories of teaching outlined in the chapter. Where do your own views lie? Now that you have seen these other views, have you changed your theory of teaching?

_____

_____

_____

Comments _____

_____

At level 1, teaching is, as it were, held constant – it is transmitting information, usually by lecturing – so differences in learning are due to differences between students in ability, motivation, what sort of school they went to, A-level results, and yes, their 'innate' approaches to learning. Ability is usually seen as the most important factor, an interesting consequence of which is that teaching becomes not so much an educative activity as a *selective* one, assessment the instrument for sorting the good students from the bad after teaching is over. Many common practices (addressed in Chapters 8 and 9) spring from this belief.

The view of university teaching as transmitting information is so widely accepted that delivery and assessment systems the world over are based on it. Teaching rooms and media are specifically designed for one-way delivery. A teacher is the knowledgeable expert who expounds the information the students are to absorb and to report back accurately, according to their ability, their motivation, even their ethnicity (see Chapter 7). The curriculum is a list of items of content that, once expounded from the podium, have been 'covered'. How the students receive that content and what their depth of understanding of it might be are not specifically addressed.

Level 1 is founded on a *quantitative* way of thinking about learning and teaching (Cole 1990; Marton *et al.* 1993), which manifests itself most obviously in assessment practices. Learning outcomes are quantified into units of knowledge of equivalent value: a word, an idea, a point. The correct ones are counted and converted by a common currency, usually a percentage, to make them interchangeable. We examine this model, its manifestations and its consequences, in Chapter 8.

Explaining the variability in student learning on students' characteristics makes this a *blame-the-student* theory of teaching, based on student deficit. When students don't learn (that is, when teaching breaks down), it is due to something the students are lacking:

*How can I be expected to teach that lot with those A-level results? They wouldn't even have been admitted ten years ago.*

*They lack any motivation at all.*

*These students lack suitable study skills. But that's not my problem, they'll have to go to the Counselling Service.*

In themselves, these statements may well be true: A-level or HSC results might be poor, students nowadays may be less academically oriented. That is exactly the challenge outlined in Chapter 1.

Blame-the-student is a comfortable theory of teaching. If students don't learn, it's not that there is anything wrong with the teaching, but that they are incapable, unmotivated, foreign, or some other non-academic defect, which it is not the teacher's responsibility to correct. Blaming the student is very common in teaching international students, as we see in Chapter 7.

The level 1 theory of teaching is totally unreflective. It doesn't occur to the teacher to ask the key generative question: 'What else could I be doing?' And until they do ask that, their teaching is unlikely to change.

### Level 2. Focus: what the teacher does

Teachers at level 2 focus on the teacher presage factors. This view of teaching is still based on transmission, but of concepts and understandings not just of information (Prosser and Trigwell 1998). The responsibility for 'getting it across' now rests to a significant extent on what the teacher does. The possibility is entertained that there may be more effective ways of teaching than what one is currently doing. This is a major advance. Learning is seen as more a function of what the teacher is doing than of what sort of student one has to deal with.

The teacher who operates at level 2 works at obtaining an armoury of teaching skills. The material to be 'got across' includes complex understandings, which requires much more than chalk-and-talk. Consider the following:

> *I'll settle them down with some music, then an introductory spiel: where we were last week, what we're going to do today. Then a video clip followed by a buzz session. The questions they're to address will be on the OH. I'll then fire six questions at them to be answered individually. Yes, four at the back row, finger pointing, that'll stir that lot up. Then I speak to the answers for about seven minutes, working in those two jokes I looked up. Wrap up, warning them there's an exam question hidden in today's session (screams of 'Now he tells us!' Yuk, yuk). Mention what's coming up for next week, and meantime they're to read Chapter 10 of Bronowski.*

Plenty of variation in technique here, probably – almost certainly – a good student response, but the focus of this description is entirely teacher-centred. It's about what *I* the teacher am doing, not upon what *they* the students are learning.

Traditional approaches to teaching development often worked on what the teacher does, as do 'how to' courses and books that provide prescriptive advice on getting it across more effectively:

- Establish clear procedural rules at the outset, such as signals for silence.
- Ensure clarity: project the voice, clear visual aids.
- Make eye contact with students while talking.
- Don't interrupt a large lecture with handouts: chaos is likely.

This may be useful advice, as we endorse in Chapter 6, but it is concerned with *management*, not with facilitating learning. Good management is important, but as a means of setting the stage so that good learning may occur, not as an end in itself.

Level 2 is also a deficit model, the 'blame' this time is on the teacher. It is a view of teaching often held by university administrators because it provides a rationale for making personnel decisions. Good teachers are those who have lots of teaching competencies. Does Dr Jones 'have' the appropriate competencies for tertiary-level teaching? If not, he had better show evidence that he has by the time his contract comes up for renewal. However, competencies may have little to do with teaching effectiveness. A competency, such as constructing a reliable multiple-choice test, is useful only if it is appropriate to one's teaching purposes to *use* a multiple-choice test. Likewise, managing educational technology, or questioning skills, or any of the other competencies tertiary teachers should 'have', should not be isolated from the context in which they are being used. Knowing what to do is important only if you know when and how you should do it. The focus should be not on the skill itself, but on whether its deployment has the desired effect on student learning. Which brings us to the third level of teaching.

**Level 3. Focus: what the student does**

Teachers at level 3 focus on all the components in the systems, in particular on what the student does at process and product, and how that relates to teaching. Level 3 sees teaching as supporting learning. No longer is it possible to say: 'I taught them, but they didn't learn.' Expert teaching includes mastery over a variety of teaching techniques, but unless learning takes place, they are irrelevant; the focus is on what the student does, on what learning is or is not going on.

This implies a view of teaching that is not just about facts, concepts and principles to be covered and understood, but also to be clear about:

1 what it means to 'understand' content in the way we want it to be understood;
2 what kind of teaching/learning activities are required to reach those kinds of understandings.

The first two levels did not address these questions. The first question requires that we specify what levels of understanding we want when we teach a topic; the second what learning activities might best be appropriate for achieving those levels. Then follow the key questions:

• How do you define those levels of understanding?
• What do students have to do to reach the level specified?
• What do you have to do to find out if they have been reached or not?

Defining levels of understanding is basic to clarifying our curriculum object-ives, the subject of the Chapter 3. Getting students to understand at the level required is a matter of getting them to undertake the appropriate learning activities, which is dealt with in Chapters 5, 6 and 10. This is where a level 3 student-centred theory of teaching departs from the other models. It's not what *we* do, it's what *students* do that is important. Finally, we need to check that their understandings and performances are what we wanted, which is dealt with in the chapters on assessment (Chapters 8, 9 and 10).

Level 3 teaching is systemic. Good student learning depends both on student-based factors – ability, appropriate prior knowledge, clearly accessible new knowledge – and on the teaching context, which includes teacher responsibility, informed decision-making and good management. But the bottom line is that teachers have to work with what material they have. Whereas lectures and tutorials might have worked in the good old days when highly selected students tended to bring their deep approaches with them, they may not work so well today. We need to create a teaching context where the Roberts of this world can go deep too.

Do the conceptions we hold affect the way we teach? Gow and Kember (1993) showed that teachers who saw teaching as knowledge transmission created classrooms where students scored very low on the deep approach, while teachers who saw teaching as facilitating student learning created classrooms where students scored very low on a surface approach. Teachers' beliefs had created teaching environments to which the students reacted by tuning their approaches to learning to suit the environment to which they were exposed. We return to the important question of changing teachers' conceptions in Chapter 12.

## Constructive alignment

Since writing the first edition of this book, I came across the following:

> Learning takes place through the active behavior of the student: it is what *he* does that he learns, not what the teacher does.
>
> (Tyler 1949: 63)

Sound familiar? See the preliminary pages of this book. Ralph Tyler, a Grand Old Man of American education said this over 50 years ago, in one of the most widely read books in the educational literature (it was into its thirtieth impression by 1970). He developed the notion that teaching should be directed at what teachers were aiming at, learning assessed according to those aims, and the whole organized suitably. He addressed four questions:

1 What educational purposes should the school seek to attain?
2 What educational experiences can be provided that are likely to attain these purposes?
3 How can these educational experiences be effectively organized?
4 How can we determine whether these purposes are being attained?

Here was constructive alignment. Thousands of education students and in-service teachers had read about it, no doubt passed their exams about it – and nothing had changed. Tyler might just as well have been farming sheep.

No doubt Thomas Shuell had Tyler in the back of his mind when he wrote:

> If students are to learn *desired outcomes* in a *reasonably effective manner*, then the teacher's fundamental task is to get students to *engage in learning activities* that are likely to result in their achieving those outcomes . . . what the student does in determining what is learned is more important than what the teacher does.
>
> (Shuell 1986: 429; emphases added)

Shuell has filled out what Tyler said. Here is a blueprint for the design of teaching, which is elaborated here as constructive alignment.

In saying what the 'desired outcomes' are, we are clarifying our objectives. In deciding if the outcomes are learned in a 'reasonably effective manner' we need to reference our assessment to those objectives and to define what reasonably effective might mean in terms of our grading system. And in getting students to 'engage in (appropriate) learning activities', we are teaching them effectively. Most importantly, we are saying that all these aspects of teaching are mutually supportive; each is an integral part of the total system, not an add-on.


**The principle of alignment**

The 3P model describes teaching as a balanced system in which all components support each other, as they do in any ecosystem. To work properly, all components need to be aligned to each other.

Apart from the students and ourselves, the critical components include:

1 The curriculum that we teach.
2 The teaching methods that we use.
3 The assessment procedures that we use, and methods of reporting results.
4 The climate that we create in our interactions with the students.
5 The institutional climate, the rules and procedures we have to follow.

Imbalance in the system will lead to poor teaching and surface learning. Non-alignment is signified by inconsistencies, unmet expectations, and practices that contradict what we preach.

Each of these components should work towards the common end, deep learning. Let us begin with institutional climate (item 5); that is a given. We have to work within or around institutional requirements as best we may. As to the classroom climate (item 4), that is more under our control. The kind of atmosphere we create – authoritarian, friendly, cold, warm – can markedly affect the effectiveness of a teaching approach. For example, problem-solving in small groups won't work with a know-all group leader who insists on telling students the answers. We cannot teach in a manner that is inappropriate for the mode of teaching we are using or that is false to ourselves. Forcing teachers into an untenable role destroys alignment.

As to the curriculum (item 1), the teaching methods (item 2) and the assessment procedures (item 3), we have to be particularly careful to seek compatibility. When there is alignment between what we want, how we teach and how we assess, teaching is likely to be much more effective than when it is not. Cohen (1987) calls alignment between objectives and assessment (criterion-referenced assessment) 'the magic bullet', so effective is it in improving learning. I am going further and, with Tyler, suggesting that teaching methods should be included in the alignment. You wouldn't lecture education students on how to teach using small groups, and then give them a written test. You would get them to participate in small groups, then run their own and see how well they did it.

Alignment itself, however, says nothing about the nature of what is being aligned. This is where constructivism as a theory of learning comes in. If we specify our objectives in terms of understanding, we need a theory of understanding in order to define what we mean. In deciding on teaching methods to use that address the objectives, we need a theory of learning and teaching. Hence, 'constructive alignment', a marriage between a constructivist understanding of the nature of learning, and an aligned design for teaching (Biggs 1996a).

It is easy to see why alignment should work. In aligned teaching, there is maximum consistency throughout the system. The curriculum is stated in the form of clear objectives, which state the level of understanding required rather than simply a list of topics to be covered. The teaching methods are chosen that are likely to realize those objectives; you get students to do the things that the objectives nominate. Finally, the assessment tasks address the objectives, so that you can test to see if the students have learned what the objectives state they should be learning. All components in the system address the same agenda and support each other. The students are 'entrapped' in this web of consistency, optimizing the likelihood that they will engage the appropriate learning activities, but paradoxically leaving them free to construct their knowledge their way. Cowan (1998) makes a similar point when he defines teaching as 'the purposeful creation of situations from which motivated learners should not be able to escape without learning or developing'. This is deep learning by definition.

At this point we should say what constructive alignment is not. It is not, as some have suggested, 'spoon-feeding'. Spoon-feeding, like the other level 1 metaphors with their curious affinity to metabolic processes – 'regurgitating', 'chewing it over', 'stuffing them with facts', 'ramming down their throats', 'getting your teeth into' – puts a stranglehold on the student's cognitive processes. Spoon-feeding does the work for the students, so that they have little left to do but obediently swallow. Constructive alignment makes the students do the real work, the teacher simply acts as broker between the student and a learning environment that supports the appropriate learning activities.

### The design of aligned teaching

Figure 2.2 depicts the constructive alignment model. There are really two systems: the teaching system, which is what the teacher constructs, and the learning system, which is how the student reacts. Actually, these are

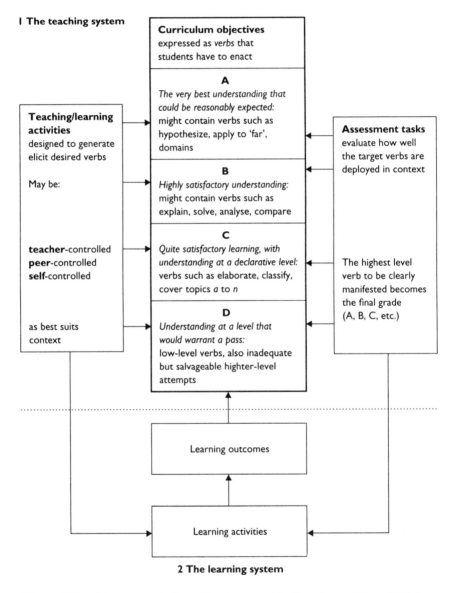

**Figure 2.2:**   Aligning curriculum objectives, teaching/learning activities (TLAs), and assessment tasks

subsystems which interact to form their own system, which in turn becomes part of the wider institutional system. But let us begin at the beginning: the institutional system has to wait until the last chapter.

Take the teaching system first. The curriculum objectives lie in the middle, which asserts their centrality. Get them right, and the decisions as to how they are to be taught and how they may be assessed, follow. We express the objectives in terms of what constructive activities are most likely to achieve the desired outcomes for the topic or unit in question. Activities are *verbs*, so practically speaking we specify the verbs we want students to enact in the context of the content discipline being taught.

Turn back to Figure 1.1, which uses verbs in this way. We see that Susan tended spontaneously to use high-level verbs such as theorize, reflect, generate, apply, whereas Robert used lower-level verbs such as recognize, memorize, and so on. Their level of engagement is expressed in the cognitive level of the verbs used: reflection is high level, memorizing low level. Note that these verbs are examples only. Precisely what is meant by 'level', and how to determine it, are key issues addressed in Chapter 3.

Those verbs take objects: the content being taught. We can now explicitly go beyond the one-dimensional notion of 'covering' the topics in the curriculum, by specifying the *levels* of understanding we want. Different levels will be differentially acceptable. The level of understanding in a bare pass is obviously less than that you would require in a high distinction. In the constructive alignment model, the first step is to arrange these levels of understanding in a hierarchy that corresponds to the grading system you use.

Exactly how this may be done is dealt with in the next chapter. For an immediate example, express the objectives as a four-tier hierarchy corresponding to grade levels. Let us use the neutral A to D letter grades. Grade A denotes a quality of learning and understanding that is the best one can reasonably expect for the unit and level of students in question. Obviously, that level will become increasingly higher from first year to higher years. B is highly satisfactory but lacks the flair that distinguishes A. C is quite satisfactory, while D denotes a quality and complexity of understanding that is passable only, and anything less is fail. You will notice that Figure 2.2 uses sample verbs which are quite general. You would of course use families of verbs to suit each level and each content area. The range here between A and D is wide for one module. And should we be awarding C principally on describing? Such matters of judgement are addressed in the next chapter.

The important thing for now is that the categories are defined by a particular *quality* of learning and understanding, not by the accumulation of marks or percentages. Judgements as to that quality are formed from the assessment tasks. Finer discriminations, within categories, may be useful for reporting grades and for other administrative purposes, but that is a separate issue. Our interest here is in stating the objectives qualitatively, and assessing student products accordingly. This notion, that the *quality* of learning is the important thing, is not new. The term 'first class honours' has been used for a long time to capture the idea that a student with first class honours *thinks differently* from a student with an upper second. This difference is not captured by saying that a first has to obtain X more marks than an upper second. This is discussed further in the next chapter and in Chapter 8.

Once we have sorted out the objectives, we design teaching/learning activities, or TLAs, that are likely to encourage students to engage the optimal verbs. ('TLA' is a better term than 'teaching method' because it captures the reciprocal relationship between learning and teaching.)

Finally, we select assessment tasks that will tell us whether and how well each student can meet the criteria expressed in the objectives. Objectives, teaching and assessment are now aligned, using the verbs in the objectives as markers for alignment.

To sum up, in an aligned system of instruction the teacher's task is to see that the appropriate learning activities, conveniently expressed as verbs, are:

1 nominated in the objectives;
2 likely to be elicited in the chosen teaching/learning activities;
3 embedded in the assessment tasks so that judgements can be made about how well a given student's level of performance meets the objectives.

Because the teaching methods and the assessment tasks now access the same verbs as are in the objectives, the chances are increased that most students will in fact engage with the appropriate verbs: by definition, a deep approach. Had Ramsden's psychology teacher included in the objectives such terms as 'theorize', 'generalize' or 'comprehend the profundities of the founders of modern psychology', an assessment task that required only paraphrasing 'a bit of factual information for two pages of writing' would immediately be seen to be inadequate.

Now to the learning system. The students' learning activities are primed by the teaching system in two ways. First, there are the TLAs themselves, what we require students to do in the learning episode. Second, there are the learning activities elicited by what the students see will be required from the assessment: 'two pages of writing', or demonstrations of understanding the objectives? This aspect of assessment is called backwash, and we come back to that in Chapter 9. The learning activities, whether elicited by the TLAs, by the assessment or by the student's own priorities, produce an outcome: that is then matched, via the assessment, to the objectives.

Constructive alignment is common sense. Mothers and driving instructors use it all the time. What is the objective? To teach the child to tie her shoes. What is the TLA? Tying her shoes. What is the assessment? How well she ties her shoes. It is so obvious, yet most university teaching is not aligned. There are several reasons for this:

1 Traditional transmission theories of teaching ignore alignment. A common method of determining students' grades depends on how students compare with each other (norm-referenced), rather than on whether an individual's learning meets the objectives (criterion-referenced). In the former case, there is no *inherent* relation between what is taught and what is tested. The aim is to get a spread between students, not see how well individuals have learned what they were supposed to have learned.
2 Some administrative factors, such as resource limitations, which dictate large classes with mass lecturing and multiple-choice testing, make alignment difficult. Some administrative requirements, such as reporting in percentages and grading on the curve, make alignment impossible.
3 People hadn't thought of it before. Many of these matters may not have occurred to teachers.
4 Others might like to use the principle but they don't know how to.

These points are addressed throughout this book. We shall see how the principle of alignment can be applied to the design of most units.

## Summary and conclusions

### Research into student learning

It is only in recent years that students of learning have studied learning as it takes place in institutions, by students. There is now a body of theory called 'student learning research' that directly relates to practice, constructivism and phenomenography being the two most influential. Both emphasize that meaning is created by the learner, but constructivism focuses on the nature of the learning activities the student uses.

### Surface and deep approaches to learning

Appropriate learning activities are referred to as comprising a deep approach to learning, and inappropriate activities as a surface approach. Surface and deep approaches to learning are not personality traits, as is sometimes thought, but are most usefully thought of as reactions to the teaching environment. Good teaching supports the deep approach and discourages the surface, but much traditional practice, for a variety of reasons, has the opposite effect. The 3P model depicts the classroom as a an interactive system in which student characteristics and the teaching context mutually determine ongoing deep or surface learning activities, which in turn determine the quality of learning outcomes.

### Levels of thinking about teaching

The 3P model helps put in place three common theories of teaching, depending on what is seen as the main determinant of learning: (1) what students are, (2) what teachers do, and (3) what students do. These foci are in ascending order of abstraction, and define 'levels' of thinking about teaching. At level 1, the teacher's role is to display information, the students' to absorb it. If students don't have the ability or motivation to do that correctly, that is their problem. At level 2, the teacher's role is to explain concepts and principles, as well as to present information. For this they need various skills, techniques and competencies. Here the focus is on what the teacher does, rather than on what the student is, and to that extent is more reflective and sophisticated. At level 3, the focus is on what the student does: do they engage the appropriate learning activities? That is what the teacher is to encourage. The task is twofold:

1 To maximize the chances that students will use a deep approach.
2 To minimize the chances that they will use a surface approach.

That is the secret of good teaching. And that is what the rest of this book is about.

### Constructive alignment

Constructive alignment is a design for teaching calculated to encourage deep engagement. In constructing aligned teaching, it is first necessary to specify the desired *level* or *levels* of understanding of the content in question. Stipulating the appropriate verbs of understanding helps to do this. These verbs then become the target activities that students need to perform, and therefore for teaching methods to encourage, and for the assessment tasks to address, in order to judge if or to what extent the students have been successful in meeting the objectives. This combination of constructivist theory and aligned instruction is the model of *constructive alignment.*

## Further reading

### On student learning from a constructivist and systems perspective

Biggs, J.B. (1993) From theory to practice: a cognitive systems approach, *Higher Education Research and Development,* 12: 73–86.
Steffe, L. and Gale, J. (eds) (1995) *Constructivism in Education.* Hillsdale, NJ: Lawrence Erlbaum.
Sternberg, R.J. and Zhang, L.F. (eds) (2001) *Perspectives on Thinking, Learning, and Cognitive Styles.* Mahwah: Lawrence Erlbaum.

The first item applies the systems approach to student learning, the second is a fairly recent summary of the constructivist positions generally and how they apply to education.

Sternberg and Zhang is a useful collection of chapters on learning/ cognitive styles, approaches and orientations. I argue in my chapter that styles are a distraction; most of the other contributors argue that they are not, while Entwistle, McCune and Walker make room for everyone in their chapters.

### On applying student learning research to teaching

Biggs, J.B. (1996) Enhancing teaching through constructive alignment, *Higher Education*, 32: 1–18.

Dart, B. and Boulton-Lewis, G. (eds) (1998) *Teaching and Learning in Higher Education.* Camberwell, Vic.: Australian Council for Educational Research.

Prosser, M. and Trigwell, K. (1998) *Teaching for Learning in Higher Education.* Buckingham: Open University Press.

Ramsden, P. (1992) *Learning to Teach in Higher Education.* London: Routledge.

Tyler, R.W. (1949) *Basic Principles of Curriculum and Instruction.* Chicago: University of Chicago Press.

The first article outlines the theoretical basis of constructive alignment with an illustrative example. Dart and Boulton-Lewis contains a collection of papers that address teaching issues from the general student learning paradigm. Prosser and Trigwell demonstrate the implications for teaching arising from the phenomenographic framework, and in a sense parallels the present book, which operates from constructivism. Ramsden's approach is his own, but derives much from phenomenography, Chapters 1 to 7 giving rather more detail on the history and development of the student learning paradigm and how it may be applied to teaching than is given here. Tyler said most of it over 50 years ago, but no one paid any attention. The book is less than 100 pages and worth a read, for old time's sake. I hope they pay attention this time round.

# 3

## Formulating and clarifying curriculum objectives

**The goal of most teachers would be that their students 'understand' what they teach them. What is meant by 'understanding', however, is not always clear. The aim of this chapter is to clarify and define different levels of understanding, and convert them to curriculum objectives, as appropriate to the content and level of the unit. A useful tool for doing this is the SOLO taxonomy, which when applied to particular content can specify objectives in terms that are clear both to us and to our students. The objectives contain criteria for the desired learnings, which the assessment tasks are designed to address, thus linking objectives and assessment. Such criterion-referenced assessment steers students' attention to what is to be learned, while their performance tells us how well they have learned it, and how effective our teaching has been.**

### What do we mean by 'understanding'?

What, in a word, do you want your students to gain from your teaching? Did you say 'understanding'? Most teachers do. They don't want their students just to memorize, they want them to *understand*. The trouble is that 'understanding' can mean very different things.

I can 'understand' what *chat* means in French, but not 'understand' the sentence 'Le chat est assis sur la natte.' My understanding is basic indeed, but is still 'understanding'. Then I can 'understand' the idea contained in a sentence, but miss the meaning of the theme of the text in which the sentence is embedded. I can 'understand' abstract concepts and principles, but here too ambiguity reigns. To say I 'understand' the law of supply and demand means what: that I can tell someone what the law is? That I can solve textbook problems on supply and demand? That I can make wise market decisions and make lots of money? A related meaning of 'understanding' – and to us the most important – is practising what I preach. I could write this book on constructive alignment, and urge you to consider what a good thing it is, while my own teaching remains embarrassingly misaligned. My own understanding of 'constructive alignment' would be crucially deficient.

Entwistle and Entwistle (1997) conducted a series of studies on what students meant by 'understanding', and then asked them how they attempt to understand when preparing for examinations. The students described the experience of understanding as 'satisfying'; it was good to have the feeling that you understood at last. It also felt 'complete', a whole, as previously unrelated things were suddenly integrated. The experience was 'irreversible'; what is now understood cannot be 'de-understood'. Students thought a good practical test of understanding was being able to explain to someone else, or to be able to adapt and to use, what had been understood.

These are pretty good definitions of sound understanding that go beyond the word and sentence levels. They probably fit most teachers' requirements: You want students to interrelate topics, to adapt and use the knowledge so understood, perhaps to explain it to others, and hopefully to feel satisfied and good about it.

Unfortunately, when it came to exam time, these hopeful indicators of understanding evaporated. Students attempted to understand in ways that they thought would meet assessment requirements. Understanding then took on much less desirable forms. Entwistle and Entwistle (1997) distinguished five:

1 Reproduces content from lecture notes without any clear structure.
2 Reproduces the content within the structure used by the lecturer.
3 Develops own structure, but only to generate answers to anticipated exam questions.
4 Adjusts structures from strategic reading of different sources to represent personal understanding, but also to control examination requirements.
5 Develops an individual conception of the discipline from wide reading and reflection.

Only the last form of understanding, described by a small minority of students, is anything like their own definitions. All others focused on examination requirements. Entwistle and Entwistle found this 'worrying', because it meant that the examinations actually prevented students from achieving their own personal understandings of the content. Many of these students were in their final year, just prior to professional practice, yet the assessment system pre-empted the very level of understanding that would be professionally relevant. Worrying indeed.

To use our learning in order to negotiate with the world and to see it differently involves understanding of a high order. It is the kind of understanding that is referred to in the rhetoric of university teaching, yet seems hard to impart.

## Understanding and institutional learning

The longer most undergraduate students (not all – not the Susans) stay in most tertiary institutions, the less deep and the more surface-oriented they tend to become, and the more their understanding is assessment-related. The tendency is almost universal: Australia (Watkins and Hattie 1985; Biggs 1987a), the UK (Entwistle and Ramsden 1983), Hong Kong (Gow and Kember 1990). Learning, in other words, has become institutionalized. Much assessment practice appears not to require any conceptual change regarding learning, and so students lose 'ownership' of their learning and become alienated from it: 'Most of all I write what "they" like me to . . . when I get the piece of paper with BA (Hons) on it then I will write the way I want, using MY ideas . . .' (Arts undergraduate quoted in Watkins and Hattie 1985: 137).

Large classes that pre-empt in-depth teaching, jam-packed curricula that attempt to cover too much, and the apparatus surrounding accreditation – the reporting of assessment results, concerns about security – all make assessment for in-depth understanding difficult (see Chapters 8 and 9). Under these conditions it seems understandable that only a few students acquire the sort of understanding that changes perspectives and drives enlightened performance.

The task for this chapter is to clarify what we mean by 'understanding', then we can explicitly foster it in our teaching methods and test for it in our assessment methods.

## Performances of understanding

The Harvard Project Zero Team (Gardner 1993; Wiske 1998) focused on the higher levels of understanding in high school science. They came up with the idea that if students 'really' understood a concept they would *act differently* in contexts involving that concept, and could use the concept in unfamiliar or novel contexts. That is, real understanding is *performative*, which echoes the constructivist or level 3 view that learning changes students' perspectives on the world, so that they behave differently.

The challenge then is to conceive our teaching objectives in terms of a variety of *performances* of understanding, rather than in verbal declarations of understanding. This implicates teaching. In Project Zero, students are required to show their understanding by interacting 'thoughtfully' with a novel task, reflecting on appropriate feedback given to them to see how they can improve. That is how students learn complex tasks outside the classroom – just watch how they learn a computer game – but in the classroom, many performances that students are required to undertake are simply routines, adequate for handling common assessment tasks, but inadequate for the deep reflection needed in handling novel situations.

The difference between meeting the requirements of institutional learning and 'real' understanding is illustrated in Gunstone and White's (1981) demonstrations with Physics I students. In one demonstration, two balls, one heavy and one light, were held in the air in front of the students. They were then asked to predict, if the balls were released simultaneously, which one would hit the ground first, and why. Many predicted that the heavy one would 'because heavy things have a bigger force' or 'gravity is stronger nearer the earth' (both are true but irrelevant). These students had 'understood' gravity well enough to pass HSC (A-level) physics, but few understood well enough to answer a simple real-life question about gravity. They could correctly solve problems using the formula for $g$ – which does not contain a term for the mass of the object falling – while still reacting in the belief that heavy objects fall faster. They didn't *really* understand gravity in the performative sense. And the reason for that is obvious. Their teaching and assessment did not require them to.

To *really* understand is to have one's conceptions of phenomena changed. These physics students hadn't changed their common-sense conceptions of gravity, but had placed alongside them a set of statements and formulae about physical phenomena that would see them through the exams. Their experienced world remained pre-Newtonian. To really understand physics, or mathematics, or history, is to *think like* a physicist, a mathematician or a historian, and that shows in how you behave. Once you really understand a sector of knowledge, it changes that part of the world; you don't behave towards that domain in the same way again.

Verbal or 'declarative' levels of understanding will suffice for some purposes, for example to explain what gravity, or the three laws of motion, are about. But is this why we are teaching these topics? Is it for acquaintance, so that students know something about the topic and can answer the sorts of stock question that typify examination papers? In that case, declarative understanding will suffice. Is it to change the way (sooner or later) students can understand and control reality? If that is the case, then a performative level of understanding is implicated. It is that level of understanding that needs to be explicit in the objectives and directly addressed in the teaching and assessing.

In teaching the laws of motion, the Project Zero researchers required students to predict what will happen in a novel situation, and to explain why. For example:

*During a space flight, the astronauts discover that moisture is condensing and forming snow. They decide to have a snow fight. Describe what happens.*

The kind and level of understanding involved in handling this problem is analogous to that required in higher education, whether academic or professional. Graduates need to face new problems and interact with them, not only competently, but also thoughtfully. Predicting, diagnosing, explaining and solving non-textbook problems are what professionals have to do, so this is what university teachers should aim to get their students to do, particularly in higher years. Building such performances of understanding into the course objectives, aligning teaching to them, and designing assessment tasks that confirm that students can or cannot carry out those performances, is a good way to start.

## A framework for understanding understanding

So far we have been talking about the end-point, 'real' understanding. However, understanding develops gradually, becoming more structured and articulated as it does so. Undergraduates will not attain the level of precision and complexity of the subject expert, but we want none to retain the plausible misunderstandings that marked Gunstone and White's physics students' understanding of gravity.

We thus need to define understanding in ways that do justice to the topics and content we teach, as appropriate to the year level taught, much more specifically than was outlined in the objectives panel in Figure 2.2. The task is to define what is acceptable for each stage of the degree programme, given a student's specialization and degree pattern. That is a highly specific matter that only the teacher and subject expert can decide, but a general framework for structuring levels of understanding helps teachers to make those decisions, and it also provides a basis for discussing levels across different years and subject areas. Once a sound understanding of the basic structural framework is achieved, adapting it to particular unit or course objectives is straightforward.

The SOLO taxonomy is based on the study of outcomes in a variety of academic content areas (Biggs and Collis 1982). As students learn, the outcomes of their learning display similar stages of increasing structural complexity. There are two main changes: *quantitative*, as the amount of detail in the student's response increases, and *qualitative*, as that detail becomes integrated into a structural pattern. The quantitative stages of learning occur first, then learning changes qualitatively.

SOLO, which stands for Structure of the Observed Learning Outcome, provides a systematic way of describing how a learner's performance grows in complexity when mastering many academic tasks. It can be used to define curriculum objectives, which describe where students should be operating, and for evaluating learning outcomes so that we can know at what level individual students actually are operating.

To illustrate, let us take some content with which you are all familiar. It is set as an assessment task (Task 3.1):

*What are approaches to learning? How can knowledge of approaches to learning enhance university teaching?*

In a few sentences, outline your answer to these questions. **Stop reading any further until you have completed the task**. Then turn to Task 3.1 and try to evaluate your own response against the model responses.

---

**Task 3.1: SOLO levels in approaches to learning question and why**

The following levels of response could be observed (the first three responses hopefully were not).

*1 Prestructural*

'Teaching is a matter of getting students to approach their learning.'

This response could have been written by somebody with understanding at the individual word level, but little understanding of what was discussed in the previous chapter. Prestructural responses simply miss the point or, like this one, use tautology to cover lack of understanding. These responses can be quite sophisticated, such as the kind of elaborate tautology that politicians use to avoid answering questions, but academically they show little evidence of relevant learning.

*2 Unistructural*

'Approaches to learning are of two kinds, surface, which is inappropriate for the task at hand, and deep, which is appropriate. Teachers need to take this into account.'

This is unistructural because it meets only one part of the task, defining what approaches to learning are in terms of just one aspect, appropriateness. It misses other important attributes, for example that they are ways of describing students' learning activities and what might influence them, while the reference to teaching adds nothing. Unistructural responses deal with terminology, getting on track but little more.

*3 Multistructural*

'Approaches to learning are of two kinds, surface, which is inappropriate for the task at hand, and deep, which is appropriate. Students using a surface approach try to fool us into believing that they understand by rote learning and quoting back to us, sometimes in great detail. Students using a deep approach try to get at the underlying meaning of their learning tasks. Teaching is about getting students to learn appropriately, not getting by with short cuts. We should therefore teach for meaning and understanding, which means encouraging them to adopt a deep approach.'

I couldn't agree more. The first part is quite detailed (but could be more so); the second part is also what good teaching is about. So what is the problem with this answer? The problem is that this response does not address the key issue – *how* knowledge of approaches can enhance teaching – not *that* they can enhance teaching. This response, if elaborated, would constitute what Bereiter and Scardamalia (1987) call 'knowledge-telling': snowing with a bunch of facts, but not structuring them as required – and do not be misled by the odd connective like 'therefore'. Here, the student sees the trees but not the wood. Seeing trees is a necessary preliminary to adequate understanding, but it should not be interpreted as comprehending the wood.

### 4 Relational

'Approaches to learning are of two kinds, . . . (etc.) . . . The approaches come about partly because of student characteristics, but also because students react differently to their teaching environment in ways that lead them into surface or deep learning. The teaching environment is a system, a resolution of all the factors present, such as curriculum, assessment, teaching methods and students' own characteristics. If there is imbalance in the environment, for example a test that allows students to respond in a way that does not do justice to the curriculum, or a classroom climate that scares the hell out of them, the resolution is in favour of a surface approach. What this means is that we should be consistent . . .'

And so on. Here we have an explanation. Both concepts – approaches and teaching – have been integrated by the concept of a system; examples have been given, and the structure could easily be used to generate practical steps. The trees have become the wood, a qualitative change in learning and understanding has occurred. It is no longer a matter of listing facts and details, they address a point, making sense in light of their contribution to the topic as a whole. This is the first level at which 'understanding' in an academically relevant sense may appropriately be used.

### 5 Extended abstract

I won't give a lengthy example here. The essence of the extended abstract response is that it goes beyond what has been given, whereas the relational response stays with it. The coherent whole is conceptualized at a higher level of abstraction and is applied to new and broader domains. An extended response on approaches to learning would be a 'breakthrough' response, giving a perspective that changes what we think about them and their relationship to teaching. The trouble is that today's extended abstract is tomorrow's relational. Marton and Säljö's original study was such a breakthrough; linking approaches to learning to systems theory was another; but now both are conventional wisdom.

The examples illustrate the five levels of the taxonomy. Uni- and multistructural levels see understanding as a quantitative increase in what is grasped. These responses were deliberately constructed to show that the higher level contains the lower level plus a bit more. The 'bit more' in the case of multistructural incorporates the unistructural, then more of the same – a purely quantitative increase. The 'bit more' in the case of relational over multistructural involves a conceptual restructuring of the components, the recognition of the systems property as integrating the components, while the next shift to extended abstract takes the argument into a new dimension. SOLO describes a hierarchy where each partial construction becomes the foundation on which further learning is built. A neat example of how teachers' conceptions of learning fit SOLO is given by Boulton-Lewis (1998).

This distinction between knowing more and restructuring parallels two major curriculum aims: to *increase knowledge* (quantitative: unistructural becoming increasingly multistructural); and to *deepen understanding* (qualitative: relational, then extended abstract). Teaching and assessment that focus only on the quantitative aspects of learning will miss the more important higher-level aspects. Quantitative conceptions of teaching and learning address the first aim only, so that the deepening of understanding is left to Susan's predilections for spontaneous deep learning activities. The challenge for us is to highlight the qualitative aim in the objectives, and support it by both teaching and assessment methods. Then Robert's understanding is likely to be deepened too.

How SOLO is used to construct particular objectives is developed in a later section, when we have clarified the kinds of knowledge we are looking for.

#### Understanding of what? Kinds of knowledge

Knowledge is the object of understanding, but knowledge comes in various kinds.

*Declarative*, or propositional, knowledge refers to knowing about things, or knowing what: knowing about what Freud said, knowing what the terms of an equation refer to, knowing what kinds of cloud formations can be distinguished, knowing what were the important events in Shakespeare's life. Such content knowledge accrues from research, not from personal experience. It is public knowledge, subject to rules of evidence that make it verifiable, replicable and logically consistent. It is what is in libraries and textbooks, and is what teachers 'declare' in lectures. Students' understanding of it can be tested by getting them to declare it back, in their own words and using their own examples. If you use SOLO, you can classify the levels of their understanding, right up to extended abstract.

*Functioning* knowledge is based on the idea of performances of understanding. This knowledge is within the experience of the learner, who can now put declarative knowledge to work by solving problems, designing buildings, planning teaching or performing surgery. Functioning knowledge requires a solid foundation of declarative knowledge, to relational level at least, but it also involves (1) knowing how to do things, such as carrying out procedures or enacting skills (procedural knowledge), and (2) knowing when to do these things, and why (conditional knowledge).

*Procedural* knowledge is skill-based: functioning knowledge without the conceptual foundation. It is a matter of getting the sequences and actions right, knowing what to do when a given situation arises, having the right competencies.

*Conditional* knowledge subsumes both procedural and higher-level declarative knowledge, so that one knows when, why, and under what conditions, one should do this as opposed to that. The combination turns procedural knowledge into functioning knowledge, which is flexible and wide-ranging. The relationship between these kinds of knowledge is given in Figure 3.1. In sum, functioning knowledge (4) involves declarative knowledge (1) (the academic knowledge base), procedural knowledge (2) (having the skills), and conditional knowledge (3) (knowing the circumstances for using them).

These distinctions tell us what our curricula might address. Curricula in most universities are overwhelmingly declarative, when really graduates are supposed to be educated so that they can interact thoughtfully with professional problems: to use functioning knowledge, in other words. We separately teach (1) and some (2), and graduates are supposed to reach (4) on their own. This criticism does not apply to problem-based learning,

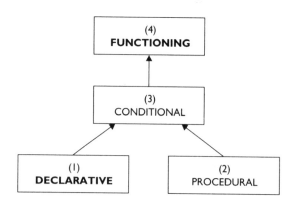

**Figure 3.1:** Relationships between different kinds of knowledge

which in fact starts with functioning knowledge (4) and works backwards – but we come to that in Chapter 11.

Leinhardt *et al.* (1995) make a similar, but more drastic, distinction between 'professional' knowledge and 'university' knowledge:

- *Professional knowledge* is functioning, specific and pragmatic. It deals with executing, applying and making priorities.
- *University knowledge* is declarative, abstract and conceptual. It deals with labelling, differentiating, elaborating and justifying.

It seems that would-be professionals are trained in universities to label, differentiate, elaborate and justify, when what they need out in the field is to execute, apply and prioritize.

Leinhardt *et al.* are making much the same point as Entwistle and Entwistle (1997): the forms of understanding that university accreditation and assessment procedures encourage are not those that are professionally relevant. The rhetoric is right, but in practice university focuses on declarative knowledge, which students often see as irrelevant, and hence worthy of only a surface approach.

In sum, if the target is *functioning* knowledge, the theoretical (declarative) knowledge needs to be developed to relational/extended abstract levels in order to provide both the knowledge of the specific context, and the conditional knowledge that enable the skills to be performed adequately. It is a matter of addressing and integrating several domains of knowledge. In designing our objectives, we should be ensuring that by the exit level at graduation, students' knowledge is alive and functioning.

## Getting the curriculum in focus

### Why use curriculum objectives?

At this point, we should distinguish between goals or aims of teaching (in this context 'aim' and 'goal' are synonymous), and curriculum objectives. All teachers have an overall aim or goal: 'to teach for understanding' is such an aim; 'to produce general practitioners with a concern for treating the whole patient in the community context' is a more specific aim, but it is still an aim.

An objective is much more specific; it not only refers to content topics, but also contains a *criterion* for the level of learning required, and that the assessment tasks can address (hence 'criterion-referenced assessment'). A 'performance of understanding' is an example of an objective.

Objectives are unpopular with some educators. They recall the bad old days of behavioural objectives, which many thought trivialized education (e.g. MacDonald-Ross 1973). Behavioural objectives were born from an exclusively quantitative conception of teaching and learning, which meant that when objectives were defined, the definition was in quantitative units of knowledge, while the assessment process amounted to counting the number of items acceptably performed. Teaching meant 'teaching to the test' (Popham and Husek 1969; Cohen 1987). The alignment was excellent, but what was aligned was a very narrow band of essentially low-level and fragmented activities.

With constructive alignment, on the other hand, objectives are defined not just in terms of content, but also in terms of the level of understanding applied to that content. The focus is not just on *what* students know, which is when teaching to the test becomes highly suspect, but on *how well* they know it.

But can complex learning be specified in advance to the degree required by curriculum objectives? Is it not like the drunk who only looks for his lost keys under the streetlight? In this case, what is interesting and important is what you can't see, not what you can.

Making the objectives up-front and salient is not to exclude other desirable but unforeseen or unforeseeable outcomes. The most interesting research is that which yields the unintended and unforeseen. Thus, being clear about what we do want in no way pre-empts us from welcoming unexpected outcomes from our students' learning. In fact, higher-level activities are open-ended, as indicated by expressions like 'generalize', 'solve unseen problems', 'develop a theory to explain why . . .'. Particular outcomes are here unspecified, it is only the process that is specified, and that allows for surprises in plenty. It is important that our assessment procedures allow students to pleasantly surprise us (see Chapter 9). Asking them questions to which we already know the answers, when they know that we know, is not only unnatural, it is asking to be bored rigid when assessing students' performances.

So we are not being rabid behaviourists, or closed or restrictive, in seeing objectives in terms of the activities we want our students to perform. Specifying objectives in this way gives us the best of both worlds. We are making it clear in what direction we want to go, but if a student wants to go further and explore the hinterland, that is even better.

### The relation between curriculum objectives and assessment

In aligned teaching, assessment after teaching has been completed is conducted to tell us how well students have learned what we intended them to learn, and at what level. This kind of assessment is called *criterion-referenced*, which is not to be confused with *norm-referenced* assessment, the function of which is to compare students' performances with each other, for example by ranking. Norm-referenced assessment should not apply in normal teaching. These two forms of assessment, the theory behind each and the procedures each generates, are elaborated in Chapter 8.

The curriculum objectives form the central pillar of teaching a unit or module, as we saw in Figure 2.2; they express what we want the students to understand after we have taught the unit, in a range of acceptability that is reflected in the grading system. Some students' understandings will be inadequate, in which case they fail. The understanding of some others will be passable, but no more than that. Yet others will display better understandings. A few, but the more the better, will have an exemplary understanding and control over what we have taught them.

The aim is to specify these levels of understanding in advance and embody them in the objectives. That is what we are going to do now.

### Steps in defining objectives

We might start by clarifying what objectives are, and what they are not. The following is not an objective, although it is sometimes mistaken for one:

> *Introduce the topic in terms of its relation to last week's lecture. Elaborate for about 15 minutes (no more! Watch the clock!), then the video* Coronary Occlusions: Part 2. *Get the students to converse in pairs, getting them to specify the links between the video's position and my lectures. Summarize and round off.*

This is a great way to remind the teacher how to conduct the class, but it is not an objective. Objectives are concerned with the students' learning activities, not the teacher's teaching activities.

But neither will it do simply to say that 'at the end of this unit, students will be able to understand the concept of muscle tone and its relation to functional activity' (taken from the objectives for an occupational therapy unit). What does it *mean* 'to understand the concept of muscle tone'? What learning activities are involved? What *level* of understanding are the students to achieve? The following further steps are needed.

*Step 1. Decide what kind of knowledge is to be involved.* Are the objectives to rate as declarative knowledge only: knowing about phenomena, theories, disciplines? Or functioning knowledge: requiring the student to exercise active control over problems and decisions in the appropriate content domains? The objectives should be clear as to what kind of knowledge you want and why.

*Step 2. Select the topics to teach.* Selecting the actual topics to teach is a matter of specific content expertise and judgement. You, as the content expert, are best able to decide on this, but note the inevitable tension between coverage and depth of understanding.

There is almost always strong pressure to include more and more content, particularly perhaps in professional faculties where outside bodies validate courses and when teachers share the teaching of a unit. All concerned see their own topic as the most important. Over-teaching is the inevitable result. We need always to bear in mind that:

> The greatest enemy of understanding is coverage – I can't repeat that often enough. If you're determined to cover a lot of things, you are guaranteeing that most kids will not understand, because they haven't had time enough to go into things in depth, to figure out what the requisite understanding is, and be able to perform that understanding in different situations.
>
> (Gardner 1993: 24)

If we conceive the curriculum as a rectangle, the area (the breadth times the depth) remains constant. Take your pick. Breadth: wide coverage and surface learning giving disjointed multistructural outcomes; or depth: fewer topics and deep learning giving relational and extended abstract outcomes. Do you want a curriculum 'a mile wide and half an inch deep', as US educators described the school mathematics curriculum following the abysmal performance of US senior high school students in the Third International Mathematics and Science Study (quoted in Stedman 1997)? Or do you want your students to *really* understand what you have taught them?

In fact, the area of the curriculum isn't quite constant. Good teaching increases the area, maintaining depth. But there are limits, and there is little doubt that most courses in all universities contain more content than students can handle at little more than the level of acquaintance. However, when modes of assessment go no deeper than acquaintance, as is likely with multiple-choice, the students are out of trouble and the problem remains invisible (see Chapter 9).

*Step 3. The purpose for teaching the topic, and hence the level of knowledge desirable for students to acquire.* Why are you teaching this particular topic? Is it simply to delineate boundaries, to give students a broad picture of what's 'there'? Is it to inform on a current state of play, to bring students up to date on the topic or discipline? Is it to stockpile knowledge, of no perceived use for the present, but likely to be needed later? Is it to inform decisions that need making now? These purposes imply different levels of understanding.

Declarative knowledge in a professional education programme may be taught for various reasons:

• As general 'cultural' content, as in the liberal arts notion of an educated person; e.g. a business management student must take an arts subject for 'broadening'. There is no functioning knowledge involved here.

- As content specifically related to the profession: e.g. the history of western architecture in an architecture degree. This is important background for architects to have, but again there may be little direct bearing on functioning knowledge.
- As content that does bear on functioning knowledge, but is not a priority. In this case, students might be taught the basic outlines and where to go for more details as the need arises.
- As content which definitely bears on everyday decision-making. High-level declarative knowledge is now not enough, but it is an essential foundation for functioning knowledge. In the past, the declarative knowledge alone has often been taught, its application being left to the students.

All these different purposes for teaching a topic or subject unit require careful thought as to the balance between coverage and depth. The curriculum is not a plateau of topics, all 'covered' to the same extent, but a series of hills and valleys. In an international phone call, you don't just chat about the weather. We need similarly to prioritize our classroom communications.

Usually, we spend more or less time on a topic according to its importance. That is one way of addressing the issue, but what we really mean by priority is that important topics should be *understood at a higher level* than less important topics. An important topic should be understood so that students can use it, or solve problems with it. With less important topics, acquaintance may be sufficient. We can signal importance by allocating a level of understanding for each topic. This is discussed below.

*Step 4. Putting the package of objectives together and relating them to assessment tasks so that the results can be reported as a final grade.* We now have a package of objectives that specifies the content and level of understanding that we address in our teaching, and that students will attempt to learn. The question remains: how do we assess these separate objectives so that we can derive a single grade category for each student?

Of the above steps, (1) and (2) are ones that teachers themselves can address, bearing in mind the points made above. Step (4) is a matter of assessment strategy, which is addressed in Chapter 9. Question 3 is what remains for this chapter: how to define our priorities as levels of understanding.

## Defining the objectives

We now look at how we may delineate the ranges of understanding we need in teaching our units, and to define our priorities in terms of levels of understanding for different topics. The levels of understanding can be

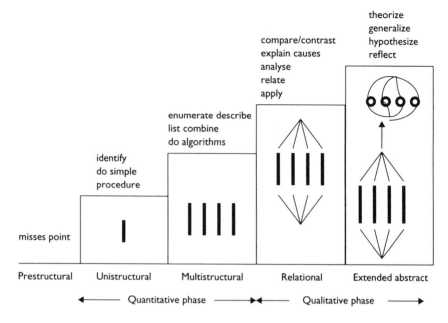

**Figure 3.2:**   A hierarchy of verbs that may be used to form curriculum objectives

described as verbs in ascending order of cognitive complexity that parallel the SOLO taxonomy. This gives us a wide range of levels that can be adapted to the levels appropriate to particular units, from first to higher years.

High-level, extended abstract involvement is indicated by such verbs as 'theorize', 'hypothesize', 'generalize', 'reflect', 'generate', and so on. They call for the student to conceptualize at a level extending beyond what has been dealt with in actual teaching. The next level of involvement, relational, is indicated by 'apply', 'integrate', 'analyse', 'explain', and the like; they indicate orchestrating facts and theory, action and purpose. 'Classify', 'describe', 'list', indicate a multistructural level of involvement: the understanding of boundaries, but not of systems. 'Memorize', 'identify', 'recognize' are unistructural verbs: direct, concrete, each sufficient to itself, but minimalistic. Figure 3.2 illustrates the point visually. A relevant component is depicted as '**I**', so that unistructural has one of them, multistructural several, relational integrates them with a concept or structure, and extended abstract generalizes them to a new area. With each step, typical verbs are associated that would be useful in formulating curriculum objectives.

The verbs in the staircase are general, indicating what each family, from lowest to highest, might look like. Particular content areas and topics would have their own specific verbs as well, which you would need to specify to suit your own unit. The following questions need addressing:

- Why are you teaching the subject? To acquaint students with the topics within an area, or as a central plank in their understanding (see pp. 45–7)?
- Is it an introductory or advanced subject? In first-year subjects taught for acquaintance, an extended abstract or theoretical level of understanding is likely to be too high for even an A grade. The answer also varies according to why students are enrolled: a pass in Anatomy I might be defined differently for students in first-year medicine, and for students in a diploma in occupational therapy.

These decisions will fall within the range definable by the four SOLO levels, which can be enormous, referring to specific terminology at one extreme, to theories and principles, at the other. It helps if we subdivide the SOLO categories. This can be done in any way that suits. An example follows, with (a) and (b) referring to simple and complex levels, respectively, within each category.

*Unistructural*
(a) Simple naming, terminology.
(b) Focusing on one conceptual issue in a complex case.

(b) is clearly more abstract and higher level, but is unistructural in that only one feature is given serious consideration.

*Multistructural*
(a) A disorganized collection of items, a 'shopping list'.
(b) 'Knowledge-telling': a strategy used in essay-writing in which the student 'snows' the marker with masses of detail, often using a narrative genre inappropriately but with the desired effect (Bereiter and Scardamalia 1987).

(a) is a simple list, which may nevertheless be adequate for some purposes, while (b) may well address abstract content and be quite impressive in its way, although in most cases the structure is simplified and wrong (see p. 40).

*Relational*
(a) Understanding, using a concept that *integrates* a collection of data.
(b) Understanding how to *apply* the concept to a familiar data set or to a problem.

(a) is a declarative understanding, (b) functioning, which requires (a) for the application to work. Many tertiary objectives require this distinction. We see an example from physiotherapy in Box 9.3, p. 183.

*Extended abstract*
(a) Relating to existing principle, so that unseen problems can be handled.
(b) Questioning and going beyond existing principles.

(a) is probably the highest level in most undergraduate work, with (b) a surprising bonus if it occurs. (b) is often called 'post-formal', the sort of understanding required to do postgraduate research (Collis and Biggs 1983).

As SOLO gives a good sense of the hierarchy in learning, it may be a useful guide for defining the grading categories as appropriate to one's own subject (Biggs 1992a). Individual teachers can use it or not as they wish, to derive their own categories. Some will found their own experience sufficient in itself.

However the levels are derived, they need to be delineated clearly, and verbs help in doing that. In particular, the use of verbs to structure the objectives emphasizes that learning and understanding come from student activity. Practically speaking, verbs are concrete, easy for you to handle and for students to understand, and they can be related to all stages of teaching: objectives, teaching/learning activities and assessment tasks. The discipline would determine what verbs would be appropriate. A useful exercise would be to list some of the key verbs in your teaching of a particular unit, at those levels you designate (see Task 3.2).

I have suggested the letter grades A, B, C, D here. Other systems refer to high distinction, distinction, credit, pass, or to number grades, 1 through 7, or 1 through 9. The degree itself might be graded first class honours, upper second, lower second third or pass. Grading categories are dealt with in full in Chapter 9.

The easiest step to decide is, what is minimally acceptable? That becomes D. This will almost certainly contain a mix of categories of verb: correct terminology, a certain amount of coverage, declarative understanding at a multistructural level for important topic concepts, but some room for misunderstandings with regard to more complex or more fringe concepts. The cocktail of verbs you decide here is a matter of judgement, but you should aim to define a certain quality of performance – a D-ness, if you like – that marks minimum acceptability.

Next, define A. What does the sort of performance look like that you would describe as 'the best you could hope to expect' in this unit, for this level, for these students? Of what does 'A-ness' comprise? Being original, using novel examples, relating to first principles, high levels of declarative understanding, demonstrated mastery over concepts and techniques – you'll have to work that out to suit the unit. But the *smorgasbord* of high-level, relational and extended abstract verbs will certainly help you to do that.

Having defined the limits, barely acceptable and marvellous, you can fill in the remaining categories of B-ness and C-ness (or whatever grading categories you use). I have put it like that, as X-ness, to emphasize that there is a flavour, a quality, that defines categories of performance, that can be captured with the mixture of verbs as applied to the unit content.

**Task 3.2: Devise a grading scheme for a focus unit**

Define grading categories in terms of levels of understanding that you think are appropriate to your grading system. Letter grades are used here (A to D), but write in whatever terms you use (HD, D, Credit, P, . . . ). Figure 3.1 suggests some general verbs to help you, see also the text (pp. 48–50).

A (or    ): _____

_____

_____

B (or    ): _____

_____

_____

C (or    ): _____

_____

_____

D (or    ): _____

_____

_____

Is it clear what you are trying to get the students to learn? How could you know if they have learned it?

The content defines *what* to teach, the verb to *what level* it is to be understood. Then, in Chapter 5, we see that the verbs also suggest *how* it might be taught.

The categories should not be defined in terms of ranges of marks along a continuum, such as 'high distinction is 85 per cent and above'. Quantitative definitions of a grade make adequate criterion-referencing difficult if not impossible. Because the target of 85 per cent is a heterogeneous sum, students have little idea as to what being 'highly distinguished' means in terms of their understanding of the subject matter. What qualitative difference can there be between 84 per cent and 85 per cent? But we are told there is a whole grade of difference: one is highly distinguished and the other only distinguished. What this tells students is to scramble for as many marks as they can rustle up. Any dispute about grading then becomes a niggling quibble about a mark extra here, a mark extra there. This can be demeaning for both student and teacher. Box 3.1 tells an extraordinary story of how badly this can go wrong.

In the case of defining grades qualitatively, the grade itself tells students something meaningful about the nature of their learning. A dispute over grading becomes a one-on-one seminar on the nature of their learning, why the level of their understanding falls short, and what they would have to do to demonstrate that it be graded higher. This is altogether a more

---

**Box 3.1:   How not to 'mark' a dissertation**

A student's postgraduate thesis, carried out at an Australian university, was submitted late, and given a mark of 76. However, during an oral examination, in which the student left the room in tears, one examiner persuaded the other two examiners that because of 'supervisory difficulties', the thesis be upgraded to 79, which meant a classification of second class honours for the degree. The student then raised other issues, including sexual harassment, and claimed her thesis was worthy of first class honours. An internal inquiry suggested that 79 be converted to 80, so the dissertation was now awarded first class honours. But the case was then referred to the deputy ombudsman, who advised that the 'real' mark should have been 73, when readjusted for lateness and the bonuses for stress.

A 'real' mark is surely that which reflects the genuine worth of the work done, but here we have a thesis variously marked at 73, 76, 79 and 80, ranging from second to first class honours. The variation is due not so much to differences in staff opinion as the intrinsic academic worth of the thesis, as to differences in opinion on non-academic matters – lateness, stress, supervisory difficulties and sexual harassment – which were factored in arbitrarily. The public, employers, other universities – not to mention the poor student – simply have no idea whether the thesis demonstrates those qualities of flair and originality that are associated with first class honours, or of the less dazzling but high competency that is associated with a good second class degree. It is ironic that a layperson, the deputy ombudsman, seems to have been the one who was least swayed by non-academic issues.

*Source*: From a flood of tears to scandal, *The Australian*, 26 January 2001, p. 4.

fruitful, meaningful and dignified encounter, in which some new learning might actually take 'place.

This chapter on deriving objectives has involved discussion of assessment-related issues, which in a criterion-referenced system are always closely implicated. We revisit some of these issues in Chapters 8 and 9, while Chapter 11 contains an example ('The learning portfolio') of deriving objectives that you might find helpful.

## Summary and conclusions

### What do we mean by 'understanding'?

While teachers universally 'teach for understanding', institutional obstacles often prevent us from assessing the level of understanding we should be assessing. 'Understanding' is a word of many values; we express one meaning, we assess another, lower-level meaning. In making our objectives clear it is essential that we unpack and make explicit the meanings we want our students to address. The very highest levels of understanding that we want students to display by the end of a degree programme – and in some cases very much before the end – are seen as performative. Students need to understand what we teach them to the extent that a particular sector of their world has changed, and is now coming under their control.

### A framework for understanding understanding

We need a way of describing how understanding grows and unfolds. As understanding develops, it becomes more structured and articulated, as described in the SOLO taxonomy. In learning a new topic, understanding moves through a quantitative phase, from uni- to multistructural, which involves finding out more and more facts. These are the 'bricks' of understanding, which form more or less elaborate and original working structures at the relational and extended abstract levels. SOLO provides a framework for formulating teaching objectives.

Knowledge is the object of understanding, but it comes in several kinds. Declarative (propositional) knowledge refers to knowing about things, and at the higher levels is about understanding theory in the abstract, but it is independent of the experience of the learner. Functioning knowledge involves not only the academic declarative knowledge base, but also the procedural skills, and conditions and circumstances for using them; it needs to be brought within the experience of the learner. These distinctions are important in sorting out whether students need to understand, as in 'know about', as in 'put to empowered use'.

### Getting the curriculum in focus

Before deciding particular objectives we need to:

1 decide what kind of knowledge is to be involved;
2 select the topics to teach. But beware: 'the greatest enemy of understanding is coverage . . .';
3 decide the purpose for teaching the topic, and hence the level of knowledge desirable for students to acquire. We need to prioritize, by requiring that important topics are understood at a higher level than less important topics;
4 put the package of objectives together and relate them to assessment tasks so that the results can be reported as a final grade.

Prioritizing objectives is done in terms of the verbs related to each level of understanding: important topics are assigned a higher level of understanding than less important ones. The SOLO taxonomy is useful for providing a 'staircase of verbs' that can be used selectively to define the ranges of understanding needed. Using verbs to structure the objectives emphasizes that learning and understanding come from student activity, while practically speaking, verbs can be used to align objectives, teaching/learning activities and assessment tasks.

### Defining the objectives

To define each grading category (A through D) qualitatively, the following steps occur:

1 Decide what is *minimally acceptable*. That becomes D. There will be a mix of categories of verb, allowing for low-level verbs and poorly enacted high-level. Aim to define a *quality* of performance, a D-ness, that marks minimum acceptability.
2 Define *the best performance you could hope to expect* in this unit. What is the nature of A-ness? Some extended abstract verbs, perhaps?
3 Define the remaining categories, B and C, using the mixture of verbs and content topic. The topic defines *what* to teach, the verb to *what level* it is to be understood.

Qualitatively defined grades tell students something meaningful. A dispute over grading becomes a seminar on the nature of their learning, not a demeaning quibble. More of that in Chapters 8, 9 and 11.

## Further reading

Biggs, J.B. (1992) A qualitative approach to grading students, *HERDSA News*, 14 (3): 3–6.

Biggs, J.B. and Collis, K.F. (1982) *Evaluating the Quality of Learning: The SOLO Taxonomy*. New York: Academic Press.

Boulton-Lewis, G.M. (1998) Applying the SOLO taxonomy to learning in higher education, in B. Dart and G. Boulton-Lewis (eds) *Teaching and Learning in Higher Education*. Camberwell, Vic.: Australian Council for Educational Research.

Toohey, S. (1999) *Designing Courses for Universities*. Buckingham: Open University Press.

Biggs focuses on using SOLO for defining grading categories and objectives, while Biggs and Collis go into the derivation of SOLO in detail. Toohey is concerned with designing courses (programmes), rather than curriculum objectives for units, but similar principles apply, and it is in any case important that there is consistency across units within the same programme.

# 4

## Setting the stage
## for effective teaching

**Effective teaching means setting up the teaching/learning context so that students are encouraged to react with the level of cognitive engagement that our objectives require. There are several aspects to this: motivation, climate, and the elicitation of the specific teaching/ learning activities that are likely to lead to the outcomes we want. The last question, what teaching methods to use, we leave to Chapters 5, 6 and 10. The present chapter is concerned with the two preliminary issues: getting students to agree that appropriate task engagement is a good and impelling idea (otherwise known as 'motivation'), and the kind of climate we create in our interactions with students.**

### The two faces of good teaching

In the last chapter we set our objectives by tying levels of understanding to the cognitive activities, expressed as verbs, most likely to realize those objectives. The function of teaching is to activate those verbs with appropriate teaching/learning activities, or TLAs. That is one face of good teaching: to encourage students to use a deep approach.

The second face of good teaching is to discourage students from using a surface approach. To do this, we need to identify any factors in our own teaching that might have this effect, and eliminate them.

There is a range of verbs from high to low cognitive level that need to be activated if our target unit is to be learned adequately. The highest would refer to such activities as reflecting, theorizing, and so on, the lowest to memorizing. In between are various levels of activity. When using a deep approach, students use the full range of desired learning activities; they learn terminology, they memorize formulae, but move from there to applying these formulae to new examples, and so on. When using a surface approach, there is a shortfall; students handle all tasks, low and high,

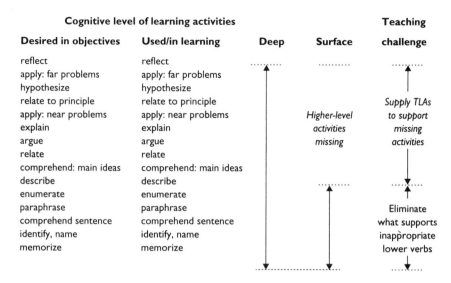

**Figure 4.1:** Desired and actual level of engagement, approaches to learning and enhancing teaching

with low-level verbs ('two pages of writing, etc. . . .'). The teaching challenge is to prevent this shortfall from occurring, or to correct it where it has occurred. This situation is depicted in Figure 4.1.

Supporting the full range of activities, the deep approach, is what the rest of this book is about. Preventing the surface approach is the main thrust of this chapter. This is a matter first of finding out what in our teaching discourages students from engaging the set learning tasks at the appropriate level of cognitive activity; and second, of doing our best to eliminate those factors (see Figure 4.1). These negative aspects of teaching are as much affective, related to feelings, as they are cognitive. They are to do with motivation, and the sort of learning or classroom climate we create in our relationships with students.

## The costs and benefits of getting involved

Level 1 thinking sees motivation as a substance that students possess in varying quantities: good students having lots, poor students little or none. Level 3 thinking sees motivation as an outcome of teaching, not as its precondition. Good teaching makes students want to engage the tasks. Two factors make students (or anyone) want to learn something:

1 It has to be important; it must have some *value* to the learner.
2 It must be possible to do the learning task; the learner has to *expect success.*

Nobody wants to do something they see as worthless. Neither do they want to do something, however valued, if they believe they have no chance of succeeding. In both cases, doing the task will be seen as a waste of time.

This common-sense theory of why students do or do not learn is called the *expectancy–value theory* of motivation, which says that if anyone is to engage an activity, he or she needs both to value the outcome and to expect success in achieving it (Feather 1982). Value and expectancy are said to multiply, not add, because both factors need to be present; if either one is zero, then no motivated activity occurs.

Expectancy–value theory is particularly relevant in the early stages of learning, before interest has developed to carry continued engagement along with it. The following true incident illustrates this clearly:

> When we got to the Psych I lectures, the Stats lecturer said 'Anyone who can't follow this isn't fit to be at University'. That was the first message I got. I *was* having difficulty with Stats and so I thought, maybe he's right, maybe university isn't for me. I liked the rest of Psych. but couldn't handle the Stats and had to withdraw.
>
> Next year, funny thing, I did Maths I and we came to probability theory, much the same stuff that I'd bombed out in last year. But the lecturer there said 'Probability is quite hard really. You'll need to work at it. You're welcome to come to me for help if you really need it . . .'
>
> It was like a blinding light. It wasn't *me* after all! This stuff really was *hard,* but if I tried it might just work. That year I got a Credit in that part of the subject.
>
> (Mature student quoted in Biggs and Moore 1993: 272)

This story has important implications for understanding what motivates students.

### What makes students expect to succeed, or to fail?

The student quoted above had initially been led to believe she had no chance of success. Her first teacher attributed success to ability, the student perceived she was not succeeding, so she naturally concluded she didn't have the ability needed. As this was something beyond her control, she concluded she had no chance of succeeding. Her second teacher attributed success instead to effort, which is something the student could control. With that came the liberating realization that what was certain failure could now be possible success. So she engaged the task, and did in fact succeed. The reasons for that transformation are instructive.

With a history of successful engagement with content that is personally meaningful, the student both builds up the knowledge base needed for deep learning and, motivationally, develops the expectations that give confidence in future success: what are known as feelings of self-efficacy and ownership ('I can do this; this is my thing'). The most direct way that expectations of success are instilled is on the basis of previous success, but only if the conditions that are believed to lead to success remain unchanged. If a student believes that a particular success was due to factors that might change, and that are uncontrollable, such as luck, or dependence on a particular teacher, belief in future success is diminished.

Westerners and Asians differ significantly in their attributions for success and failure. Westerners tend to see success as being attributable more to ability than to effort, while ethnic Chinese see effort as more important. This is possibly one reason why Chinese students do so well in international comparisons of attainment (see Chapter 7).

Norm- and criterion-referenced assessment send different messages about likely performance. In norm-referenced assessment, students see the game as competitive; to get a high grade they have to beat other students, which puts a premium on the importance of relative ability as determining the outcome. In criterion-referenced assessment, students see the situation as a designated learning experience; to get a high grade they have to know the goals and learn how to get there, with a premium on attributions involving effort, study skill and knowing the right procedures. The results of norm-referenced assessment depend on the abilities of other students, over which there is no control, while in criterion-referenced assessment, the results depend on each student learning the appropriate knowledge and skills: the ball is in the student's court.

These attributions are also sensitive to teacher feedback, as the student's story on learning statistics makes very clear. The psychology teacher's comment pre-empted student control; the maths teacher made students see that it was up to them. Feedback about process also encourages beliefs in future success, which again is easier with criterion-referenced assessment: 'This is what you did, this is what you might have done, this is how to get a better result.' How does norm-referenced feedback, such as 'You are below average on this . . .', help? What does Robert do with that information? This is not to say that some students don't want to be told where they stand in relation to their peers, but that information has little to do with teaching and learning. It is nice to be told that you're cleverer than most other students, but not very helpful for learning how to improve your performance. To be told, directly or indirectly, that you're less intelligent than most others is simply destructive.

To instil expectations of failure, as did our psychology lecturer with consummate skill, is easy to do. This is classic blame-the-student activity: attributing success to ability, and failure to lack of ability, or to some other entity that lies fixed within the student. A valuable act of self-reflection as a teacher is to monitor what you say, how you say it, and what comments you write in students' assignments. What does the subtext say about future failure? Task 4.1 asks you to think of the hopeless and hopeful messages you might convey.

## What creates value?

Next, we look at the second term in the expectancy–value formula. What makes a task worth doing? How can we enhance the value of the task to the students? The general answer is clear enough: make their work

---

**Task 4.1: What messages of success and failure do I convey to my students?**

Hopeful messages: *success is due to ability, failure to lack of effort or skill.*

Hopeless messages: *success is due to luck, failure to lack of ability.*

Think back on some recent communications to students, such as comments in class, body language, handling questions, writing comments on assignments, describing what it takes to succeed, descriptions of tasks, readings and so on. Do you think you convey hopeful, or hopeless, messages? Write down a couple of telling examples:

1 _____

_____

_____

2 _____

_____

_____

_____

important to them. Work can be important in various ways, each one producing a familiar category of motivation:

1 What the outcome produces (extrinsic motivation).
2 What other people value (social motivation).
3 The opportunity for ego-enhancement (achievement motivation).
4 The process of doing it (intrinsic motivation).

### 1 Extrinsic motivation

When students are motivated extrinsically they perform the task because of the value or importance they attach to what the outcome brings. There are two subcategories:

1 *Positive reinforcement,* where the student performs in order to obtain something positive following success, such as a material reward.
2 *Negative reinforcement,* where the student performs in order to avoid something negative, a punishment, that would follow failure or non-engagement.

The student's focus in both cases is not on the process, or even on the product, but on the consequences of the product: obtaining the reward that a pass will bring or avoiding the punishment that will follow from failure. The quality of learning is usually low under extrinsic conditions, particularly negative reinforcement. The task itself is instrumental; the focus of attention is on getting what you want, or on not getting what you don't want. The task is only something to be got out of the way. Extrinsic motivation is a standing invitation to students to adopt a surface approach. Negative reinforcement is worse than positive, because if the learning is not successful, punishment is implicated, which introduces a range of side issues.

### 2 Social motivation

Students learn in order to please people whose opinions are important to them. If the processes of studying, or the fruits of a good education, are valued by people important to the student, education may take on an intrinsic importance to the student. This is evident in some families, particularly Asian families, who have a high regard for education. In these circumstances, children are likely to accept that education is a good thing, to be pursued without question. Motivation here is not focused on material consequences, and indeed social motivation is a good precursor for intrinsic motivation itself. We can usually trace the beginning of our interest in something to someone else who exhibited that interest to us. We then want to be like them. This process is called modelling, where the models are admired and readily identified with. University teachers can be models, as was evident in the Oxbridge tutorial system, and often still is in postgraduate supervision. At the undergraduate level in today's crowded universities, however, many students are unlikely to have a significant, life-changing, one-to-one discussion with an academic.

### 3 Achievement motivation

Students may learn in order to enhance their egos by competing against other students and beating them. It makes them feel good about themselves. This can often lead to high achievement, and tends even to be associated with deep learning (Biggs 1987a), but the aims of deep learning and of achievement motivation ultimately diverge. The one is concerned with handling the task as appropriately as possible, the other as *grade-effectively* as possible. Achievement motivation in the raw is not a pretty sight, killing collaborative learning. Other students become competitors, not colleagues, and so steps are taken to disadvantage others: key references are hidden or mutilated, hints are not shared, misleading advice is given. Achievement motivation needs competitive conditions in which to work, and while that suits the minority of students who are positively motivated by competition, it actually damages the learning of those who perceive competition as threatening. Achievement motivation, like anxiety, changes the priorities of students because content mastery plays second fiddle either to winning or to avoiding the appearance of losing. More students are turned *off* and work less well under competitive conditions than those who are turned on and work better.

### 4 Intrinsic motivation

Here there are no outside trappings necessary to make students feel good. They learn because they are interested in the task or activity itself. They do mathematics for the intellectual pleasure of problem-solving and exercising their skill, independently of any rewards that might be involved. The point is to travel rather than to arrive. Intrinsic motivation drives deep learning and the best academic work.

Such motivation has a long history, which includes successful and rewarding engagement previously in the same content area. Susan does not turn up at university to study mathematics without a long and successful previous involvement in mathematics; she has not only a solid background of content knowledge, but also that extra spark that causes her to question, to wonder, to hypothesize alternatives. She is already motivated and presents few problems.

The problem is created by students like Robert. They will have their own, largely pragmatic ways of valuing their studies, but these values will be broad, lacking the focus on particular topics that interest creates. Their motives will 'derive from the meal-ticket, parental and other social pressures, possibly a generalized need for status, maybe lack of employment alternatives. Of course they want to graduate, in the long term, but that is marginally related to the here-and-now of getting involved with an academic task. In the absence of an immediate felt need, that need has to be created, and that is where selling the cost–benefits positively is so important. How can one create the value in the task if it is not already felt by the students?

We are quickly back to assessment. A common cry is that students will not spend time learning a topic if they think it is not going to be assessed. Therefore, the word goes out that the topic *will* be assessed, and so they had better study it. This is a double-edged strategy. If that is the topic's only value, then this is an excellent way of *de*valuing it. The subtext says: 'the only value of this topic is that I have decided to test you on it.'

In a criterion-referenced or aligned system of instruction, this does not happen. The reason why the topic is being tested is because it was thought important enough to be overtly included in the objectives in the first place. The fact that it is there establishes its value, even if the student at this stage cannot see why. Our conclusion must be: unless assessment tasks mirror the official curriculum they will erode it. Assessing outside, or below, the curriculum gives irrelevant or counterproductive tasks a false value, such as 'saying who said what on two sides of paper'.

It also depends on the kind of climate that has been created. I was told of one teacher who informed his senior undergraduate class: 'You're going to hate the next couple of weeks; I know I am. I see absolutely no point in this form of linguistic analysis, but there it is, it's in the syllabus and we've got to cover it.' Amazingly, the student who told me this had found that topic to be the most interesting part of the course, and was designing a dissertation proposal around it. Susan can of course cope with this kind of thing; she has her own reasons for valuing the topic. But Robert, who has nothing but the teacher's word for it, will see the topic as valueless, hence not worth learning, except for the most cynical of reasons.

Using social motivation is a far superior strategy than sternly advising students that 'it's in their best interests'. Teachers who love their subject, and show it, can be inspirational. The fact that here is someone who does perceive great value in it will cause the students to be curious, to seek some of that value.

Students need to find academic activities meaningful and worthwhile. Nowhere is this clearer than in problem-based learning, where real-life problems become the context in which students learn academic content and professional skills. When faced with a patient with a suspected broken leg whom they have to help, learning all the necessary knowledge leading to the diagnosis and treatment of the patient is manifestly a worthwhile activity for a medical student, and learning is usually very enthusiastic (see Chapter 11).

Teachers might worry less about motivating students and more about teaching better. That, in a nutshell, is what this section means. When they teach in such a way that students build up a good knowledge base, achieve success in problems that are significant, and build up a feeling of ownership of their learning, motivation follows good learning as night follows day. It is a matter of getting the causes and the effects right. 'Motivation' is best dealt with by avoiding what not to do. This is where the expectancy–value model is useful. Devaluing academic tasks by encouraging cynicism destroys motivation.

Teaching better is what the book as a whole is about. Establishing a productive classroom climate is taken up in the next section.

## The teaching/learning climate

Teachers create a learning climate through formal and informal interactions with students. This climate is about how we and they feel about things, and that naturally has positive or negative effects on students' learning.

### Theory X and theory Y climates

McGregor's (1960) distinction between theory X and theory Y assumptions about human trustworthiness is a good way to characterize a learning climate. Teachers operating on theory X assume that students cannot be trusted. They assume students don't want to learn, they will cheat if given the slightest opportunity, and so must not be allowed to make any significant decisions about their learning. They need to be told what to do and what to study, attendances need to be checked every lecture, invigilated examinations must make up most of the final grade, self- and peer assessments are quite out of the question, deadlines and regulations need to be spelled out with sanctions imposed for failing to meet them.

This way of thinking leads very quickly to a working climate based on anxiety. Theory X is in essence a blame-the-student model of teaching, and with that goes all the other baggage associated with the level 1 view of teaching.

Teachers operating on theory Y assume that students do their best work when given freedom and space to use their own judgement, that while bureaucratization of the classroom and of the institution may be necessary to run a tight ship, it may be counterproductive for good learning. Consequently, theory Y teachers take the opposite view on such matters as take-home assessment tasks, self- and peer assessment, class attendance, allowing students freedom to make their own decisions, and so on. You give the benefit of the doubt. Sure, some students may be more likely to cheat when assessed on projects than on invigilated exams, but the educational benefits outweigh that risk. Theory Y is a meta-theory that is compatible with the level 3 view of teaching. The important thing is to support student learning, not to beat student deviousness.

I have described pure cases here. An all-theory-X environment would be intolerable for students, while all-theory-Y would be near impossible to run efficiently. Elements of both exist in the learning climates we create, but in our individual philosophies we tend to lean towards one theory or the other. Our leanings may be because of our personalities, our own educational history, but hopefully most of all, because of our worked out philosophy of teaching. We should create the sort of learning climate that we believe strikes the right balance for optimal learning, given our conditions, our subject and our own students.

The way we lean translates into action at virtually all levels of student–teacher interaction. For example, when I told colleagues at the University of Hong Kong, where English is the official language of instruction, that I allowed students to use Cantonese in group discussions, because group interaction was then much livelier, a not uncommon reply was, 'But they could be discussing the Happy Valley race results for all you know.' True, they could have been. On the other hand, they could have been engaged in fruitful learning. It is a question of balancing trust, risk and value. Theory X operates to produce low trust, low risk, but low value; theory Y to produce high trust, high risk and high value – if it works. This book is about making it work. It can, as the following from an erstwhile theory X teacher suggests:

> The biggest point I have learned from this course is my biggest flaw as a teacher, that is, I did not trust my students to be able to behave themselves . . . [or to be] capable of being responsible for their own learning . . . I made numerous rules in class for them to follow so as to make sure that they 'behaved', did all the preparations and planning for them, giving them mountains of homework and short tests to make sure that they revise for their lessons and so on – all rooted from my lack of trust in them! And I dared to blame them for being so passive and dependent when all along I helped to encourage them to be so!
>
> (B.Ed. student, University of Hong Kong)

### How climate affects learning

The effects of classroom climate on student learning come about in several ways. Cognitively, theory X restricts the range of potentially useful ways of learning, particularly self-directed learning, as the above quotation illustrates. In terms of affect, theory X generates negative feelings, which distract from proper task engagement, directly encouraging a surface approach. The aim is to get the task out of the way. Theory X generates two counterproductive emotions in particular: anxiety and cynicism.

Anxiety, produced for example by intimidation, sarcasm, threats of failure, or heavy use of sanctions, simply creates an intense need to get out of the situation. The student's behaviour is therefore directed towards that end rather than towards proper task engagement. Anxiety makes a mess of a student's priorities.

Cynicism works in a more coldly cognitive way. Perceptions that the teacher is somehow degrading the task or belittling students by requiring them to behave in a demeaning manner, evoke cynicism, the reaction to which is a deliberate decision not to engage the task honestly. If the teacher doesn't take the task seriously, why should the student? There are many ways in which teachers convey cynicism:

- Showing lack of interest or dislike of a topic ('You'll hate this, but we've got to cover it!').
- Playing games with students when they can't play back, such as setting facetious distractors in multiple-choice test items.
- Theory X by numbers, for example drawing a line after the 2000th word in a 2000 word-limit essay, and marking only to that point. One can attribute all sorts of theory X subtexts to this practice, from a blame-the-student theory, to the delirious joy of exercising power. But the consequence is that the student's work is devalued. If a student exceeds the limit, it is surely to make the argument more clearly. Marking to the 2000th word tells the student not to bother with making cases in future, just list isolated points within the word limit.
- Discounting grades or marks for being late, or some other offence. Subtext: meeting a deadline is more important than trying to create a product of quality. This practice makes genuine criterion-referencing impossible. Issues of learning should not be confused with issues of discipline (see also Box 3.1, p. 52).
- Busywork: insisting on trivia, making quality performance secondary to bureaucratic demands or to personal convenience.

This last category is extremely wide. For example, refusing to accept student criticisms or suggestions as to content or teaching method, assessing for trivial content, being 'too busy' to attend to reasonable student requests. As a teacher educator and a teaching developer, I have to mention our own particular occupational hazard and come-uppance: not practising what we preach. As one student quoted to a teacher educator: 'Faculties of Education should not be advocating things for teachers or schools that they are not capable of practising themselves' (Fullan 1993).

*Time stress: coverage*

A particular source of both anxiety and cynicism is time stress brought out by an obsession with coverage. There are too many topics, yet each is taught with equal emphasis. Students are grossly overloaded, pre-empting deep engagement with any topic. There are many reasons why students are subjected to time stress:

• Lack of coordination between teachers in setting assignment deadlines.
• Insisting on the prime importance of what you teach yourself.
• Lack of knowledge or even concern about the students' perspective on the workload.
• Shared teaching and particularly shared assessment, where each teacher thinks their own contribution the most important.
• Generally, a lack of care and forethought in designing the curriculum initially.

Deep engagement in a task takes time. If you don't provide the time, you won't get deep engagement.

**Climate and direction: summary**

Let us bring the two sections on motivation and climate together. A theory Y climate is a necessary but not a sufficient condition for the cultivation of positive motivation. The teacher must further demonstrate that the task is intrinsically worthwhile and valued.

Expectations of success and failure depend critically on what students are most likely to attribute their success and failure to. How these attributions are built up is partly cultural, partly upbringing and partly what goes on in the classroom. Communicating the message that failure is due to factors that aren't going to go away, and that aren't controllable (such as low ability), is to instil an expectation of failure. Attributing failure to factors that can be changed, such as lack of the appropriate skills (these can be taught), or to insufficient effort (this can be increased next time), help remove the crippling incapacity that failure may induce. Likewise, attributions of success to a special interest, or competency, is likely to increase feelings of ownership and hence positive motivation. Attributing success to luck or to help from someone is likely to decrease feelings of ownership.

Finally, a theory Y climate does not necessarily mean a disorganized teaching/learning environment. An organized setting, with clear goals and feedback on progress, is important for motivating students, and to the development of deep approaches (Hattie and Watkins 1988; Entwistle *et al.* 1989). Knowing where you are going, and feedback telling you how well you are progressing, heightens expectations of success. Driving in a thick fog is highly unpleasant and so is learning in one.

## Improving teaching by avoiding the negatives

No doubt there are many other ways in which teaching can encourage surface learning, but the previous section gives the general idea. The first step towards improving teaching is to find out the extent to which these surface-inducing features exist in your own teaching, and who controls them. Those that are under your own control can be minimized or removed, while those that are under the control of others you may or may not be able to do something about.

### Finding out what might be wrong

Three possible sources could provide information on what might be encouraging students to react with a surface approach:

1 Your own reflections on your teaching.
2 The students themselves.
3 Informed advice from a colleague in the role of 'critical friend', or from a staff developer.

Much can be achieved by self-reflection. We can reflect on objectives, on alternative TLAs and on different modes of assessment, which is exactly what this book is hoping to encourage. The Approaches to Teaching Inventory (Prosser and Trigwell 1998; see also Chapter 12) is a useful instrument for clarifying your conceptions (views) of teaching and how consistent your practices are with those conceptions.

However, there are limits to what we can ourselves see as wrong with our teaching. We are likely to be blind to the more personal aspects, the kind of learning climate that we establish with our students. For example, what we intend as humour might come across as sarcasm; attempts at being friendly, as patronizing. Both are fertile breeding grounds for anxiety and cynicism. We need somebody to tell us such things.

Our students are probably the most direct source of this kind of information. It is, after all, their perceptions that structure the intention to use a surface approach. Obtaining student feedback is best done anonymously, provided you are capable of putting up with the jibes of the facetious, and the negativism of the genuinely disgruntled. You can use an open question: 'What aspects of my teaching do you like most? What would you like to see changed?' A positive note is better than: 'What do you see wrong with my teaching?' You are likely otherwise to invite all sorts of destructive criticism.

A structured questionnaire in which you specifically ask about aspects on which you want feedback, and which allows for positive as well as critical feedback, is a useful tool. Aspects of teaching that are likely to lead to surface approaches are listed in Table 4.1, while constructing a questionnaire to suit your context forms part of Task 4.2. We return to

**Table 4.1:** Aspects of teaching likely to lead to surface approaches

*Motivation*

**1 Conveying expectations of a low probability of success:**

- Oral and written comments suggesting failure is due to lack of ability, success due to luck or other factors outside the student's control; not suggesting how a poor result might be remedied
- Norm- rather than criterion-referenced assessment
- Lack of clear direction, no feedback, no milestones of progress

**2 Conveying low evaluations of tasks, cynicism:**

- Playing games with students at a disadvantage, especially in the context of assessment ('funny' multiple-choice alternatives; busywork)
- Displaying personal dislike of content being taught
- Assessing in a trivial way: low level tasks requiring memorizing only, marking only to the literal word limit, discounting grades for non-academic or disciplinary reasons, assessments not based on content taught
- Emphasizing rules and regulations beyond their functional utility. *Subtext*: Rules are more important than learning.
- Not practising what is preached. *Subtext*: You lot can do it, but it's not worth me doing it.

*The learning climate*

**3 Aspects suggesting theory X:**

- Negative reinforcement, use of anxiety to 'motivate'
- Blame-the-student explanations of student behaviour
- Time stress: failure to consider or appreciate student workload, no time available to students for reflection
- Students given little input in decisions that affect them
- Anxiety: engendered by harsh sanctions, bullying, sarcasm, lack of consideration of students' perspective, work/time pressure
- Cynicism: engendered by students feeling that you are not playing straight with them, that you don't believe in what you are telling them

Task 4.2 in Chapter 12, by which time you'll have a lot more information that will help you to change what needs changing.

Another perspective on teaching can come from colleagues. In this respect, a 'buddy system' is useful, in which two teachers in the same department, who trust each other, visit each other's classes as critical friends. They will need a common framework and a common set of assumptions about what is good teaching in order to do this well. We return to peer reviews also in Chapter 12.

Yet another perspective is provided by the teaching development centre, if your university has one. Teaching developers have the expertise

---

**Task 4.2: How can I improve my teaching? Eliminating the negative**

Construct a questionnaire for your students to complete that will tell you what you should know, but would probably prefer not to know, about your teaching. The focus is on those aspects that are likely to lead to surface approaches. What this really means is: what is it about your teaching that students might react to negatively, but for the right reasons? Table 4.1 is a source of possible foci. You might regroup under subheadings that you worry about, for example:

- *Interaction with students in class.* Do they feel free to answer questions? Do they perceive you as censorious, sarcastic, . . .
- *Direction.* Are they clear about expectations of what to do, for example in completing assignments? In carrying out group discussions?
- *Commitment.* Do they perceive you as playing straight, practising what you preach?

And so on. There are many headings you could use. There are some points about giving questionnaires to students:

1 Avoid the 'Kick Me' message. Try to work your questions positively; students can then rate them negatively if they wish. For example, don't ask: 'When I ask questions in class does my manner make you feel very anxious/anxious/not very anxious/not at all anxious?' Ask rather: 'How do you feel when I ask questions in class? – Very glad to be asked/somewhat glad/anxious/very anxious'.
2 Use open-ended questions at the end, so that they can tell you things that you didn't think to ask about.
3 Questionnaires should be anonymous. Making it optional, though, could distort the results.

---

to act as critical friend and to provide important insights on all stages of teaching where your own perspective might be limited.

**What can be set right?**

Having found out what the problems are, the next step is to minimize them. Some problems may be located in your personal style of teaching, which is what we are concerned with here. Others will lie in the institutional system and will be addressed as they arise in following chapters. Of those that reside in yourself, some will be within your power to remove, but others may not. The present task is to look at those aspects of our teaching that we can control.

Table 4.1 summarizes the aspects of your teaching that might lead to surface approaches. The list falls under the two headings of motivation and learning climate, although they do interrelate. Some of these things I list here as leading to surface learning – and therefore to be removed – you might think to be necessary, such as deducting marks for late submissions of assignments. I would make two points. The first is that while this is a common solution to the problem of late submission, it can get out of hand, as Box 3.1 tells us. There are other solutions. It is a matter of being consistent.

This raises the second point. Theory X and theory Y are meta-theories, like the level 1, level 2 and level 3 views of teaching. In other words they provide an overall framework that generates consistency across most teaching decisions. If you are committed to level 3, then it follows that you need to structure a predominantly theory Y learning climate where student learning is the top priority. This means using such features as criterion-referenced assessment, time for reflection, trying to eliminate anxiety and cynicism, and adopting the principles and practices of constructive alignment. Some teachers are more committed than others and will lay more or less stress on different aspects of their learning climate, but basically we are dealing with a package. In that case, individual components that don't fit the package have to go. Sorry, but you'll have to think of another way of handling late submissions.

Given that, the first set of decisions is to remove those aspects of your teaching that are encouraging surface approaches in students but of which you are unaware. Using some form of reflection, with appropriate student and peer feedback, it would be possible to at least lessen some of the things that are not right with your teaching.

Discouraging surface approaches and creating the right climate is to set the stage for effective teaching. The next and more important step is to develop those TLAs that promote deep learning. We take up that theme in following chapters.

## Summary and conclusions

### The two faces of teaching

Effective teaching involves maximizing the chances that students will engage the full range of verbs needed to achieve the desired outcomes. When students use a surface approach they engage only at the lower end of the range. The teaching challenge is therefore to prevent the shortfall of higher-level cognitive activities. There are thus two facets to teaching: (1) identifying and removing those features of our teaching that encourage the use of those surrogate lower level verbs, and (2) supporting what might encourage students to use the legitimate higher-level verbs instead. Much of the trouble of the first kind lies in the affective area: motivation and classroom and institutional climate.

### The costs and benefits of getting involved

Motivation has two meanings: it refers to initiating learning and to maintaining engagement during learning. To initiate learning, students need to see the cost–benefits: that engaging in learning has evident value, and that engagement is likely to realize that value. Value accrues to a task for a variety of reasons: extrinsic, where the consequences are desirable, either because they bring something we want or they avoid something we don't want; social, where the value comes from what people important to us think; achievement, where the value is ego-enhancement; intrinsic, where we don't even think to ask where the value comes from.

Some of these aspects of value are difficult to do much about, others are not. If you must use extrinsic reinforcement, let that reinforcement be positive rather than negative; you can show enthusiasm for what you teach and act as a role model; you can use norm-referenced assessment if you want to get the juices of high-need achievers flowing, or you can use criterion-referenced assessment if you want to address the *learning* needs of students. And if you want to get your students intrinsically motivated, teach properly.

### The teaching/learning climate

The quality of the relationship set up between teacher and students, or within an institution, is referred to as its climate: the way the students feel about it. A theory X climate is based on the assumption that students cannot to be trusted, a theory Y climate on the assumption that they can. If level 1 and level 3 views of teaching describe two cognitive views of teaching, theory X and theory Y climates are their affective counterparts.

If students cannot be trusted, tight formal structures with sanctions for non-compliance need to be established. Anxiety and cynicism are the result, both leading to surface learning. Anxiety distracts students: the point is to avoid the threat, not to engage the task deeply. Cynicism simply devalues academic work in the students' eyes: 'If you have to have all these rules, rewards and sanctions to get people to work, then the results cannot be worth much.'

### Improving teaching by avoiding the negatives

The two big questions for any individual teacher are: 'What do I believe in, a theory X or a theory Y climate?' 'What am I doing, unwittingly, that might be creating the opposite climate to what I want?' Teachers trying to implement aligned teaching must answer the first question with theory Y. Information on the second question may come from one's reflections, from the students, from informed advice such as that of a colleague, or of a staff developer. Each source provides a different perspective, but reliance on your own reflections isn't likely to be a productive source of information on those aspects of your teaching of which you are unaware. These can be supplemented with questionnaires, observations, and interviews, their focus on aspects of teaching discussed in this chapter. The factors that are likely to lead to poor motivation and surface learning are summarized in Table 4.1.

### Further reading

#### On expectancy–value theory of motivation

Feather, N. (ed.) (1982) *Expectations and Actions.* Hillsdale, NJ: Lawrence Erlbaum.

#### On classroom climate

McGregor, D. (1960) *The Human Side of Enterprise.* New York: McGraw-Hill.

#### On both

Biggs, J. and Moore, P. (1993) *The Process of Learning.* Sydney: Prentice Hall.

Further reading for this chapter is a tough one. There is plenty of theoretical material on motivation, but readers who don't know this literature already will have no time to read it now and transform it into functioning knowledge. Feather's book is there for those who would like to delve further. Most of the work on climate is directed either at school classroom level or at big business. The recent literature addressed to businesspersons is of the macho achievement motivation kind, not level 3 oriented at all. The exception is McGregor's original work on theory X and theory Y, which is well worth reading, but it needs translating into the tertiary context. The general principles of both foci of this chapter are given a more in-depth treatment in Biggs and Moore.

# 5

## Good teaching: principles and practice

**Now the stage has been set, we look at the action. Successful teaching is a construction site on which students build on what they already know. Teaching requires much relevant activity from students, interaction with others, and self-monitoring to check everything is proceeding according to plan. The teacher's role varies, from highly directive, specifying procedures and correcting errors, to supervisory, to consultant, to group leader. The role adopted defines the nature of different teaching/learning activities (TLAs), each of which is best suited to achieve different purposes. We visit a range of teacher-directed, peer-directed and self-directed TLAs. The focus in this chapter is on TLAs suitable for classroom situations of around 40 students or less, and in the next chapter, on TLAs for large classes.**

### Characteristics of rich teaching/learning contexts

In Chapter 1, good teaching was defined as getting most students to use the high-level cognitive processes that the more academic students use spontaneously. Traditional teaching methods – lecture, tutorial and private study – do not in themselves provide much support for higher learning processes. They work for Susan, but leave Robert floundering with a pile of lecture notes; a lot of trees but no wood. The challenge for teaching, then, is to select teaching activities that will encourage Robert to reflect, to question, to analyse and to do those other things that Susan does anyway.

Our search for good rich TLAs might well start by looking at good teaching/learning environments. Some general principles of good teaching emerge, which we illustrate in this chapter for the situation of up to about

40 students in the class, and in the next for the increasingly common case of the large class.

A few years ago, I attended a mammoth educational research conference: 40 parallel sessions over five days. There were hundreds of studies relevant to this very question of what contexts seemed to support good learning, and what did not. I attended as many as my spinning head would allow, and then read the abstracts of all the rest. On the flight back home, all that noise began to harmonize into a rough and ready factor analysis. Four factors floated into my ken. I haven't been able since to find any instance in the literature that gainsaid them. They are as follows (Biggs and Moore 1993):

1 A well-structured knowledge base.
2 An appropriate motivational context.
3 Learner activity, including interaction with others.
4 Self-monitoring.

The first two, a well-structured knowledge base and an appropriate motivational context, are at the same time prerequisites of good learning and outcomes of it. The need to know more arises from knowing a lot already; that's how the burning questions are defined. Answering them leads inevitably to deeper knowledge still. The better you have learned, the better you will learn. When that happens to students we call it deep learning, and when to teachers we call it research.

Creating an appropriate motivational context was addressed in the previous chapter. In this chapter, we look at building a knowledge base, learner activity, including interaction with teacher and peers, and students monitoring their own learning and teaching themselves. The use of educational technology in creating a teaching environment is of course very important, but it raises other matters that are best dealt with separately (Chapter 10).

## Constructing a base of interconnected knowledge

Sound knowledge is based on *interconnections*. Everything that has been written so far in this book about understanding, deep learning, the growth and development of knowledge, and intrinsic motivation reiterates this. Understanding is itself the realization that what is separate in ignorance is connected in knowing. Cognitive growth lies not just in knowing more, but also in the restructuring that occurs when new knowledge becomes connected with what is already known. Four general precepts arise out of this recognition.

## 1 Building on the known

The physics professor is greeting the new intake of freshers, still glowing from their A-level successes.

> '*Now. You remember the physics you were taught in sixth form?*'
> *Two hundred heads nod enthusiastically.*
> '*Well forget it. You're here to learn* real *physics, not the simplicities you were taught in school!*'

That took place many years ago in my old university, a perfect example of how not to teach. Teaching builds on the known, it must not reject it. In deep learning, new learning connects with old, so teaching should exploit interconnectedness: make the connections explicit ('Last week we... Today, I am taking that further...'), choose familiar examples first, get students to build on their own experiences, draw and explain parallels while teaching, use cross-references, design curricula that draw out cross-connections, and so on.

## 2 Maximizing structure

Connections are best drawn hierarchically, not horizontally. That is, we should help students to *reconceptualize* so that what are seen as differences at a subordinate level become related at a superordinate level. Let us take an example from the previous chapter: the concept of motivation. Extrinsic and intrinsic motivation have different, sometimes opposite, effects on learning; one is associated with poor learning, the other with high quality learning. Two different phenomena. Not so: each is incorporated within expectancy–value theory. The different effects are not because they are different forms of motivation, but because the student reads the value component differently: in one case the task itself is valued, in the other the task is only a means of acquiring what is valued.

In all curricula, there must be many specific concepts that seem irreconcilably different to students but which are actually different exemplars of the same higher principle. It is the trees and the wood all over again. In teaching, we should see that the shape of the wood becomes clear; that the students understand what the nodes in the structure are.

One can mazimize the chances of students coming to grasp the structure in many ways. New information should not be just dumped on the learner, in rambling lessons, or in poorly constructed texts. Good teaching always contains a structure, hidden away, but there to be found. Teaching from lists is like sawing the branches off a tree, stacking them in a neat pile and saying, 'There! See the tree?'

In some circumstances, it is appropriate to present the structure up-front. An 'advance organizer' is a preview of a lecture that mentions the main topics to be dealt with, and the overriding conceptual structure to which they may be related (Ausubel 1968). The student then has a conceptual framework from the start: as material is intro-duced, it can be fitted into place. For example, a diagram based on expectancy–value theory could be used as such an organizer to a lesson on motivation.

A 'grabber', on the other hand, elicits interest in the topics to follow: a cartoon, or an interesting slide or video clip. Whereas the advance organizer is conceptual, the grabber is affective, based on interest and familiarity. Both have their place.

Some teachers fall into the trap of talking down to students with an in-your-face conceptual structure, all answers and no questions. Lessons that are too well structured encourage students simply to take on board the given structure and memorize that, thereby establishing one of the lowest of the forms of understanding mentioned by Entwistle and Entwistle (1997; see above, p. 35). The student must do the structuring in the end; it's what the student does that is important. The challenge is to strike the right balance between presenting students with chaos on the one hand, and with cut-and-dried conclusions on the other, where all the interesting conceptual work has been done. The question of how much structure to present, given your students and their existing knowledge base, comes through reflective experience.

## 3 Using error constructively

In the course of knowledge construction, students inevitably create misconceptions, which need to be corrected: but first, you have to find out what they are, by *formative assessment*. This does not necessarily mean formal testing, although trial runs on final assessments can be useful. It means probing students' knowledge as it is being constructed, so that any misunderstandings can be set right, literally in the formative stage. To do this requires a theory Y climate, where students will feel free to admit error. If they think they might be graded on the result, they will be very defensive.

In a tutorial or group session where the tutor is censorious, or sarcastic, students will keep quiet, preferring not to make themselves vulnerable. This is independent of any particular teaching method. In an otherwise fine problem-based learning (PBL) course at a particular university, one tutor completely wrecked the process. The aim in PBL is for students to pose questions and to follow up plausible answers to a given problem. This they do by reference to theory, past experience, similar cases, etc., asking questions and testing possible answers in discussion. In this particular case, the tutor replied to every question put to her, all-knowing and sneer-ing: 'That's for me to know, and for you to find out.' So the students in this group gave up asking questions, and PBL acquired a bad name. So did the tutor.

Some teachers feel awkward about drawing attention to students' errors. In wanting to create a theory Y climate, where students can feel free to explore possibilities and ask far-out questions, these teachers allow misconceptions to pass uncorrected or even unquestioned.

The dilemma is: do I correct mistakes and risk discouraging students from expressing their understandings in public, or do I let them go uncorrected in the interests of maintaining a productive working atmosphere? Not to correct is abdicating from an important teaching function. One technique is to smile encouragingly, with 'Yes, not bad. Can anyone else elaborate on that?' This signals that there is a problem, and that we are getting on to a better reply, but not exactly what the problem is. The answer must lie in the interpersonal chemistry, the rapport, that a teacher can create, so that public correction is cheerfully accepted and appreciated (see also Anderson 1997).

Japanese teachers use a technique Hess and Azuma (1991) call 'sticky probing', which to westerners might seem a little drastic. A single problem is discussed for hours by students, with teacher adjudicating, until a consensus acceptable to teacher and students is reached. The focus of the probing is a particular student's error, which the teacher believes would be instructive to publicly unpack and reconstruct, with the student the focus of public correction. Japanese students, however, don't appear to see this as a punishment for making a mistake but as part and parcel of learning.

Learning from error thus presents two problems:

1 To get students to expose their erroneous thinking without risk of ridicule, loss of face or low grades.
2 To correct them nicely.

How one resolves this dilemma is obviously an individual matter, but it does need addressing.

### 4   Maximizing students' awareness of their own knowledge construction

Constructing a knowledge base is done not by the teacher as masterbuilder, but by the students using the materials supplied both by their teacher and by their experience. That being so, the students need to be aware of what they are doing, and checking how well they are doing it.

Monitoring the 'construction site' is another name for those study skills that involve self-management, including self-assessment. This is best discussed under the heading of self-directed TLAs (below).

## Learner activity and interaction

The last two characteristics of rich teaching/learning contexts, learner activity and interacting with others, provide some general principles of teaching, and a basis for classifying TLAs.

### The fact of activity

Being active while learning is better than being inactive: activity is a good in itself. Wittrock (1977) outlines one study in which students were required to learn from text in increasing forms of activity: reading silently, underlining important words, writing out the key sentences containing those words, rewriting sentences in one's own words, to the most active, teaching somebody else the material. There was a strong correlation between extent of activity and efficiency of learning.

In a quite different vein, MacKenzie and White (1982) devised an excursion on coastal geography in which each of the objectives was linked to quite dramatic actions, such as chewing mangrove leaves, wading through a muddy swamp, jumping across rock platforms, and so on. Recall on a written test three months later was near perfect. Spiegel describes a similar approach of 'adventure learning' to legal studies (see Box 5.1).

There are two factors at work here. The first is a matter of attention and concentration. Activity simply heightens arousal, which makes performance more efficient. Even physical exertion has quite dramatic effects on mental performance. Typically, four minutes of brisk exercise, such as running or pedalling on a bicycle, improves performance in such tasks as

---

**Box 5.1: Adventure learning in the School of Law**

Nadja Siegel, lecturer in law at Queensland University, is the winner of the law section of the Australian University Teaching Awards. Through adventure learning she tries to develop in students the skills they will need to apply professionally . . . She creates activities with an element of risk – physical, social or emotional – so that the experience is more real. Crossing a river using blocks as rafts, with one team missing equipment, forces them into deciding whether to adopt a competitive or cooperative approach. But she says adventure learning is not just games . . . 'you really need to be aware of how you're using the activity and be able to direct the students' experiences to the focus of their learning . . .'

*Source: The Australian Higher Education*, 26 November 1997.

mental arithmetic, after which time performance worsens in the unfit, continuing to improve in the fit (e.g. Tomporowski and Ellis 1986). It is obvious what is happening: Getting the adrenalin to flow increases alertness. This is one very good reason for breaking up long periods of lecturing with interspersed activities (see Chapter 6).

The second and more powerful factor is when activities are keyed to academic objectives. In this case, you get the benefit of activity, but it is *relevant* activity. For example, the role of salt in the ecology of mangrove swamps was an objective, so chewing mangrove leaves for their salt content was integral to that objective. Cooperating in building a raft is relevant for team management (Box 5.1). Declarative and functioning knowledge are linked, reinforcing each other.

We learn through different sense modalities, and the more one modality reinforces another, the more effective the learning. It is like trying to access a book in a library. If all you know is the author, or the title, or the publisher, or the year of publication, you could be in for a long search, but the more those 'ors' become 'ands', the faster and more precise the search becomes. Just so in accessing or remembering what has been learned. The more TLAs tie down the topic to be learned to multiple sensory modes, the better the learning.

Table 5.1 puts this very neatly. Don't take the percentages mentioned too literally, but the messages are clear, simple and basically right. Some sensory modalities are more effective for learning than others; the more they overlap, the better; and best of all, you learn through teaching. We shall be exploring the practicalities and logistics of that later.

Think of learning as stored in three memory systems (Tulving 1985):

1 *Procedural memory* – remembering how to do things. Actions are learned.
2 *Episodic memory* – remembering where you learned things. Images are learned.
3 *Semantic memory* – remembering meanings, frequently from statements about things. Declarative knowledge is learned.

**Table 5.1:** Most people learn . . .

| | |
|---|---|
| 10% | of what they read |
| 20% | of what they hear |
| 30% | of what they see |
| 50% | of what they see and hear |
| 70% | of what they talk over with others |
| 80% | of what they use and do in real life |
| 95% | of what they teach someone else |

*Source*: Attributed to William Glasser; quoted by *Association for Supervision and Curriculum Development Guide 1988*.

When we learn something, each system is involved; we learn what we did, where it was and how to describe what it was. However, they are not equally easily accessed. Actions are easiest to remember (do we ever forget how to ride a bicycle?), and semantics, what was actually said, are hardest. That sequence probably reflects the sequence of biological development: first actions, then images, then semantics. Be that as it may, recalling the context or the actions can often bring back the semantics; once we picture where we learned it, we are more likely to recall what it was that we were supposed to have learned. It's like accessing the book in the library. Thus even learning straight declarative knowledge is best done in association with a rich store of images. The adventure learning studies do exactly that.

### The kind of activity

Some activities are more relevant to our course objectives than others. MacKenzie and White's and Siegel's adventure learning contexts do not only provide powerful images to associate with declared objectives, those contexts require relevant actions. The TLAs address the objectives.

Lecture rooms might offer less scope for activity than wilderness areas, but the same principles apply. Students can be required to do more than just listen and take notes, but to do things that directly address what we want them to learn. One activity resource is increasingly plentiful in tertiary classrooms: other students. The kinds of activities that are elicited when students interact with each other greatly increase our options even in large classes, as we see in the following chapter. The problem is not a shortage of possible TLAs, but selecting those that will do what you want them to do, in your teaching context. For some purposes, lecturing is better than problem-based learning: not many, perhaps, but there are some. So any TLA is chosen because:

1 it is the most suitable for realizing your objectives;
2 it is practical to use within your context and resourcing.

### A classification of teaching/learning activities

Let us simplify by classifying TLAs according to who is in major control. TLAs can be *teacher*-directed, *peer*-directed and *self*-directed. Each typically elicits a different kind of engagement from the learner.

1 Teacher-directed activities include most formal teaching situations: lectures, tutorials, laboratories, field excursions, and much interactive software. These TLAs are by far the most common in undergraduate teaching, for obvious and very good reasons, but they are not the only valuable ones. Some are quite subject-specific, others suitable across subjects.

2 Peer-directed activities include both formal TLAs that the teacher may have initially set up and then left to the students to run, and activities set up by the students outside the classroom, including web-based activities such as ICQ ('I seek you'). Teachers may initiate peer activities and then withdraw so that the role of peers becomes increasingly important, but retain control in report-back sessions, and in orchestrating conclusions.

3 Self-directed activities include all independent learning and study activities. Flexible learning provides an instance where the context and materials are set up by the teacher, but the learning itself is self-directed. Lifelong learning is now generally regarded as a goal of tertiary education. Students need to know how to learn without specifically having to be taught.

Each kind of TLA best addresses a particular form of learning.

1 Teacher-controlled activities are best suited to dealing in depth with a topic; the teacher is the expert and can correct misconceptions and present the 'official' view. These TLAs are particularly useful for focusing on prioritized content; imparting, explaining and clarifying information; providing feedback; deepening understanding through interaction with students.

2 Peer-controlled activities are particularly useful for elaborating, broadening understanding, providing different viewpoints and perspectives, and obtaining self-insight by comparison with others like oneself.

3 Self-controlled activities are useful for developing in-depth understanding, monitoring and self-assessment, and independent learning. Self-direction is surely included in most tertiary aims, and is surprisingly underutilized despite the rhetoric and despite recent increases in class size.

## Teacher-directed TLAs

### Lecturing and class teaching

Lecturing is the standard tertiary method. The subject matter expert tells the students about the major topics that make up the discipline or professional area, and what the latest thinking is. The assumption is that the flow of information is one-way, student contribution usually being limited to questions and requests for clarification. Elaborating the material, removing misconceptions, applying to specific examples, comparing different interpretations, are left to the complement of the lecture, the tutorial.

Lecturing is used over an enormous range of class size. In classes of about 12 students and less, most teachers change from a straight lecturing style and become more interactive, deliberately eliciting contributions from the students, while for their part, the general run of students begin commonly to participate at about 12 in a group, the more so as the group becomes smaller. Of course there are large individual differences in how teachers react to class size, some managing to teach 40 and more in an interactive way, and by the same token, there are students who will happily respond interactively with a large audience looking on. There is, however, no doubt that class size has a crucial influence on teaching style.

The distinction between expository and interactive teaching is basic. Expository teaching is one-way, involving minimal interaction from students. It is appropriate whenever the teacher wants to tell the students something from a position of expertise. It is endemic in large classes, however, not because it is the most appropriate way to teach, but because many see it as the *only* way. We see in the next chapter that there are in fact many alternatives to lecturing. Interactive teaching is two-way, occurring more readily in smaller classes.

## The interactive presentation

The class presentation is a more interactive version of the lecture, more suited to small-class delivery. All the principles of good teaching apply: structuring, using the knowledge base, a suitable climate and so forth.

It is essential that the presentation has an implicit structure. This is where some 'inspirational' lecturers need to be careful. They talk well, they have brilliant ideas on the run, all the better for their freshness and spontaneity. They like students to ask unplanned questions, so they can think up answers on the spot: the lightning riposte, that's the stuff of good teaching! Possibly, in some cases, but probably not in most. There could be a role confusion between stand-up comic and serious academic.

Research into teaching expertise has emphasized two apparently opposed aspects: teaching as *management*, and teaching as *improvised conversation*. One requires meticulous planning and preparation, the other on-the-spot responding to events as they occur (Berliner 1986; Biggs and Moore 1993: ch. 16). The conversational metaphor is misleading if it suggests that spontaneity is marred by tiresome preplanning and schedules. It is not. You do not get relevant and high-level spontaneity without content knowledge, preparation and experience. The two aspects – deep preparation and spontaneity – are complementary, not alternatives.

Good improvisation is crucial in making the best of interactive teaching; questions and comments from students can be the basis for rethinking and reconstructing new and exciting ideas, if the ball is picked up and taken in an appropriate direction. The experience gives the phrase, 'the social construction of knowledge', real meaning. Papers have originated that way.

*Dealing with student questioning*

An important skill for the presentation is dealing with student questioning. This requires a knowledge of topic structure that is sufficiently rich and flexible that you can recognize the students' perspective of it and their access to it. It is not only a matter of having expert knowledge of your subject – that goes without saying – but of having 'pedagogic content knowledge' (Shulman 1987), which is jargon for understanding your students' perspectives on that knowledge; how they see it, and how their contributions can be orchestrated in harmony with your own expert knowledge.

Questions may be of different kinds. Important distinctions are:

- *Convergent or divergent.* Convergent questions are asked with a correct answer in mind, divergent are genuinely seeking student input.
- *High-level or low-level.* High-level questions probe the high-level verbs: theorizing, reflecting, hypothesizing. Low-level questions seek factual answers and tend therefore to be convergent.

Convergent questions are not necessarily low-level. Socratic questioning is a case in point. The teacher goes round the class asking questions that lead subtly to an answer the teacher already has in mind. This comes across as the social construction of knowledge: all contribute and agree on the picture the individual answers have painted.

Divergent questions are obviously useful for probing student experiences and incorporating them as examples of the case-in-point, and for student reflection. Divergent questions are best for high-level learning activities, but they can just lead to aimless rambling, and that needs to be controlled. In professional programmes, where the students have hands-on experience, there is a wealth of functioning knowledge to be tapped, located in a conceptual structure and generalized. But it can also be extremely boring and unproductive. Good questioning skills are required.

High-level questions need *wait-time* if they are to be answered satisfactorily. Thinking takes time, and high-level thinking takes more time than low-level thinking. Whether out of fear of silence, of impatience or just bad judgement, the fact is that in most classrooms nowhere near enough wait-time is allowed. When tertiary students were allowed unlimited time to answer, they averaged 9 seconds to answer a convergent question, and over 30 seconds to answer a divergent question (Ellsworth *et al.* 1991). The quality of response increased the longer students took. You might feel embarrassed by 30 seconds of silence, so work out ways of not being embarrassed.

*Concept maps*

Concept maps were designed both to present a structure, and to find out how students see the structure (Novak 1979). This makes it a very flexible device: it can be used by teachers for both teaching and assessment purposes, and by students for organizing their ideas, for example for reviewing the semester's work, for planning and writing essays, or for clarifying difficult passages.

In creating concept maps, students singly or in groups can be presented with a central concept or principle and they then generate sub-concepts that relate to it, or the sub concepts can be supplied. A taught unit could be the target. They then arrange the sub-concepts, either drawing them or arranging cards on which they have been written, in a way that makes best sense to them, the distance between sub-concepts reflecting their perceived degree of interrelation. Lines are then drawn linking sub- and central concepts with a brief explanation of what the link or relationship is. It is not necessary to use cards; once the nominated concepts are decided, they can be written directly onto a sheet of paper, and the connecting relation lines drawn in.

Creating concept maps is a learning experience for the students, helping them to explicitly structure their thinking, and at the same time the resulting maps give an indication of how the student sees the way in which individual concepts relate to each other. They can therefore be used for assessment purposes. Concept maps present an overall picture and, as holistic representations of a complex conceptual structure, are best evaluated by judging the complexity of the arrangement and the correctness of the interrelations rather than by analytic 'marking' (see Chapter 9). They can be used as feedback to see how teaching might be adjusted, or as part of the final assessments of student learning, or for students in their studying.

Let us look at two concepts maps based on the content of the previous chapter (Task 5.1), and then decide which is the better, map 1 or map 2. (Don't look at my analysis until you have made yours.)

The maps in Task 5.1 might be the work of students, or the teacher. A good strategy would be to get students to tell their versions, then for you to tell yours, and they can compare. It may well be that some students will come up with a different central focus, which could be as good as or better than that intended. Comparing different versions could result in some interesting learning all round.

In one study with first-year science and agricultural students, Santhanam *et al.* (1998) obtained mixed results. Students saw the value of the procedure but not its relevance: they thought memorization was the best approach to study in first year, and so did not adopt concept mapping in their own studying; a depressing finding, suggesting that the students obtained the wrong cues from the teaching or assessing contexts (see also Ramsden *et al.* 1986).

*Think-aloud modelling*

When presenting new tasks or problems it can be very helpful for the teacher to think out loud so that the students are clearer about what they are supposed to be doing. The teacher is doing the self-analysis and

### Task 5.1: Two concept maps of Chapter 4

Look at these two concept maps and see what you think. How would you evaluate them?

I

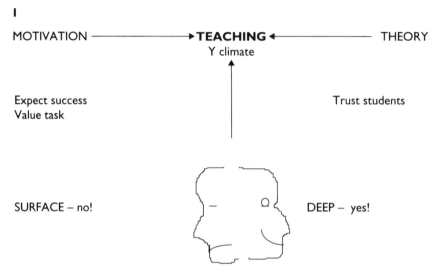

MOTIVATION ─────────→ TEACHING ←───────── THEORY
Y climate

Expect success                                    Trust students
Value task

SURFACE – no!                                     DEEP – yes!

**The two faces of teaching**

2

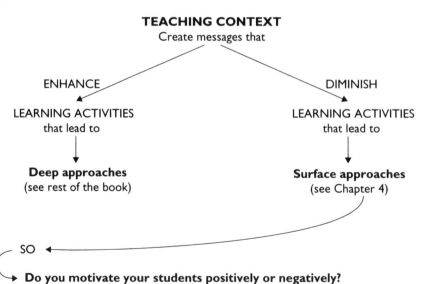

**TEACHING CONTEXT**
Create messages that

ENHANCE                                    DIMINISH

LEARNING ACTIVITIES                        LEARNING ACTIVITIES
that lead to                               that lead to

**Deep approaches**                        **Surface approaches**
(see rest of the book)                     (see Chapter 4)

SO ←

→ **Do you motivate your students positively or negatively?**

*What* messages do you send about . . .

• Chances of success – attributable to controllable factors?
• Value of the content – worthwhile, encourage 'ownership'?

*How* do you send these messages?

• Climate – personal relations with students, practise what you preach
• Assessment practices – comments, feedback, criterion-referenced

How do you find out *what* you do?

• Self-monitoring, reflection?
• From student feedback?
• From peers, staff development?

**Analysis of concept maps**

Figure 1 sees teaching as the central focus of the chapter, with motivation, a theory Y climate, and encouraging deep and discouraging surface as being essential for good teaching. Motivation comprises expecting success, and a task that is valued, while trust is the essential characteristic of a theory Y climate.

This is a distorted simplification. The giveaway is the overall structure: a 'star-burst', a central focus (which isn't quite correct, the focus isn't teaching as such) and sub-concepts radiating out from it. There are no connections between each of the sub-concepts, which makes it multistructural at best, in SOLO terms. What it says is that 'teaching is this, and this, and this . . .'. One more thing: it picks up the words of a subhead, 'the two faces of teaching', and makes that a dominating feature without explaining what those two faces are. Then the map itself is about the smiling face only: success, value, theory Y. In fact the message of the chapter is that motivation also has a dark side: expecting failure, devaluing, theory X. Which way are you as a teacher going to go? How will you find out? What will you do about it when you have found out? Map 1 completely misses these points, and shows that the chapter has been misunderstood; the student who created this one is in need of conceptual therapy.

Figure 2, on the other hand, links this chapter with the rest of the book, then goes on to say what the chapter is about, addressing those questions that figure 1 glossed over. The central focus is that messages that students receive from the teaching context affect their learning activities. Aligned teaching is one part of that: reflecting on the sorts of message we send that discourage appropriate learning the other part.

---

reflection publicly, letting the students know how an expert does it, so that eventually they do so themselves. Many teachers think aloud for their students automatically, but many others do not. Modelling is handy whenever you get the inevitable, 'But what are we supposed to do?'

In written tasks, using an overhead projector is an advantage because it enables you to face and interact with the class while at the same time thinking out loud, showing your notes and revisions, and mistakes, as you go. A writer can think out loud while planning, composing and revising, thus demonstrating the purposes of the various techniques that academic writers use. Students are brought face to face with processes and possibilities that they themselves would not think of, and, if the class is not too large, the students can call out contributions to the ongoing composing or problem-solving process. In large classes, you could nominate the front two rows to do this.

### The tutorial

The tutorial is meant to complement the large lecture. In the lecture, the expert delivers the information, the learners are passive. In the tutorial, the students should do much of the work, the tutor's role is to see that they do. They should set rich tasks, ask probing questions, challenge misconceptions, and overall manage the proceedings appropriate to the students' levels of understanding. Basically, tutors are there just to chair the proceedings. Students see 'good' tutorials as those that promote active learning, where tutors are able to set up a good theory Y atmosphere, to facilitate good debate, to open out the quieter students and to quieten the too open, and to provide a focus for discussion and interaction that requires students to prepare in advance (Anderson 1997).

Tutors should therefore be aiming to seek elaboration, criticism of given interpretations, and to develop different interpretations and applications of lecture material. Particularly valuable are the opportunities for students to see how others interpret the material, and to judge, with discreet adjudication from the chair, what are the best interpretations so that misconceptions are also corrected. Tutorials in the sciences often deal with public problem-solving, which calls for other skills.

If these are the aims, tutorials often do not achieve them. A poor tutorial is where the students are inactive. This can be because of group size. As the group exceeds about 12 or so, the tutor increasingly will take centre-stage. It is difficult to see how 'tutorials' of 30 and 40, as happens in many universities, can possibly do what they are supposed to do. Other universities solve the problem by scrapping tutorials, which they might as well under these circumstances.

Inadequate preparation, poor tutoring, or even the decision to go 'democratic' so that all the questions come from the floor, can result in the tutor conducting a question and answer session, with tutor as instant expert delivering an off-the-cuff and inexpert lecture. This situation is more likely perhaps where tutors are junior, insecure and desperate to impress. It is obviously important that tutors should be given clear training and guidance as to the purpose of tutorials and how to conduct them. Tutorials must be understood as the complement, not the supplement, of the lecture.

*One-to-one tutoring*
The classic tutorial situation derives from Oxbridge, where it was once the main teaching method. The Oxbridge model is too expensive for wide use in today's universities, but good one-to-one teaching may arise in two contexts: in the early stages of senior undergraduate and postgraduate supervision, and in some forms of interactive software, which could be used in flexible learning. Indeed, the paradigm for many computer games, where the computer responds to the player's last response, thereby increasing the level of difficulty as skills are mastered, is so effective as to be addictive. In general, this guided conversational style of tutoring is highly effective, but it requires deep and flexible knowledge on the part of the tutor to anticipate the tutee's responses.

## The seminar

The seminar is usually a student presentation on a topic that each student has researched. With senior or graduate students, these can be very effective, particularly if combined with peer assessment of the presenter (see Chapter 9). Unless this is conducted carefully, however, the seminar can become a surface approach to teaching, particularly in undergraduate years. It seems all very student-centred, but all the teacher need do is to allocate the topics and then sit back, the presentation also doing the work of the assessment. The major, if not the only, beneficiary is the presenter, and then only with respect to learning the topic presented. What the audience get is yet another lecture given by someone with even more hazardous lecturing skill than the teacher.

## Laboratories, excursions

These are usually intended as hands-on experiences and are subject-specific regarding intent and design, so I will not dwell on them here. Increasingly, there are virtual laboratories as mentioned in Chapter 10. Just one point: MacKenzie and White (1982) warn that if the excursion is not to become 'a bus tour', the activities need to be specifically and overtly linked to the declarative knowledge they relate to. Similar considerations apply to the laboratory.

## Peer-directed TLAs

There is much evidence that student–student interaction, both formally structured and spontaneous, can enrich learning outcomes (Collier 1983; Johnson and Johnson 1990; Topping 1996). The following outcomes are likely in effective student–student learning interactions:

- Elaboration of known content. Students hear of different interpretations, things they themselves hadn't thought of. This facilitates:
- Deriving standards for judging better and worse interpretations.
- Meta-cognitive awareness of how one arrives at a given position. How did the other person arrive at that conclusion? How did I get to mine? Which is better?

The meta-cognitive aspects are sharpened because students readily identify with each other's learning in a way they do not do with top-down teacher-directed learning (Abercrombie 1969).

Then there are the motivational and social outcomes:

- Interacting with peers is usually more interesting than listening to lectures.
- Increased self-concept, communication skills, self-knowledge ('I can teach!'), getting to know other students better out of which friendships may arise.

There are very many ways in which student–student interaction can be utilized.

### Peer groups (other than tutorial)

*Buzz* groups are ad hoc groups of students that are given a question or topic to discuss in the course of a class. The success of this technique, and of many multi-person group structures, depends on the size of the class, and making absolutely sure it is clear to them what they have to do. A question in writing is highly advisable. Brainstorming groups have a topic and no rules, except to say whatever comes to mind.

If the architecture permits, students can be allocated to groups of ten or so in the same room, but it can be awkward where lecture rooms are tiered, with fixed seats. Try outside under the trees. When the groups have reached their conclusions, one person speaks to the plenary session on their behalf, making sure that the spokesperson is nominated in advance. When reporting back, individuals then need not feel shy about saying something others might criticize: it comes from the group.

*Syndicate groups* are formed out of a class of 30 or so into 4 to 8 students each (Collier 1983). Each group has an assigned task. The heart of the technique is the intensive debate that is meant to go on in the syndicates. The assignments are designed to draw on selected sources as well as on students' first-hand experiences, so that everyone has something to say. The syndicates then report back to plenary sessions led by the teacher to help formulate and to consolidate the conceptual structures that have emerged from each group. Collier reports that student motivation is very high, and that the higher-level skills are enhanced, as long as they are addressed in assessment. Otherwise, students tend to ramble.

*Jigsaw* is somewhat similar to syndicates, except that the groups are more clearly allocated sub-tasks, and the plenary is to put the finished sub-tasks back together to solve the main task. This is a good way of getting a complex task handled where every person has had some active input into the solution. The downside is that each group only gets to see the working of their own sub-task and may miss the whole. Again, assessment is the answer: the assessment task must address the whole (concept maps are useful here, as they are what the whole complex is about, not just the sub-concept).

*Problem-solving groups*

Abercrombie (1969) worked with medical students in problem-solving groups. Her groups consisted of ten or so students, and the task was diagnosis, mostly using X-ray plates as content (about what the X-ray may be of and what it might mean). The principle is applicable to any situation where students are learning to make judgements and where there is likely to be a strong difference of opinion. Students have to construct a hypothesis where the data are insufficient to reach an unambiguous conclusion. Different individuals typically seize on different aspects of the data, or use the same data to draw different conclusions, so that astonished students find themselves at loggerheads with others equally convinced of the correctness of their own interpretations. The shock of that discovery can be powerful, forcing students to examine closely the basis of how they arrived at their own conclusions. Students taught in this way made better diagnoses, based more firmly on evidence, and they were less dogmatic, being more open to consider alternative possibilities (see also Abercrombie 1980).

In the School of Experimental Psychology at the University of Sussex, there is an interesting mixture between student-led tutorials and teacher support. Students give a 15 minute presentation that has been assessed by the teacher beforehand, each tutorial has assigned questions for discussion, and each student must put to the group at least one point in the lectures they didn't understand. Beyond that, the students run the main proceedings themselves, except that it was found useful for the teacher to turn up for the last 10 minutes. This has a good effect on morale, and allows unresolved issues to be put to the teacher (Dienes 1997).

In all group work, the students must have sufficient background to contribute, either from reading enough to have an informed discussion, or where the topic relates directly to personal experience. Above all, the group leader needs to be able to create the right sort of atmosphere so that students can discuss uninhibitedly. Some teachers find it hard not to correct a student, or not to be seen as the expert and the one to arbitrate in disputes. But to become expert arbitrator kills the point of the exercise, as students then tend to sit back and wait to be told what to think.

As to the optimal size of a group, there is no set answer as it depends on the nature of the group task and the group dynamics. The principle is that each member should feel responsibility and commitment. The larger the group, the more likely 'social loafing' will take place, one lazy student leaving it to the others to do the work. Interestingly, this is a western phenomenon. In ethnic Chinese groups, members work *harder* in larger groups (Gabrenya *et al.* 1985). This issue of group size and contribution is important when using group tasks for assessment purposes (see Chapter 9).

*Learning partners*
Students select, or are assigned, a partner for the unit. This technique is particularly useful in large-class teaching and is elaborated in Chapter 6.

*Learning cells* are dyads formed not so much for mutual support but for working jointly on a problem or skill. The justification is simply that students work better when working in pairs (McKeachie *et al.* 1986). This is particularly useful in laboratory situations, learning at the computer terminal, or question–answer on set tasks as in reciprocal questioning (see below).

*Reciprocal questioning*
Students are trained to ask generic questions of each other, following the teaching of a piece of content (King 1990). Generic questions get to the point of the content; in SOLO terms they are relational. Examples of such questions are:

- What is the main idea here?
- How would you compare this with . . . ?
- But how is that different from . . . ?
- Now give me a different example . . .
- How does this affect . . . ?

King compared these kinds of questions with equal-time open-ended discussion, and while the latter often gave longer answers, they were almost all low-level. On critical thinking and high-level elaboration, the questioning groups were far superior. Reciprocal questioning emphasizes that, when getting students to interact in order to reach specific cognitive objectives, make sure there is a clear, and high-level, agenda for them to address.

Forms of *peer teaching* specially suitable for large-class teaching are described in the next chapter.

## Self-directed TLAs

The aims of all tertiary institutions would refer, implicitly or explicitly, to the development of self-management skills. When the basic bodies of knowledge, and knowledge relating to professional practice, are changing as rapidly as they are, it no longer makes sense to teach students all those things they will need to know in their professional careers. While there are still vestiges of the old 'fill up the tanks' model of education (see Chapter 11), our aims at least recognize that the old model is impractical. Students should be taught how to learn; how to seek new information; how to utilize it and evaluate its importance; how to solve novel, non-textbook, professional problems. They will need high-level meta-cognitive skills and an abstract body of theory on which to deploy them so that they can judge how successfully they are in coping with novel problems and how they may do better (Schon 1983). Action learning for life, if you like (see Chapter 1).

We are dealing with three levels of self-directed learning, discussed next.

## 1   Generic study skills

Study skills are ways of managing time and space. They include:

- keeping notes and references neatly and systematically so that they can be found when needed;
- apportioning time and keeping track of deadlines so that all topics and subjects are given adequate time, and in proportion to their importance.

Generic study skills might be thought to be the job of high school, or of the counselling or learning assistance centre. Certainly they seem to be well learned in the university of hard knocks: adults are much better at such foresight, organizing and planning than are students straight from school (Candy 1991; Trueman and Hartley 1996), and women are generally better than men at such organizational skills (Trueman and Hartley 1996). Teaching generic study skills, particularly long term planning, has positive effects on performance (Hattie *et al.* 1996).

## 2   Study skills that relate to learning particular content

These skills include:

- underlining/highlighting the key words in a passage;
- reading for main ideas, not details;
- taking notes properly, by capturing the main idea of several sentences in own words, rather than copying every second or third sentence ('copy–delete');
- using concept maps to derive a major structure;
- composing essays according to a preplanned structure; using review and revise, not first drafts;

Consider this experiment, though. Ramsden *et al.* (1986) taught study skills to first-year undergraduates from a variety of faculties, focusing on reading and note-taking, examination preparation and writing skills. The effects were the opposite of what was intended: in comparison to a control group, the students increased their use of *surface* approaches. Subsequent interviews with the students revealed that they believed that to be successful in the first year you needed to retain facts accurately, so they selected from the study skills course just those strategies they believed would help them to memorize better. You will recall first-year students rejected concept maps for the same reason (Santhanam *et al.* 1998). Students get these ideas from hints dropped in lectures and from the general culture of the class. It is therefore important that teachers not only say that reproduction of lecture or text material will be counterproductive, but also show that it is not required in the assessment tasks. Again, alignment is the key.

Chalmers and Fuller (1996) recommend teachers embed useful study skills in their teaching so they are not only teaching *what* they want their students to learn, but *how* to learn it. They suggest sections of strategies for *acquiring* information (note-making, memorizing, skim reading), strategies for *working with* information (explaining ideas, organizing ideas, writing summaries), strategies for *confirming* learning (handling assessment tasks), and so on. These are adapted to suit the particular unit or course content.

The same applies to other study skills, such as the well-known heuristic SQ4R, used for reading text (Thomas and Robinson 1982):

- *Survey* – What is it about? What are the headings, subheadings, figures, etc.?
- *Question* – Set questions to be answered after reading.
- *Read* the text with a view to answering the questions.
- *Reflect* – How does it relate to what you already know? Are your questions answered? What else should it have said?
- *Recite* the important facts, quotes, that you will need.
- *Review* – Can you answer the questions in future?

SQ4R is as good as the use to which it is put. If the students think they need factual answers to simple questions, that's what they'll get from SQ4R. However, if the teacher models the method to the class, showing how to focus on themes and main ideas, and how to extract them from text, it can be helpful. It has to be done in interaction with particular content, where the teacher can explain the main ideas, and why they are important.

In sum, study skills are part of the teaching system and therefore should be supported by the context in which they will be used. It then becomes clear why those strategies are useful. Building knowledge is so much more effective when the tools needed for building are used on the spot, thoughtfully.

### 3 Meta-cognitive learning skills

Finally, there are those self-management skills that are focused on what the learner does in new contexts, which is the ultimate aim of university teaching. Perkins (1991) characterizes the difference between the study skills of the previous section and those of this section as the difference between 'going beyond the information given' (BIG) and 'without the information given' (WIG). In BIG teaching, direct instruction is followed by thought-oriented activities that challenge students, so that they come to apply, generalize and refine their understanding: conventional teaching at its best. WIG teaching goes beyond direct instruction in that the students are encouraged by questioning and support to find their own way out, as in the best examples of problem-based learning (see Chapter 11).

So in WIG we are not dealing with heuristics or other specific study tips, but with managing the problems and questions that have not been previously addressed:

- This is a 'fuzzy' problem; how can I reformulate it in a way that relates to first principles, and leads to good solutions?
- What do I know that might be relevant? What problems like this have I met before? What did I do then?
- How can I find out further information? From where? How do I test it?
- Let's try this solution. Does it work? How could I improve it?

These constitute a different order of question, using both generic (1) and content (2) skills, in order to organize and conceptualize what is known (BIG), prior to (3) reconceptualizing it (WIG). The verbs involved here are mostly open-ended: planning, theorizing, hypothesizing, generating. We return to this in Chapter 11 when discussing problem-based learning, and the sorts of problem that encourage WIG learning.

Alongside these divergent WIG processes, it is also necessary to monitor what is going on, and the testing of ongoing outcomes for adequacy, to see that learning is on track, which is more of a convergent process. Evaluating one's own work, of prime importance in everyday professional life, is one skill that graduates feel their university education least prepared them to do (Boud 1986). Self-evaluation or self-monitoring skills therefore need to be addressed. This is where self- and peer-assessment is so important, not only as an assessing but also as a learning experience. We deal with this in Chapter 9.

## Summary and conclusions

### Characteristics of rich teaching/learning contexts

If we are to devise and implement effective teaching/learning activities (TLAs), it makes good sense to see what there is in common between contexts in which good learning takes place. We find that they embody the construction of a good knowledge base, the perception by students of a felt need to learn, student activity, including social interaction. The power of a teaching method or TLA depends on the extent to which it embodies these characteristics.

### Constructing a base of interconnected knowledge

A powerful knowledge base is complex in structure and error-free, built on accessible interconnections. Creating such a base involves for teaching purposes: building on the known, making use of students' existing knowledge, emphasizing structural interconnections between topics, and confronting misconceptions students may have. These points should infuse teaching whatever the particular method, and can be helped with such techniques as advance organizers and concept maps to outline overall structure. Most important is to maximize students' awareness of their own knowledge construction, largely by placing them in situations that require them to self-monitor and self-direct their own learning.

### Learner activity and interaction

Knowledge is constructed through learner activity and interaction. Activity has two main roles. The fact of being generally active in and of itself provides general alertness and efficiency. Second, and more particularly, activity specifically keyed to objectives, using different sensory modes of learning to provide multiple access to what has been learned, is a very powerful way of learning.

Learning may be directed by teacher, peers or self. Each agent best serves different purposes. These agencies of direction provide a convenient way of classifying TLAs.

### Teacher-directed TLAs

Lecturing is the main TLA at university, although the size of class offers plenty of interactive modifications available within the basic 'lecturing' mode: student questioning, think-aloud modelling, concept mapping, and – to anticipate the next section – use of student–student interaction.

Other teacher-directed sessions include the tutorial, in which student–student interaction addresses those verbs that the related lecture could not permit; the seminar, which is nominally teacher-directed although most of the work is done by students; laboratories and excursions provide selected first-hand experience for students but require good teacher guidance to be successful.

Teacher-directed TLAs using educational technology are discussed in a separate chapter.

**Peer-directed TLAs**

Student–student interaction brings a different range of outcomes: elaboration, awareness of others' interpretations, deriving standards of acceptability, and meta-cognitive awareness. Student–student interaction can take many forms. Different results emerge according to the group structure and purpose. Peer teaching and learning partnership are particularly well suited for high student–staff ratios and are considered in the next chapter.

**Self-directed TLAs**

Self-directed learning is what university is ultimately about. There are three levels:

1 Generic study skills that apply to managing and organizing one's time and space.
2 Study skills that relate to learning particular content: of being given information and then proceeding paradigmatically beyond it.
3 Meta-cognitive learning skills of high generality that enable one to handle new situations where teacher-provided information is lacking.

In traditional university teaching, the teacher has been directly concerned with none of these, (1) being the province of school or specialist intervention, (2) and (3) being learned by osmosis. That position is no longer tenable: students need contexts that require independent thinking, and that allow them to flex their meta-cognitive muscles.

## Further reading

**On good teaching/learning contexts and principle of good teaching**

Biggs, J. and Moore, P. (1993) *The Process of Learning.* Sydney: Prentice Hall, chapters 16 and 17.
Fuller, R. (1998) Encouraging active learning at university, *HERDSA News,* 20(3): 1–5.
Jackson, M. (1997) But learners learn more, *Higher Education Research and Development,* 16: 101–10.
Ramsden, P. (1992) *Learning to Teach in Higher Education.* London: Routledge, chapter 6.

Biggs and Moore describe rich learning contexts and the conditions for good learning, and summarize research on expert teaching. Ramsden deals with six key principles of effective teaching. Fuller's article is very rich yet practical. Jackson's title comes from Comenius: 'The main object is to find a method in which teachers teach less but learners learn more . . .'. Exactly.

### On good teaching practices

(On lecturing – see next chapter.)

Brown, G. and Atkins, M. (1988) *Effective Teaching in Higher Education.* London: Methuen.

Chalmers, D. and Fuller, R. (1996) *Teaching for Learning at University.* London: Kogan Page.

*HERDSA News.* The newsletter of the Higher Education Research and Development Society of Australasia. There are three issues a year, each containing at least one highly practical article of the 'it worked for me, why don't you have a go?' variety.

Race, P. and Brown, S. (1993) *500 Tips for Tutors.* London: Kogan Page.

Society for Research into Higher Education newsletter.

Just a sample of the many books on good teaching practice. The 'tips for . . . ' genre contains useful collections of procedures but you must use your own judgement as to their applicability to your own problems. There is a danger of falling into the level 2 mode: tell me what are good teaching techniques and I'll use them. You know by now it doesn't work like that. Chalmers and Fuller remind you to teach students how to handle the information you are teaching them.

### On using groups

Abercrombie, M.L.J. (1980) *Aims and Techniques of Group Teaching.* London: Society for Research into Higher Education.

Collier, K.G. (1983) *The Management of Peer-group Learning: Syndicate Methods in Higher Education.* Guildford: Society for Research into Higher Education.

Johnson, D.W. and Johnson, R.T. (1990) *Learning Together and Alone: Co-operation, Competition and Individualisation.* Englewood Cliffs, NJ: Prentice Hall.

The first two are practical accounts of using groups effectively. Johnson and Johnson is the latest edition of a classic on setting up cooperative learning groups.

# 6

# Enriching large-class teaching

**The lecture is the standard method for teaching large classes. Its strengths lie in communicating (1) information, and (2) the teacher's personal interpretations, but it makes demands on concentration that drastically undermine its value if not properly handled. This chapter suggests how the lecture can be made more effective, using periodic pauses, changes in activity that clarify and elaborate the lecture content, and active review by students. Other large-class TLAs are peer-directed, such as learning partners, various kinds of group work both in and out of class, and peer teaching; and self-directed, particularly in conjunction with teacher-prepared flexible learning materials used on- or off-campus. Class size, although constraining, is no reason to abandon the principle of alignment. It is a different context for learning, not necessarily a worse one.**

## The ubiquitous lecture

In the early 1970s, a celebrated lecturer, a Dr Fox, did a circuit of several US university medical faculties. He was hugely successful wherever he went; the student ratings were highly positive, praising him particularly as an inspirational teacher, and a master in total command of his subject matter. It turns out that Dr Fox was a professional actor, whose only knowledge of the field was supplied by a *Reader's Digest* article (Ware and Williams 1975). This study has been used:

1 to call student ratings of teaching into question, on the grounds that a clever presentation can mask real deficiencies in substance;
2 to support the idea that lectures may motivate, and even inspire students.

Both conclusions are inappropriate.

Very few teachers are professional actors, or have any training in public speaking. The normal class lecture is not a one-off event with a billed guest speaker, but the regular method of teaching throughout the semester. The majority of academics do not have the personal gifts, or the rhetorical skills, to be able to perform centre-stage, inspiring students day after day. Those who think that they can do so are likely to be deluding themselves. My point is not that large-class lecturing should be subcontracted to professional actors, but to seek how we can best use the situation, one teacher/ many students, more realistically.

We look at ways of enriching the teaching of large classes from two points of view: (1) examining ways of increasing the cognitive range of the lecture, and (2) looking at alternatives to the lecture for handling these high student–staff ratios. First, let us see what the lecture can do, and what it cannot do.

## Advantages and limitations of the lecture

One attraction of the lecture is that it accommodates large fluctuations in student numbers. It has therefore become the method for all seasons. It is assumed that if you know your subject, and do not have any speech defects, you can deliver a passable lecture. That assumption needs examining closely.

Classic reviews of the lecture method were conducted by Bligh (1972), and (McLeish 1976). Bligh reviewed nearly a hundred studies comparing lecturing with other methods, mostly group discussions or reading, and found the following:

1 Lectures are as effective as other methods for *teaching information*, but not more effective. Forty studies suggested that unsupervised reading is better than lecturing.
2 Lectures are quite ineffective for stimulating *higher-order thinking*. Examples of the latter included: amount of outside reading, considering more than one authority, problem-solving, decision-making, application of principles, creativity, undertaking higher degree work. Of 26 studies reviewed, not one favoured the lecture over other methods on any of these highly desirable criteria.
3 Lectures cannot be relied on to inspire or to change students' attitudes favourably. One study did favour the lecture, but that only reiterates the point that while exceptional orators might inspire (see Box 6.1, no. 2), most teachers do not but many believe that they do.
4 Students like really good lectures, but as a rule prefer well-conducted group-work.

So, if lectures do not inspire students, and are only as good as other methods for passing on information, how can they be justified? What can the lecture do that books and groups cannot?

Many university teachers, through their research and scholarship, have developed a perspective on their field of expertise that is not to be found in textbooks. Textbooks do not usually have an 'angle', a perspective, but are more often a multistructural list of things that every first-year student might ever need to know. Who better to provide a critical perspective on that bland display of knowledge than the teacher at the cutting edge of the topic, and in person? Through sheer publication lag between a paper appearing in the journals, textbooks are easily two or more years out of date, and active researchers are not. The best defence of the lecture, particularly in senior undergraduate years, thus lies not in doing what other media do as well or better, but in exposing students to the most recent developments in the field, and to the ongoing workings of a scholarly mind. Where does that leave lecturers who aren't front-line researchers? Hopefully, looking for alternatives to the lecture.

The unique contribution of the lecture thus derives from the nexus between research and teaching. This role is most recognizable today in supervising research students. In the undergraduate years, sheer student numbers have weakened that role of active scholar-cum-mentor, but not entirely. It is still possible to provide that personal perspective on knowledge, both on the process of constructing and validating knowledge and on interpreting the outcome. Heaven forbid that teachers have reached the demeaning point where all that remains is to tell students content that they can read more effectively.

In short, the teacher should be an agent for *transforming* knowledge, helping students to interpret and to construct their own knowledge, not a passive substation that relays pre-formed messages to them. The teacher is, as it were, a master craftsman, the student an apprentice in the craft of scholarship. This is where modelling might come in, and where the word 'inspire' becomes relevant.

The lecture is therefore as good as the lecturer, not as crowd-pleaser but as scholar. So, if you want to use the lecture as your predominant method, the question is: can you offer your students something that the textbook or other sources cannot? If the answer to that is in the negative, and you are not a highly skilled orator, you should, if you can, use the lecture sparingly. Box 6.1 gives examples of two successful lecturing styles.

## Psychological constraints

Many of the lecture's limitations arise from certain facts about human learning:

---

**Box 6.1:    Two prize-winning approaches to lecturing**

*1 Conceptualization through questions and relevance*
Judy Cowie, lecturer in economics at the University of Adelaide, National
CAUT Fellow 1996 pioneered the 'Adelaide method', where workshops and
tutorials are held before lectures, so that students can approach lecture
material with increased confidence. Ms Cowie never presents text book
material in lectures and allows question-and-answer time, even with hundreds of students, . . . relating key concepts to newspaper articles and television reports.

*Source: The Weekend Australian, 26–27 July 1997.*

*2 Conceptualization through infectious enthusiasm*
Dr Alastair Greig, lecturer in sociology, Australian National University, won
the Australian University Teaching Award in the social science section, with
the 'highest student approval ratings the panel had seen' – and with a Glaswe-
gian accent so broad 'my students think I stepped off the boat yesterday'. His
style is described as 'infectiously enthusiastic'. He starts each lecture with
appropriate cartoons, poems, or songs and distributes typed lecture notes
'so students . . . can concentrate on listening.'

*Source: The Australian Higher Education, 26 November 1997.*

---

1 Sustained and unchanging low-level activity lowers concentration. Sitting
  listening to a lecture is such an activity. Yet it requires concentrated
  effort to follow lecture content.
2 The attention span of students under these conditions can be maintained
  for about 10 to 15 minutes, after which learning drops off rapidly (see
  Figure 6.1).
3 A short rest period, or simply a *change* in activity, after about 15 minutes
  leads to a restoration of performance almost to the original level (see
  Figure 6.1).
4 A brief period of consolidation after prolonged learning greatly en-
  hances retention. Getting students to review at the end of the lecture
  what has been learned leads to much better and lasting retention than
  simply finishing and dismissing the students (see Figure 6.2).
5 The low-level outcomes usually gained from the lecture are in large part
  due to the unbroken activities of listening and note-taking.

Figure 6.1 shows, first, the rapid drop-off in attention and therefore in
effective learning as a function of time into the lecture, then the recuper-
ative effect of a rest or change of activity after about 20 minutes. That 20
minutes might be 10, 30, or even longer. It depends on the students, the

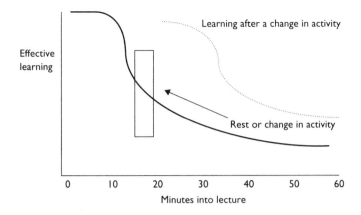

**Figure 6.1:**   Effect on rest or change of activity on learning
*Source:* After Bligh 1971.

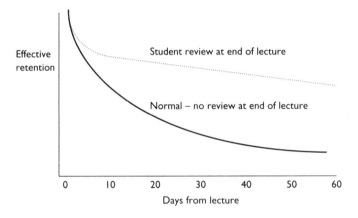

**Figure 6.2:**   Effect of testing at end of lecture on retention
*Source:* After Bligh 1971.

skill of the lecturer, the pace of the lecture, the difficulty of the material, the use of educational technology (which involves a change of activity), the time of day, and so on. But the basic point remains: do not talk longer than 15 or 20 minutes without a pause, unless you are certain you still have the students' attention. When you do pause, get the students to change their activity.

Figure 6.2 suggests that you should *consolidate* what has been dealt with in a learning session if it is to be retained for a significant period of time. In the original study on which the figure is based, the consolidation was determined by asking students about the lecture content at the end of the lecture. They were required to *actively review* what they had just learned. That does not mean that you tell them what you've just told them, as in the conventional summary (although you can do that too); if means that you get them to tell you, or a neighbour, what you have just told them. They need to be active in reviewing what they have been exposed to in the previous 50 minutes or so.

Interposing breaks with a different focused activity during the lecture, and active review after, helps to lift the quality of learning outcomes, as in (5) above.

We arrive yet again at the fundamental premise of this book: 'it's what the student does . . .' And that is the basic problem with the lecture. Both teacher and students see the lecture as a matter of teacher performance, not of learner performance. It is a perception that has to be reversed.

In sum, while lectures can convey information to students, the usual form – talking on the one hand, listening and note-taking on the other – does not get students to think critically or creatively, nor does it motivate them. Yet as budgets get tighter, and student–staff ratios larger, the lecture is likely to become even more entrenched.

Think of the large-class situation as a plenary session, rather than as a 'lecture', where the session chairperson is not endlessly talking. When lectures are scheduled, think of it as a timeslot that has been fixed for the plenary session. What happens within that slot need not be lecturing. The question is how to use the time most usefully. There are two rather different aspects to this:

1 *Managerial,* dealing with large numbers of people at a time.
2 *Educational,* using that space for effective learning.

## Management skills for large-class teaching

Management issues are paramount in large-class teaching (see, for example, Gibbs *et al.* 1984; Brown and Atkins 1988; Gibbs and Jenkins 1992; Davis and McLeod 1996a). Davis and McLeod define large-class teaching from two points of view:

1 The teacher's, when the group size, about 40 students or more, prevents the use of strategies that depend on close contact.
2 The student's, when the individual begins to feel anonymous.

This implies two almost contradictory sets of management strategies:

1 'Close contact' strategies won't work, so that specific large-class strategies will need to be acquired.
2 The anonymity the students feel needs to be counteracted.

Paradoxically, we use large-class techniques so that students don't feel that they are in a large class. In meeting this challenge, we are cheerily assured that large-class teaching isn't just making the best of a bad job, but holds its 'own delights and advantages'. Large classes actually allow a teacher to achieve quite easily some things that are more difficult to achieve in small groups' (Davis and McLeod 1996a: 3). This is an important realization. On the other hand, large-class teaching is difficult and requires self-assurance and experience. It is quite irresponsible to allocate the largest classes of first years to the least experienced and junior staff members, as so often happens.

Following are some suggestions for managing large classes. Many of the skills needed are different from the presentation skills mentioned in the previous chapter.

## Preparatory

Large classes need much more meticulous preparation than small classes. The larger the class, the slower things get done. A spur-of-the-moment change of direction, perhaps in response to a student question, highly desirable and manageable with a group of 30, becomes perilous with 300.

Preparation includes planning the academic content, the management procedures, and preparing mentally. Most people find large-class teaching more of a performance, with the increased likelihood of stage-fright, than teaching smaller classes. Even experienced teachers need time beforehand to collect themselves.

### Academic structure

You should make the purposes of each session clearly explicit well in advance. Is it to outline the boundaries or coverage of the topic/unit, to go in depth into a particular topic or series of topics, to make a case or argument in depth, to use as an outline or summary session, or to challenge previously accepted points?

### Materials

Notes, handouts, overhead transparencies, etc. need to be organized before the class, ready to be used. If you are using overheads and you suddenly decide to change the order it can be fatal. Don't sort material on the run.

### Procedural rules

This slow, heaving hulk needs to be carefully directed, otherwise it will crush your plans. Establish your procedural rules at the outset, in writing where appropriate: signals for silence, signals for starting and stopping; if you are going to use buzz groups, who is to discuss with whom, who is to be spokesperson on report back. How do you bring the students back to order when it's time? Davis and McLeod (1996a) suggest playing lively music to accompany discussion; when it stops, it's back to the lecturer. Establish the rules in the first session.

*Questioning*

Questioning in a large group needs quite different procedures from that adopted in a small group. Some teachers allow questions only at the end of the lecture, some at any time, some only one-to-one afterwards. Do the students know your rules/expectations about questioning? Are you going to pause and ask: 'Any questions?' How are you going to deal with the forest of hands; or with the clown who always asks questions to class groans? What about those students who irritatingly wait behind to ask you a terrific question that should have been aired in class, or to point out that the deadline won't work. These are whole-class matters. You should discuss these issues and design a procedure for dealing with questions.

Dealing with questions requires large-class technique. Questions provide a welcome break that many students perceive as chat-to-neighbour time while the swot has a heart-to-heart with the lecturer. To prevent this, the whole class must be included and involved. This means *distancing* yourself from the questioner, not doing the personable thing and leaning towards the questioner. Move back so that the questioner is part of the class, and the question then becomes a whole-class question. Repeat the question loudly into the microphone while looking at the 'U' (the back and side rows), not the 'T' (the front and middle rows), whence the question almost certainly came. In a very large class, it may be better to ask students to write down their questions and pass them up to the front, rather than shouting them at you. You could take them on the spot or answer them in the introduction to the next session. You might even use the large-meeting technique with microphone stands in the aisles.

**Starting the lecture**

Again, the size and buzz of a large class make different demands on getting started smoothly.

1 Don't just sail straight in. Signal that class has started and wait for quiet.
2 Start with a proper introduction: 'Following from last week when we . . . What we are going to do today . . .' Then *brief* them (Gibbs *et al.* 1984): explain what the lecture is supposed to be doing that some other activity cannot. Why lecture when the topic is in the textbook? Hopefully because you are going to do something the textbook can not. Tell the students what that is; what they should be getting from this particular lecture.

3 Preview with an overhead slide giving the subheadings of the lecture, and some explanation of the sequences of subheadings, or a diagram that is appropriate.

**Structuring the lecture**

The structure of the lecture is ideally a reflection of the structure of the topics or content being taught. Brown and Atkins (1988) refer to several lecture structures:

1 *Classical* – the lecture addresses several broad areas, each of which is subdivided. This is the easiest method of structuring, and 'potentially the most boring'. If not prepared and structured properly it can become a rambling monologue: 'I'll tell them about this, then that, and then wind up.' It is in this situation that one needs to be very clear about structure both for oneself and for the students. The topic structure needs to be clearly emphasized, and keyed in to the subdivisions.
2 *Problem-centred* – a problem is presented and alternative solutions suggested. It could be left with alternatives there for students to sort out, or the lecture closed with an argument for one of them. Do not confuse this with problem-based learning (Chapter 11).
3 *Comparative* – two or more theories, views, perspectives, etc., are offered and compared. Students need to know the different theories or positions first.
4 *Thesis* – a position is taken and then supported with evidence, argument, hypothesis.

Whatever the structure, explain it specifically on an overhead slide or handout.

**Delivering the lecture**

Following are a few points to watch during lecturing:

1 Make eye contact with students while talking; no head buried in notes.
2 Ensure clarity: project the voice, check it can be heard at the back. Cordless radio microphones are best.
3 Focus on the 'U' rather than the 'T' of the geography of the lecture room, as when asking or repeating questions. Susan and her friends tend to sit along the front row and up the middle, Robert and his friends at the back and down the sides. Focus on grabbing Robert, and you will automatically include Susan.
4 Any points you want students to get verbatim in their notes, signal and dictate, or put on overhead. Allow sufficient time.
5 Clear visual aids, notes, handouts. Handouts are important in large classes.

6 Provide the handouts at the beginning or the end of the lecture, so students can collect them on entry or exit. If possible, organize the schedule at least a week ahead so that the end of the previous session can be used for handouts. Distributing handouts during class (of 100+ say) is messy and time-wasting.

7 Consider tape-recording the lecture and making cassettes available in the library, possibly with a clear copy of your own notes. This is particularly useful for international students who may have difficulty in comprehending and keeping up with note-taking. Best not to record live, but in your office using good equipment.

8 When changing activities, explain why: Gibbs calls this flagging. For example, in the event of a break, don't just say 'OK stop. Get up and stretch.' They and you will look and feel silly. Rather: 'We've been hard at it for 20 minutes. We'll all feel better for a break. Stretch, yawn and walk around a bit. I'm going to. OK, we've got one minute.' The same applies to all changes in flow or activity.

**Personalizing the class**

One of the features of large-class teaching that students dislike most is the impersonality; it is a short step from there to a cold theory X climate. How you handle that is a personal matter, but the following are possibilities (Davis 1993):

1 Stand in front of the lectern not behind it, which also means don't read from your notes. Walk about, up and down the aisles if feasible. Get students to leave a few rows empty, so you can move along them. Such ploys give the impression of accessibility, not distance. Stand still, however, when delivering important points.

2 If the session is a whole-class activity, such as lecturing, do not in your friendly wandering allow yourself to be seduced by a *sotto voce* conversation with a nearby student, in answer to a quick informal question. It must be treated as a question coming from the whole class (see above).

3 At the beginning of the class get neighbouring students to introduce themselves to each other. These may or may not lead to formal learning partnerships (see below).

4 Get students to complete a short biographical questionnaire, with names, reasons for taking the unit, hobbies, etc. You can then refer to students by name occasionally, and select examples to illustrate points in your lectures to match their interests. They'll feel good about that, even though not everyone will get a mention.

5 Arrive early, and/or leave late, to talk with students. Let them know you'll be there. Similarly, make your hours of availability in your office known, and keep those times sacred. Some teachers may be comfortable

with inviting groups of students, in circulation to cover everyone, to coffee.

6 Where tutors mark assignments, make sure you read a sample, and discuss in class. Let them know you are not delegating entirely.

7 Use humour, topical references (but careful where there are large numbers of international students, who are likely to be confused by topical references, colloquialisms and culturally specific jokes: see Chapter 7).

These points focus on what the teacher does. We now focus on the more important issue of what the student is doing.

## Active learning in the large class

There is nothing wrong with someone with expert knowledge explaining important and useful aspects of that knowledge to someone else. In normal communication, if the listener's attention seems to wander, you do something to haul it back: a brush of eye contact, a question. Listeners, for their part, can clarify difficult points as they go, comment on aspects that strike them, and signal they are not following with a facial expression.

In a small class, these props for understanding are relatively easy to arrange. The challenge is to arrange them when there are hundreds of people listening.

### The teacher's task, the students' tasks

We teachers have one task – sharing our recent thinking in an erudite and stimulating lecture – but the students have two: to comprehend what they are hearing, and to write their notes and commentary for later reference.

Many students find it difficult to do both tasks, so they alternate them. This results in a 'copy–delete' strategy. They listen to one sentence, and while writing the gist of that one down, the lecturer is saying at least two more, and these sentences are missed. Using this inefficient note-taking strategy, students have on record less than one-third of the ideas that make up the lecture. And with only a fraction of the trees, they have to reconstruct the whole wood. Students need a chance not just to check that their notes are accurate, but more importantly to see that their notes actually do address the plot. They need time to reflect on the bigger picture.

The solution is simple: separate comprehension time from recording time. Give them a timeslot to check their notes. Gibbs *et al.* (1992) suggest setting a timer to ring every 15 minutes; when it rings, stop talking and get students to consolidate the process the lecture has set in train. If your lectures are such that any stopping point is as good as any other, fair enough, but I would prefer the timer to be audible only to me, to remind me to stop at the next logical break. Students can then swap notes with their neighbour, discuss differences and rewrite their own notes. They can thus repair the holes in the notes with the main ideas about what has been said, not the sentence-by-sentence details.

The pause can also be used to engage students in other, higher cognitive level, activities that use the content:

- To reflect, individually or in pairs, on what they think they have just learned, telling each other what they saw as the most important point in the preceding 15 minutes of lecturing.
- Each student writes down a question or a comment sparked by the previous 15 minutes. Their neighbour is asked to respond. Students can hand in their question/comments sheet at the end of the session; it will be useful for feedback (and for attendance check).
- You put a question on a transparency. They discuss with their neighbour.
- You set a problem for them to work on, either individually or in pairs.
- You answer their questions.
- You get a break, to reflect on any points that might need clarifying or elaborating, to sort out notes, or just to catch your breath.

Near the end of the lecture, you might allow five minutes for each student to tell their neighbour or learning partner what they think was the thrust of the session. This achieves the active review, and also gives them a different perspective to think about, other than their own interpretation of yours.

Linking diagrams and key points can be achieved by handouts using PowerPoint software, so that overheads can be copied and distributed, with the overheads reduced so that three or so can be placed down one half the page and the students can write their notes and comments beside each. This gives students accurate basic notes and diagrams but requires them to actively search for the main idea and put it in their own words with an example or two. Chalmers and Fuller (1996) recommend the integration of the two sets of task, the teacher's and the students', by actively incorporating note-taking into the lecture.

### Self-addressed questions

Any particular lecture is only one episode in a long story. Students can be helped to focus on the story, rather than just on the episode, by seeing that they have the schedule of lecture topics at the commencement of the unit, then getting them to respond to self-addressed questions (Fleming 1993) such as:

1 What do I most want to find out in the next class? Before each class the students have to read around this question and note down their

response. Five minutes or so before that session is due to finish, ask them to address question 2.

2 What is the main point I learned today?

3 What was the main point left unanswered in today's session?

These are then handed in, with names. The actual writing is a matter of very few sentences per question, and they can be read in a couple of minutes. The answers can be used as formative assessment both for them and for you – and as an attendance check. The cumulative record gives a very good, and quick, indication of the development of student's thinking through the course.

This forces students to actually *do* the pre-reading, and to reflect on it, as in question 1. Question 2 can tell you something about their learning and your teaching: if some quite minor aside is seen as 'the main point', either you or they have a problem. The last question allows you to address in next week's class misconceptions derived in today's class, and to discuss differences between what you and they saw as the important points. All this provides students with feedback on how their thinking is in line with other students' and with your own. For this purpose, only a sample need be read. Question (2), called 'the three minute essay', can also be used for assessment purposes, graded or ungraded.

These are not, of course, the only questions that could or should be asked. You can no doubt think of others that would better suit your objectives.

Techniques of informed note-taking, pauses, swapping lecture notes with neighbours, discussing key questions, and so on, taken singly or in combination, meet many of the objections raised about the lecture, both improving the efficiency of the lecture itself, by keeping students alert and their notes relevant, and getting students involved in the high-level activities the lecture itself usually does not evoke. In particular, the interspersed activities address monitoring, structuring and consolidating the information presented in the lecture.

## Student–student interaction in the large-class setting

The preceding activities are teacher-directed, with incidental use of students interacting with each other. As we saw in the previous chapter, peer interaction leads to valuable outcomes of its own: elaboration of knowledge, awareness of standards of knowing, reflection leading to meta-cognitive awareness and various social benefits such as improved social skills and self-concept. Students also like learning from peers.

## Learning partners

The initiative for forming partnerships comes from the teacher, but choosing partners is best done by the students. Partnerships are not so much for working towards a goal, such as a group assignment, as for mutual support. The larger the class, the more likely students will feel alienated. They need someone to talk to: to share concerns, to seek clarification over assignment requirements, to check their own insecure interpretations of procedure or of content (Saberton 1985).

Partners could be matched by the teacher: alphabetically, or on the basis of the way students complement each other (high performing/at risk, international/local, mature age/straight from school, those with access to desirable resources/those with little access). Alternatively, students could each choose their own partners, and that probably is the best way. Partners then agree to sit next to each other in class, and to consult out of class, exchanging telephone numbers, email, etc. They can also collaborate on suitable assessment tasks: we deal with that issue in Chapter 9. Partnerships that do not work because of the personal chemistry should be reformed. Some students may prefer to remain loners; that should be respected.

Learning partners permanently sitting next to each other makes life much easier for you when implementing the kinds of note-swapping, active review and so on mentioned above. It is also easier for two students to seek clarification from you than for one to do so. Your out-of-class time in dealing with queries is more than halved, because the chances are one partner can put the other partner straight.

## Peer teaching

There is no single best method of teaching – 'but the second best is students teaching other students' (McKeachie et al. 1986: 63). Peer teaching is a powerful method of learning that is greatly underutilized, although it is highly effective for a wide range of goals, content and for students of different levels and personalities, and is easily adapted for large-class teaching, transforming a class of 500 students into 500 teaching assistants. The research on peer teaching finds that both tutor and tutee benefit academically, the tutor more than the tutee, as you would expect on the grounds of active learning. The tutor is also likely to have increased social skills and attitudes to study and self (Goodlad and Hirst 1990; Topping 1996). The reasons are clear:

1 The content to be taught is viewed not from one's own perspective but from that of someone whose conceptions of the topic to be taught are different and less satisfactory.

2 The teacher reflects on how they learned the topic, which means that peers, being closer to that process and more aware of the traps and difficulties than the expert, can teach more empathically.
3 The teacher 'owns' the material, publicly taking responsibility for it and its validity. There is heavy loss of face if they get it wrong, so they are more careful about getting it right.

Such are the presumed benefits of peer tutoring in terms of enhanced learning and development of tutoring skills that two New Zealand tertiary institutions give course credit for peer tutoring, the practical work being carried out tutoring secondary school students (Jones *et al.* 1994). No, not education students, destined for a teaching career, but law, science and business students. The assumption is simply that teaching the subject deepens students' cognitive understanding.

*Student-led groups*
The most common patterns of peer teaching/tutoring are not with pairs but with groups. There are two main types: where the groups comprise students from the same class, and where the tutor is of a higher year level than the tutored.

Same-class groups may be initiated by the teacher or spontaneously by the students. Both kinds can work well. A common finding is that, compared with teacher-led groups, student-led groups range wider in their discussion and produce more complex outcomes (McKeachie *et al.* 1986; Tang 1998). However, it is not the technique, but how it runs, that is important. It may be necessary to provide some training and a structured agenda. This is something that individual teachers would need to experiment with in their own circumstances. The cost–benefits of student-led groups in classes with high enrolments are attractive.

Cross-year tutoring is closest to traditional instruction, in that the tutor is either a senior undergraduate or a postgraduate. The most general findings from many studies are that both tutors and tutees like the process, and that achievement of the tutees is little different from conventionally taught (Topping 1996), which is a very positive and cost-effective finding, when you think about it.

*Supplemental instruction (SI)*
Variously known in Australia as the Peer Assistance Supplementary Scheme or Peer Assisted Study Sessions (PASS in either case), SI is a variant of cross-year tutoring that originated at the University of Missouri in 1975. It is now used in over 300 US institutions, 15 British universities and several Australian ones. It is designed to alleviate the problem of large first-year classes.

The tutors are second-year or third-year students who passed the first-year subject exceptionally well and are judged to have appropriate personal qualities. They are trained to 'model, advise and facilitate' rather than to address the curriculum directly, and are either paid or given course credit. Data involving 295 courses in the US show improved achievement, and higher re-enrolment and graduation rates (National Center for Supplemental Instruction 1994). Outcomes in the UK are likewise encouraging (Topping 1996). At the University of Queensland, over ten thousand students a year have attended PASS, regular attendees averaging a whole grade higher than students who did not attend, while of the students gaining high distinctions, 85 per cent attended PASS, 14 per cent did not (Chalmers and Kelly 1997).

PASS employs two tutors or student leaders per group of 25 first years, and they are paid also to attend at least one lecture that the tutees receive (Watson 1996, 1997; Chalmers and Kelly 1997). Leaders receive one full day of training and ongoing weekly meetings with the staff coordinator. Attendance from the first-year classes is voluntary, ranging from 20 per cent of the class to over 80 per cent. The agenda is up to the students, frequently involving a review of what has gone on in class that week. No new material is presented; PASS is not in any sense a substitute for other teaching. Chalmers and Kelly (1997) list the following benefits to students:

1 A friendly environment where they can comfortably ask 'the dumbest questions'.
2 Weekly study keeps them up to date.
3 Insight into the range of material other students are covering, and the difficulties they have.
4 A mentor can give information and inside knowledge of how they coped.
5 International students particularly like the opportunity to discuss without staff present.

Leaders are required to keep a reflective diary, with which they provide feedback to the departmental staff coordinator. This ongoing information is far more useful to lecturers in meeting problems than end-of-semester course evaluations.

PASS is considered particularly useful in subjects having:

• large classes, particularly when unsupported by other group-work;
• highly technical content;
• a failure rate of more than 10 per cent;
• high international student enrolments;
• a service role as a core subject for a number of degree courses.

*Spontaneous collaboration*
Some student groups are unofficial, formed spontaneously to focus on coping with specific tasks, such as set assignments (Tang 1996). Tang studied spontaneous collaborative learning amongst physiotherapy students,

who, after the announcement of an assignment, formed their own groups, deciding who would check out what set of references, what ideas might be included, and so on. The collaborative effort extends variously through the planning phase of the assignment or project, but the final detailed plan and write-up is conducted individually. Over 80 per cent of Tang's students collaborated to some extent, and those that did showed greater structural complexity (higher SOLO levels) in their assignments. Such a high proportion of spontaneous collaboration may not occur with western students, but Goodnow (1991) reports that Australian students at Macquarie University formed syndicates, mainly for the purpose of exchanging wisdom on examination questions. An interesting question is how far teachers might encourage, or have any interaction with, these groups (Tang 1993).

## Self-directed TLAs

We have dealt with self-directed TLAs in the last chapter, and as we are talking about individual learners, the question does not arise in the same form in the case of the large class. Self-direction does, however, become an issue in flexible and lifelong learning, and we return to that in Chapter 10.

## Summary and conclusions

### The ubiquitous lecture: advantages and limitations

The lecture has become a generic term for tertiary teaching, an authority it does not deserve. Virtually the only advantage lecturing has over other methods is that it exposes students in person to a scholar's ongoing thinking. Even so, care is needed. A low-activity task like listening requires concentration; attention diminishes rapidly after 15 minutes or so. The challenge of large-class teaching is to restore the supports for learning that the context diminishes:

1 Interpose changes of activity during the course of the session. It is a very special lecturer who can keep students continually and fully attentive for the whole of the session.
2 Use these breaks to get the students to monitor their notes and to do some high-level cognitive work with what they have heard.
3 Make sure there is a review activity at the end of the session.

Task 6.1 gets you to incorporate all of these supports in your next large-class lecture.

### Task 6.1:   **Redesigning your next large-class 'lecture'**

Take your next large-class session, which you would normally regale with a long and carefully prepared lecture. Now is the time to have a go at restructuring the session. I am assuming the time period is one hour. If more than this, make allowance in your plans.

1 Stage a striking introduction that will grab their attention and be relevant to what follows.

 

 

 

2 Allow for three breaks after 10–15 minutes of solid talk by you. What will you do, or rather, what will they do, in each break? One of the activities should involve something you collect at the end and ponder for the next session.

Break 1 _____

_____

Break 2 _____

_____

Break 3* _____

_____

\* If applicable

3 Consolidate with an active review in the last five minutes by getting students to do something.

 

 

 

## Management skills for large-class teaching

A large class needs carefully planned management. Students must be aware of what to do when changes of activity are required. In large-class teaching you need to learn different management strategies, based on the fact of distance, while overcoming students' dislike of the alienation of being an anonymous face in the crowd. It is a familiar dilemma in the caring professions: reconciling efficient impersonality with the appearance of the personal touch.

## Active learning in the large class

To properly understand a lecture, students need to juggle two tasks simultaneously: comprehending the message, and recording its gist. Most can't do this adequately, so we should separate the presentation and consolidation sections, then students can focus on the one task, then on the other. Breaks can also be used to ensure the students have good notes, for exchanging interpretations with neighbours, for solving problems, and in general for using the content just expounded. The links across lecture episodes can be created with self-addressed questions given out in advance to students. The structure of plenary sessions thus focuses on two basic strategies: presenting content efficiently to students, and getting them to work on it. The two strategies aim at different objectives and can be incorporated in teaching even the largest classes.

## Student–student interaction in the large-class setting

The most prolific resource in large classes is the students themselves, and using them appropriately engages a different range of verbs that address a range of objectives scarcely touched by teacher-directed TLAs. Creating semi-permanent learning partnerships can make life easier for both you and them, providing a continually accessible resource for discussing, reciprocal questioning and mutual support in an otherwise anonymous environment. Groups of various kinds extend the range of activities even further. Probably the most powerful is peer teaching, where the research evidence is very strong and positive, for both the learners and teachers. In resource-starved times, it is amazing that peer teaching in its various forms, including the use of paid students as in PASS, is not used more widely.

## Matching TLAs with objectives: an overview of Chapters 5 and 6

This and the previous chapter are concerned with the fundamental question of choosing TLAs that match your objectives. We first looked at some

**Table 6.1:** What activities are teaching methods most likely to elicit?

| Teaching/learning activity | Form of learning elicited |
| --- | --- |
| **Teacher-controlled** | |
| lecture, set texts | reception of selected content |
| think-aloud | demonstrate conceptual skills |
| questioning | clarifying, seeking error |
| advance organizer | structuring, preview |
| concept mapping | structuring, overview |
| tutorial | elaboration, clarification |
| laboratory | procedures, application |
| excursion | experiential knowledge, interest |
| seminar | clarify, presentation skill |
| **Peer-controlled** | |
| various groups | elaboration, problem-solving, meta-cognition |
| learning partners | resolve differences, application |
| peer teaching | depends whether teacher or taught |
| spontaneous collaboration | breadth, self-insight |
| **Self-controlled** | |
| generic study skills | basic self-management |
| content study skills | information handling (BIG) |
| meta-cognitive learning skills | independence and self-monitoring (WIG) |

basic principles of teaching, and then at a range of TLAs that can be linked with high-level learning-related verbs. The research relating TLAs to particular verbs is so far incomplete, but personal and collegial experience will help fill gaps. Table 6.1 suggests some TLAs and the sort of learning they are likely to encourage.

The important thing is to be clear about the sort of learning you want, and then to set up TLAs that are most likely to get it. Usually the lecture and the tutorial are the givens, and in practice we bend our objectives to suit. What I am suggesting is precisely the opposite: we tune our teaching methods to elicit from students the learning activities most likely to produce the desired learning outcomes.

## Further reading

### On lecturing in large classes

Andreson, L.W. (1994) *Lecturing to Large Groups: A Guide to Doing it Less . . . But Better*. Birmingham: Staff and Educational Development Association.

Bligh, D.A. (1972) *What's the Use of Lectures?* Harmondsworth: Penguin.

Cannon, R. (1988) *Lecturing*, HERDSA Green Guide No. 7. Kensington, NSW: Higher Education Research and Development Society of Australasia.

Elton, L. and Cryer, P. (1992) *Teaching Large Classes*. Sheffield: University of Sheffield Teaching Development Unit.

Gibbs, G. and Jenkins, A. (eds) (1992) *Teaching Large Classes in Higher Education*. London: Kogan Page.

Gibbs, G., Habeshaw, S. and Habeshaw, T. (1984) *53 Interesting Things to Do in Your Lectures*. Bristol: Technical and Educational Services.

McLeish, J. (1976) The lecture method, in N. Gage (ed.) *The Psychology of Teaching Methods*, 75th Yearbook of the National Society for the Study of Education. Chicago: University of Chicago Press.

O'Neill, M. (1997) *Teaching in Large Classes*. A very comprehensive CD-ROM showing examples of expert teachers in action at all stages of teaching, from preparing to lecture to closing elegantly. Has interviews with novice teachers, expert teachers and students at each teaching stage. Email jfoo@ecel.uwa.edu.au

Concerns about large-class teaching are obviously reflected in the plethora of publications on this matter. I have included a large selection so that interested teachers can obtain at least some of those available.

**On peer tutoring**

Goodlad, S. and Hirst, B. (eds) (1990) *Explorations in Peer Tutoring*. Oxford: Basil Blackwell.

Saberton, S. (1985) Learning partnerships, *HERDSA News*, 7(1): 3–5.

Topping, K.J. (1996) The effectiveness of peer tutoring in further and higher education: a typology and review of the literature, *Higher Education*, 32: 321–45.

The first book provides case studies of peer tutoring, while Topping provides a useful classification of different types of peer tutoring and a summary of research results. Saberton's short article suggests how learning partnerships may be set up and used.

# 7

## Teaching international students

**Many university teachers report difficulties in teaching international students. These complaints refer not only to deficient language skills, but to learning-related problems that are seen as 'cultural' in origin, such as reliance on rote learning, passivity, teacher dependence, lacking creativity, and so on. These perceptions are, like most stereotypes, distortions of the real situation. This chapter reviews some of the evidence for these cultural differences, and how they might affect teaching and learning. We find that teaching international students develops in the same way as teaching generally, from a level 1 blame-the-student view of teaching, to an inclusive level 3 view that engages students in effective learning whatever their ethnicity. This is not to say that misunderstandings will not arise when teachers and learners come from different cultural backgrounds, but that an inclusive view of teaching will minimize them.**

### Who are international students? What kinds of problem do they present?

International students (ISs) are students who have gone to another country in order to enrol full-time in a university course. The numbers of such students in UK universities have remained amazingly constant. The figure has ranged in the past 60 years from a low of 10.4 per cent in 1939 to a high of 11.6 per cent in 1963 (Perraton 1997). What has varied is the make-up. Students from the EU have risen from 4 per cent of all international students in 1979 to 43 per cent in 1994, students from the Commonwealth having dropped from 54 per cent to 31 per cent in the same time.

British and Australian universities are not becoming more international, but more regionalized. In Australian universities, an average of 8 per cent come from overseas, mostly from Asian countries on the Pacific Rim, and they range from none at all in a few single-purpose institutions, to 17 per cent at the Royal Melbourne Institute of Technology (Department of Employment, Education, Training and Youth Affairs 1998).

Whatever the overall figures, teachers experience the student mix in particular classes, and that ranges widely. The proportion of ISs in the humanities is low, but in architecture, business, engineering, paramedical studies, science and mathematics, ISs could be in the majority in some classes. Local teachers are reported as seeing this as a problem for their teaching (see below). While a problem perceived is a problem experienced, need it be so? What is the nature of this seeming problem? What can be done to address it? These are the concerns of this chapter.

### 'Cultural' problems

American students studying in England, or New Zealand students studying in Australia, are technically ISs, but they are not thought of as presenting any different teaching problems from those already presented by local students. The perceived problems arise with students from a non-Anglo-Celtic background, for example from African, Middle Eastern or Far Eastern countries. The problems are thus said to be cultural in origin (Ballard and Clanchy 1997; Harris 1997).

But is this in principle different from the 'cultural' problem when Anglo-Celtic students move from the more protected and passive culture of secondary school to the academic culture of university? At university, class attendance is not compulsory, independent study skills are important, and teachers do not sit on you to see you attend classes, or are up to the mark with deadlines and schedules. Many local students find bridging these two teaching cultures difficult. The view taken in this chapter is that, language issues aside, the problems presented by the cultural gap between school and university are different from those experienced by non-Anglo-Celtic ISs only in extent, not in kind.

An 'international' student can for present purposes be defined in terms of (1) differences in ethnicity between home and university cultures, and (2) the kind of problem experienced. Problems are typically of three kinds:

1 *Social–cultural adjustment.* A major problem experienced by ISs is the stress created by adjusting to a new culture. While this is not strictly the concern of the teacher, there is an obligation on the university to supply strong support structures, particularly now that universities are vying with each other to attract the full student fees that ISs have to pay, which results in some universities offering cheap 'no frills' education, student support services being one of the expendable frills (Harris 1997). Our concern in this chapter is not, however, with the learning problems

that flow indirectly from more general adjustment difficulties, but 'how culture itself shapes cognition and learning', which is said to present problems in teaching and learning (Harris 1997: 78).

2 *Language.* Despite language prerequisites, many ISs undoubtedly have language problems that need attention; you cannot learn if you are not fluent in the language medium of instruction. Who is to deal with these language-related issues: content teachers or language specialists? While most content teachers would say that language for academic purposes is not their expertise or their business, language and learning interact deeply. But more than language is at stake: 'many of the difficulties international students experience in their study derive not from "poor English" (though lack of language competence is in many cases a real problem), but from a clash of educational cultures' (Ballard and Clanchy 1997: vi).

3 *Learning/teaching problems due to 'culture'.* In short, the cultural background of many ISs is thought to make it difficult for them to adapt to the *style* of tertiary teaching adopted in the host country. In particular, many ISs are too teacher-dependent, too uncritical of material they have been taught, prone to rote memorization; they misunderstand the cardinal sin of plagiarism, and lack knowledge of the genres of academic writing (Ballard and Clanchy 1997; Harris 1997). How to cope with this is the problem. If it is a problem. Certainly many Australian university teachers see that it is:

> Students from Malaysia, Singapore, Hong Kong appear to be much more inclined to rote learning. Such an approach does not help problem solving. (Dentistry)
> [Asian students] tend to look on lecturers as close to gods. Often they are very reluctant to question statements or textbooks. (Parasitology)
> It can be difficult to cope, in small (graduate) classes, with overseas students who are reluctant to discuss, criticize reading and express an opinion. (Commerce)
>
> (Quoted in Samuelowicz 1987: 123–5)

And in the UK:

> Many overseas students now originate in Pacific Rim countries, whose educational cultures characteristically value a highly deferential approach to teachers and place considerable emphasis on rote learning. This approach, of course, promotes surface or reproductive learning, which is at variance . . . with officially encouraged teaching innovations . . . to ensure deep transformational learning.
>
> (Harris 1997: 78)

There seems to be quite a consensus that there is a lack of 'goodness of fit', to use Harris's term, between the ISs' backgrounds, especially those

---

**Task 7.1: Teaching international students**

Do you have significant numbers of international students in your
classes? _____

Does this worry you? _____

Why? List the main problems. _____

_____

_____

_____

**After you have read this chapter . . .**
Review the problems you noted above. Do you see your way clearer now for
dealing with these problems? Explain how. _____

_____

_____

_____

_____

---

from Asian countries, and the style, ethos and task demands that British
and Australian universities typically make.

Do you see yourself as having problems in dealing with ISs? Go to
Task 7.1.

**Teaching across cultures from three perspectives**

Let us bring to bear the views of teaching developed in Chapter 2 (pp. 20–
5), which were in fact generalized from how expatriate teachers adapt to
teaching in a new system (Biggs 1996c). In that situation, what often
happens first is a kind of colonial phase: the way things are done at home
is the yardstick by which the new environment is measured, from shopping,

TV programmes, to students. Here's the initial reaction of an expatriate teacher to teaching in Hong Kong:

> I found the deathly silence that preceded the start of the lecture quite unnerving, the more so when my open-ended questions met with no response. I had to plough on, and if, as was likely, I ran out of pre-pared material, I had to *ad lib* until the scheduled end of the lecture.
>
> (Biggs 1989b: 3)

The students apparently weren't behaving like students should. They just sat there, passively. They didn't even ask questions. This comment reflects pure level 1, blame-the-student thinking. It became the students' fault, not mine, that the approach to teaching that I was using was ineffectual for them.

The next phase is accepting that the new environment has developed its own system, and the teacher's task is to adapt to that. This is level 2 thinking: good teaching involves the teacher doing all the right teacherly things.

The final phase is level 3: focusing on getting students to learn. Cultural factors might well mean that there may be different ways of doing this to best effect, but the focus is not on cultural or pedagogical difference, but on the universality of learning processes. The model is by now familiar to you, but let me illustrate how it applies to teaching across cultures (see Figure 7.1).

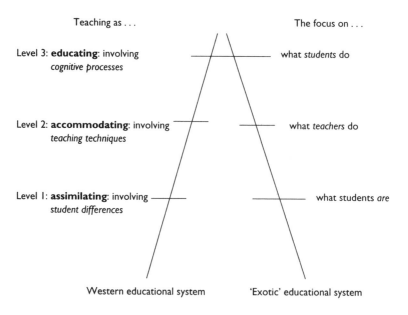

**Figure 7.1:** The focus in cross-cultural teaching

As we ascend the cross-cultural teaching ladder, the differences between our own (western) educational system and the exotic systems from which our students come, become less important. Differences are greatest on the bottom rung, where all we observe are differences between the way ISs behave and how we think students should behave. ISs have to assimilate in accordance with our definition of what constitutes a good student.

Ascend the ladder another rung, and we focus on adapting our teaching techniques to accommodate to the students. We lecture, but speak more slowly, dropping the witty word-play; they are still different but our responsibility is to teach by allowing for the differences. At the top rung, we find that ethnic students – surprise! – use the same cognitive processes as locals, and if we aim to engage those processes, teaching ISs is little different from teaching locals.

In the context of teaching across cultures, the three different foci of teaching at each level create convenient labels: teaching as assimilation, as accommodation and as education.

## Level 1: teaching as assimilation

Applying level 1 thinking to the situation of ISs, we arrive at a view remarkably similar to that adopted by the governments of countries receiving immigrants in pre-multicultural days: they must assimilate, they must be like us. The focus is on how ISs differ from local students; and because ISs do differ in some ways from local students, it is easy to stereotype them. When that happens, misconceptions and self-fulfilling prophecies occur.

The following generalizations about ISs derive from personal experience (Harris 1997), from research into lecturers' perceptions of ISs (Samuelowicz 1987; Chalmers and Volet 1997), and from recommendations on how to handle ISs (Ballard and Clanchy 1997). Some are supported by evidence; some apply equally to local and to international students; some are simply wrong.

### 1 'They rote learn and lack critical thinking skills'

This generalization is typically used to describe students from Confucian heritage cultures (CHCs) such as China, Korea, Japan, Hong Kong and Singapore. This is one of the definitely wrong generalizations, yet is the most widespread.

This criticism is voiced while CHC students are walking off with the first class honours and gold medals in huge disproportion to locals in such subjects as architecture, business studies, engineering and science. Do they achieve this on the basis of rote learning? If so, it doesn't say much for our assessment criteria. Or is it that these are the very bright ones, specially selected to study overseas? But then CHC students on their own turf, taught in their own fierce and overcrowded classrooms, consistently outperform western students, as established both in controlled international comparisons of school performance in maths and science (International Association for the Evaluation of Educational Achievement 1996), and in more fine-grained studies of Stevenson and his team in China, Taiwan, Japan and the United States (Stevenson and Stigler 1992), and in videoing maths classrooms in the United States, Germany and Japan (Stigler and Hiebert 1999; see also pp. 276–7).

CHC students achieve better and with more understanding than US students for a very good reason: they are taught better (Hess and Azuma 1991; Stevenson and Stigler 1992; Stedman 1997; Stigler and Hiebert 1999). Not only that, but the levels of thinking assessed in public examinations in Australia (the NSW Higher Schools Certificate) rely more on rote memorizing than do the Thai and Japanese equivalents (Baumgart and Halse 1999). It thus turns out that when you look at the hard evidence, as opposed to level 1 perceptions, western countries teach and assess in a way that encourages rote learning more than do many East Asian countries.

In support of this conclusion, the approaches to learning of CHC students are typically lower on surface and higher on deep than those of western students, both in their own culture (Hong Kong and Singapore) (Biggs 1991; Kember and Gow 1991; Watkins *et al.* 1991), and overseas in Australian institutions (Biggs 1987a; Volet and Renshaw 1996). A major exception, amongst dozens of studies, was that western medical students were higher on deep and lower on surface approaches – but it turned out that these students were taught by problem-based learning (PBL), while the CHC medical comparison students were (then) in a highly traditional medical school (Biggs 1991). That medical school is now committed to PBL.

So where does the 'rote learning' myth come from? It is true that CHC students engage in much repetitive activity and memorization. The culture demands it. Learning the several thousand characters in common use requires more memorization than learning the 26 letters in the alphabet. But memorization in these circumstances is in service to understanding. You learn a communication system in order to communicate with understanding. There is a CHC saying: 'repetition is a route to understanding' (Hess and Azuma 1991), which makes obvious sense not only with respect to language but to learning any complex structures, such as classical music. Every repetition affords the opportunity to increase our understanding of it. Sections begin to fall into place; the big picture unfolds.

Repetition is also used as a strategy to ensure correct recall, where it works alongside meaning, not against it. Actors learning their lines or students studying for an exam need to eliminate any cognitive load involved in verbatim recall so that they can concentrate on the meaning at the time of performance. Tang (1991) refers to this strategic use of repetition as 'deep memorizing'. Neither of these instances – repetition as a strategy of coping with complexity, or as a strategy for verbatim recall – has anything to do with rote learning and using a surface approach. Repetitive learning is a good way of coping meaningfully with the world.

Western educators distinguish between rote learning and meaningful learning (Ausubel 1968), but not so easily between rote learning and repetitive learning. Rote learning is defined in common language as 'the mere exercise of memory without proper understanding of the matter in question' (*Shorter Oxford English Dictionary*). Hence, we use the term 'rote' memory as characteristic of the surface approach, where it is used deliberately to circumvent understanding.

But that is not what CHC students are doing when they use repetition in order to reduce complexity or to ensure recall. However, westerners with a level 1 view see only the repetition, which is stereotypically labelled as mindless rote learning. Thus, Harris's (1997) comment that the educational systems of the Pacific Rim countries strongly promote surface or reproductive learning is to misunderstand those Pacific Rim countries – unless he means Australia and the United States, in which case the evidence is fairly clear that these systems do promote rote learning (Biggs 1991; Stedman 1997; Baumgart and Halse 1999). But I don't think Harris did mean this.

## 2 'They are passive; they won't talk in class'

This is partially true of CHC students but not of Asians from the Indian subcontinent or of West Indians. Even with CHC students the evidence is contradictory, although the *perceptions* of western teachers, including my own initially, are that they talk with great difficulty (see above). On the other hand, Volet and Kee (1993) found that the mean number of contributions in tutorials was no different between Singaporeans and Australians, but that the variance was: local (Australian) students either held the floor or said little, leaving an overall impression that locals did all the talking.

The 'inside/outside' rules, that determine when it is proper to talk, provide a useful slant on this (Scollon and Wong Scollon 1994). Westerners are often puzzled by the contrast between café and classroom behaviour of Chinese students: so demure and shy in the classroom, so noisy and boisterous in the café. The difference lies in what is implicitly defined as 'inside' (appropriate) and 'outside' (inappropriate). Normally, talk inside the class is outside, but outside the class talk is inside. So students tend to be quiet inside the class, but outside even academic talk is inside – as the spontaneous collaboration noted by Tang (1993) shows. However, if you turn the outside in – for example, by setting up learning partners, which makes it very difficult to attack academic tasks *without* talking to your partner – talking is now inside, and in my experience is very enthusiastic. Watson (1997) found that Asian, and especially female Asian, students attending the student-led tutorial system PASS (see previous chapter) were much more likely to participate orally than in teacher-led groups, commenting that they particularly appreciated this chance to talk. The conclusion is obvious. Talking was outside in class, but inside in PASS.

There's also the point that it is outside to talk inside the classroom when you are self-conscious about your oral language ability. I would certainly find that to be outside.

### 3  'Progressive western teaching methods won't work with Asians.'

So far as Far Eastern (China, Japan, Korea) students are concerned it is a *truism* that, raised in a conformist educational system, they are happier with memorizing and reproducing information than with problem-oriented and more active teaching strategies.

(Harris 1997: 87, emphasis added)

This not only shows a fundamental misunderstanding of Far Eastern educational methods (Stevenson and Stigler 1992; Lee 1996), it sends all the wrong signals to teachers of ISs. Thus, too, another expatriate teacher in Hong Kong:

Students in Hong Kong . . . expect lecturers to teach them everything they are expected to know. They have little desire to discover for themselves . . . They wish to be spoon fed and in turn they are spoon fed . . .

(McKay and Kember 1997: 55)

The speaker's self-fulfilling prophecy had served him well, and his students badly, over many years. He was speaking against a proposal to introduce PBL into his department; he lost and PBL won. Several Hong Kong universities now use PBL, where it works as well as it does anywhere else (McKay and Kember 1997; Whitehill *et al.* 1997).

The trouble with these misinformed stereotypes is that they exacerbate any teaching problems. They encourage teachers of ISs to continue lecturing and to assess reproductively, because teaching more innovatively 'would be unfair on the international students.' It would not. It would be unfair to continue lecturing – for everyone.

The issue of using active teaching methods with ISs is quite central and I return to it in a later section.

## 4 'They appear to focus excessively on the method of assessment'

It would be a foolish student who didn't focus on the assessment. The answer is the principle of alignment: make sure the method of assessment contains the content you want them to learn (see following two chapters).

## 5 'They don't understand what plagiarism means'

Neither do western students, to many of whom plagiarism (as opposed to cheating) is a new concept at tertiary level. They simply do not see it as a moral issue or that it undermines assessment (Ashworth *et al.* 1997). Indeed, many software packages actively encourage students to cut-and-paste from CD-ROM or web sources. The extent of plagiarism in western universities is enormous – up to 90 per cent of all students in some universities (Walker 1998). Walker also deals with definitions of plagiarism, and how students, staff and institutions deal with it. The issue of plagiarism may, however, be more complex with ISs from cultures where students are taught that it is disrespectful to alter the words of an expert (Ballard and Clanchy 1997).

This suggests, on both local and international fronts, that teachers need to be extremely clear about what constitutes plagiarism, and what the rules of referencing are. Plagiarism may, however, be difficult to define. Wilson (1997) points out that plagiarism proceeds in stages that interestingly follow the SOLO levels:

1 *Repetition* – simple copying from an unacknowledged source. Not confident of the content area. Unistructural and unacceptable.
2 *Patching* – copying, with joining phrases, from several sources. Some general, non-specific, acknowledgement. Weak multistructural and still unacceptable, but harder to spot.
3 *Plagiphrasing* – paraphrasing several sources and joining them. All sources are in the reference list, but page unspecified. Still multistructural and still unacceptable, technically, but it merges towards the next level.
4 *Conventional academic writing* – ideas taken from multiple sources and repackaged to make a more or less original and relational type of synthesis. Quotes properly referenced, general sources acknowledged, quite confident of what is being said. The package may be new, but are the *ideas?* This is relational.

Wilson does not mention an extended abstract level, but it would involve a 'far' transformation from the sources – genuine originality – which conventional academic writing should, but does not necessarily, incorporate.

Of these levels, patching is clearly unacceptable, but students writing in a second language (of whatever cultural background) find it hazardous to attempt to 'put it in your own words' when they are not confident in their use of the language. Lack of rhetorical confidence can easily lead to patching when in fact the student has good *content* understanding. Such cases might need augmented modes of assessment, such as a brief interview, or a less verbal medium such as a concept map. Even the shift from plagiphrasing (unacceptable) to conventional academic writing (presumably acceptable) is not always clear, even to academics. And where that leaves textbook writers I dare not contemplate.

In short, it is not always easy to decide what is plagiarism, after the definite no-noes of repetition and patching. But we can at least be clear about those. *The rules of citation must be made crystal clear.* All too frequently, teachers take a level 1 view: 'Of course students know what plagiarism is and what it is not. It's not my job to explain such basics.' Not so. It is precisely the teacher's job, no matter what is the ethnicity of your students.

### 6  'They stick together . . . won't mix with locals'

This is often true, both socially (which is not an issue here), and educationally (which is). Volet and Ang (1998) studied mixed groups and found stereotypes were challenged and attitudes changed positively, yet both locals and ISs preferred like-with-like tutorial groupings next time.

What are your views? Do you deliberately mix ISs and locals in tutorial/ laboratory groups, or let them decide (which inevitably means unmixed groups)? Or do you do both at different times? Mixed groups mean intercultural learning; homogeneous groups probably mean better content learning. There are value judgements here that each teacher will have to decide (Task 7.1).

### 7  'They do not easily adjust to local conditions'

Wrong, as far as *teaching* is concerned. One characteristic of CHC students is precisely their adaptability. They are very good at spotting cues and picking up coping strategies (Singaporean: Volet and Renshaw 1996; Japanese: Purdie and Hattie 1996; Chinese generally: Watkins and Biggs 1996). Volet and Renshaw's (1996) Singaporean students studying in Australia in one year changed from strategies that were adaptive in Singapore to those that were adaptive in Australia. 'Always aim to get the correct answer', and 'learn lecture material by heart', adaptive in Singapore, dropped from first to last in importance, and were replaced after a year in Australia by 'evaluate different ideas and give own opinion'. 'Make sure you understand main ideas' was adaptive in both contexts and didn't change. These students quickly got the idea, which shows that helping them to get their current priorities straight is much better than blaming them for having previous priorities.

## 8 'They tend to look on lecturers as close to gods'

Authority relations are very different between many western and non-western societies. Westerners tend to play down the authority they have 'which leaves Asians confused as to just who is in charge' (Scollon and Wong Scollon 1994: 22). Asian teachers, on the other hand, usually do not hesitate to make their authority quite clear. CHC teacher–student interaction is not lubricated with the democratic oil of first names and contrived warmth; in a hierarchical, collectivistic culture the oil of respect is a more effective lubricant. Many ISs are uncomfortable with being on first-name terms with their teachers. Such issues should not be forced.

The teacher may be seen as a sort of powerful uncle, bought with gifts: 'I'll be a loyal and diligent student; in return, your obligation is to ensure that I pass' (Ballard and Clanchy 1997). Western teachers find gifts embarrassing, and unacceptable if there is an implied bargain. It is difficult, however, to gauge whether or not an obligation is implied. Some cultures, like Korea, have a tradition of bringing gifts to the teacher on a special Teacher's Day. I recall a similar tradition that existed years ago when I taught in an English secondary school, but there was no suggestion of bribery. But maybe I missed something.

### On the other hand . . .

While ISs come to our western system of tertiary education, many come from cultures that have a rich educational heritage, particularly Confucian heritage societies (Lee 1996). Indeed, there is a closer link in those countries between common beliefs, values and socialization practices, and the demands of formal education, than there is in the West (Biggs 1994). Thus, some characteristics of CHC students make teaching them easier, rather than more difficult.

- Success is attributed to effort, and failure to lack of effort, whereas westerners believe success requires ability more than effort, and failure is attributed to lack of ability (see also Chapter 4). The CHC bottom line is optimistic: 'If I fail I can do something about it', whereas attributing failure to lack of ability engenders hopelessness.
- Motivation tends to be complex and stronger than for western students. Pressures to succeed are collectivist – familial, peer – as well as personal. Socialization practices 'create a sense of diligence and receptiveness that fit uncomfortably into . . . concepts of intrinsic and extrinsic motivation' (Hess and Azuma 1991: 7).
- As a result, CHC students are highly adaptable, as already discussed.

Study strategies, and knowledge of genres and plagiarism rules, are not written in the genes. They are learned – and can therefore be taught. A major responsibility of teachers is clearly to see that they are taught, whether the students are international or local.

## Level 2: teaching as accommodation

The level 2 view of teaching cross-culturally sees the important thing as accommodating to the cultural context. In the case of expatriate teachers, this means learning the teaching techniques that work for that system. In the case of local teachers teaching ISs, level 2 thinking means adapting one's teaching towards meeting the preferred ways of ISs. In both cases, it's what the teacher does that is the important thing:

> Lecturers in Australia teaching classes with half or more students from East Asia are likely to . . . be put psychologically off-balance and become indignant and confused. It will be difficult for the bulk of lecturers to learn good lecturing practice for Asian students. Few academics have interest in learning an alien technology . . .
>
> (Robert M. March, Professor of International Business, University of Western Sydney. Letter to the Editor, *The Australian*, 9 September 1996)

Professor March is suggesting that to teach ISs successfully you have to know what works in their system. To teach aliens, you need to know the right alien technology. But apply this to teaching ISs, and every local academic may need to learn many alien technologies. In the Faculty of Commerce and Economics at the University of New South Wales, there are over eighty mother tongues amongst the 1800 students. Teachers could not possibly accommodate to such diversity. Practicalities thus force level 1 assimilation. It's the aliens who 'must undergo an intellectual and cultural sea-change if they are to succeed' (Ballard and Clanchy 1997: ix).

Teachers can, however, accommodate to some extent, without going so far as to learn alien technologies. For example, that colloquial and humorous interpersonal style that works very well with the right students is clearly inappropriate with ISs and should be dropped (Burns 1991). Ballard and Clanchy (1997: viii) suggest

> minor modifications in current teaching practice, and in almost all cases the changes should be of benefit to all students . . . The problems of teaching students from other cultures are very often a more acute expression of the common problems of teaching our own students.

Such modifications include the following, some familiar from Chapter 6:

- Tape lectures and make tapes available.
- Speak slowly, avoid colloquialisms.

- Provide as much *visual* back-up as possible: overhead slides, diagrams as advance organizers, notes, handouts.
- Model, using 'think-aloud' to socialize students into tutorial and discussion group desired behaviour; model how you would read material for subsequent discussion.
- Place preferred names in front of people including you.
- Pair an IS with a local; latter introduces IS to class.

These are useful management tips, but they are not about teaching itself.

Level 2 suggests that teachers accommodate their teaching strategies to their students' cultural expectations. This means minor accommodation in class management techniques; accommodation beyond that, to learning alien technologies of teaching, is impractical.

In sum, levels 1 and 2 are deficit models. The deficit in level 1 belongs to the student: they lack the skills and background to study in our system, language aside. The deficit in level 2 belongs to the teachers: they lack a range of appropriate teaching skills. We examine the deficit model itself in a moment.

Meantime, we might ask: is there not such a thing as good teaching that works anywhere?

## Level 3: teaching as educating

To the above question, the answer is yes. It is to be found at level 3, with what the student does, not with what the teacher does, or what the student is. Differences between students, and differences between how teachers teach, are not universal, but the cognitive processes students use to learn with are. The argument is exactly the same as that throughout this book. The strategy is to focus on activating students' learning processes as appropriate to the objectives, as does good teaching anywhere. The *means* of activating those learning processes, however, could well differ between cultures.

Let us then turn to stereotype no. 3 above: 'Progressive western teaching methods won't work with Asians', and to the 'truism' that 'they are happier with memorizing and reproducing information than with problem-oriented and more active teaching strategies' (Harris 1997: 87). That argument is disproved if Asians can learn effectively and with enjoyment with our more active teaching strategies.

Whitehill *et al.* (1997) report on the introduction of PBL with speech therapists in Hong Kong. They comment on how the task demands of PBL seemed to conflict with Chinese cultural beliefs. For example, conflict resolution – argument – was required in PBL, but:

> To discuss with our dearest classmates is very difficult because we
> always out of track and shift to another topics but today is quite okay
> in our discussion and we work in harmony.
> (Whitehill *et al.* 1997: 137)

The problem was to resolve conflict in a culturally acceptable manner.
The students worked out possible strategies for arriving at consensus:
voting, formal debate or seeking further information. They settled on the
last strategy, which is the most adaptive, and came to realize that this
strategy led to an appreciation of theory: 'otherwise, it's difficult to make
it proof and make other people believe you' (p. 138).

The issue of working with friends – a difficulty when disagreement was
present – turned out to be 'one of the most exciting aspects of the course.
As one student said, "Problem-based learning gives me a sense of release
for I will no longer be like a clammed duck"' (p. 138). The positive side of
resolving the problem of conflict:

> We are working to our limit, without any reluctance – through coopera-
> tion, all our group members have developed deep friendship, sense
> of trust and confidence. This is very precious.
>
> (p. 138)

As for motivation, students did not mention grades or teacher approval,
only their desire to learn to be an effective speech therapist. Student
ratings of the course were overwhelmingly positive. But there is a problem.
It is to reconcile this experience with the truism that these students would
have been happier memorizing.

Tang *et al.* (1997) report the adoption of PBL in six departments
at the Polytechnic University of Hong Kong. Full-time students had
initial difficulty in adjusting to PBL, having come directly from an extremely teacher-centred and examination-dominated school system. The
strategy was therefore to modify PBL, giving more teacher-direction at
first than would usually be the case. After that, these ducks too became
unclammed.

So there may be 'cultural' problems at first, as there are with western
children moving from secondary school to university. In both cases, they
need to adapt from a strongly teacher-directed culture (school) to a self-
directed one (PBL). The issue is not moving from an 'Asian' to a 'western'
teaching culture, but a matter of adapting from one context to another.
Ethnicity is beside the point.

Another instance where Chinese students were happier with active
teaching strategies and problem-oriented assessment than with memorizing is my own use of a learning portfolio at the University of Hong Kong
(see Chapter 11). Briefly, the programme required minimal exposition,
student-centred small and large groups, often with no teacher present, no

set questions for the students to answer, the opposite of what these students were used to, and initially wanted. In fact, reactions at first were highly negative. Out came the cultural arguments: 'Constructivism is fine in the West, but unworkable in Hong Kong', several students told me.

Several students objected to the procedure adopted in plenary report-back following group discussions. My procedure was to list points on the board as the various group leaders summarized their discussions, leaving it to the students to come to their own conclusions. But:

* We were not told what we were supposed to have learned.
* Lecturer's opinion is not clear enough. Discussions can't draw up a conclusion.
* When we are reporting in one big group, our lecturers seem to accept every opinion but seldom criticize them or give a conclusion. Are all our ideas right? This makes me puzzled . . .

Teachers are supposed to give leadership and draw matters to the correct conclusion. There is One Right Way, into which the teacher guides the students (Gardner 1989). By the end of the unit, however, the comments changed drastically:

The reason why our lecturers seldom criticized our opinions for there are no fixed answers. One really has to find one's own way out. There are no fixed routes of becoming an expert teacher . . . That was why they kept throwing us a lot of questions to stimulate our thinking.

Is this last conclusion 'western' or 'non-Chinese'? Or is it simply a reflective response that is entirely reasonable in that learning context?

The following comment on the use of the portfolio suggests that there are more things to be thought about than the One Right Way.

I found lots of fun [in making my portfolio] . . . it led me to think about many questions that I never think of . . .

The learning portfolio is discussed in Chapter 11 as an example of aligned teaching. My point here is simply that the teaching/learning activities associated with the portfolio accessed the higher cognitive processes of students despite assumed cultural impediments. Using groups, and particularly learning partners, provided culturally acceptable ways of allowing the portfolio to do its work, just as the speech therapy students worked out their fruitful ways to deal with the unpleasant business of handling conflict amongst friends. That is the key to teaching across cultures; the cultural differences become instrumental in engaging in appropriate learning.

If Ah Hung, with his alleged propensity for rote learning, can be encouraged to behave more like Susan, I don't see why Robert can't.

## Approaches to teaching international students

Two methods of dealing with ISs have emerged: the deficit and the contextual models. As noted, level 1 (and level 2 in practice) refers to a deficit that lies in the students: their lack of knowledge of and skill in handling learning in the One Right Way – that is, the western way. Level 3 produces the contextual approach to teaching.

### The deficit approach

In the deficit approach to teaching, the strategy is to identify the skills and procedural knowledge that the target students 'lack' and that mainstream students are presumed to have already. The target students are then given separate out-of-class remediation, after which, their deficit duly repaired, they rejoin the mainstream. This model is common in special education and in dealing with ISs (Ballard and Clanchy 1997).

A successful example of an apparent deficit program is reported by Pearson and Beasley (1996). These writers searched the literature for ways in which South East Asian and Australian students might differ, and then devised an 'integrative learning strategy' taught in six classes halfway through the semester. The intervention comprised communication-based strategies: planning and writing essays and reports, reading critically, oral reporting, exam strategy and so on, using 'collectivist' (group) techniques, and content from the course (Management). Attendance at the intervention classes was voluntary and available to both locals and ISs. It worked well for all students who attended. In fact, the Australian/IS differences were irrelevant.

Deficit models proceed along the following lines, here specified for ISs:

1 Asian students memorize and are therefore 'surface learners'.
2 Hence, the way Asian students learn is inferior to that used by mainstream local students.
3 Therefore Asian students have a deficit to be remedied.

All three assumptions are incorrect. Memorizing is not surface learning. The evidence for both (1) and (2) is strongly the other way: Asians are likely to be deeper learners than westerners. In (3), we have students with learning-related deficits performing better than those without these deficits.

But do local students show similar 'deficits'? That we don't know; that question is not asked. The deficit approach to teaching is thus methodologically, and perhaps even ethically, hard to justify (Volet and Renshaw 1996).

### The contextual approach

The Volet and Renshaw study (1996; see p. 130) redefines the issue as a matter of *learning in context*, not as one of deficit. Thus, in Singapore you learn one set of adaptive strategies, in Australia you learn another set, but there will be some overlap ('searching for main ideas' is adaptive in both contexts). The teacher's task is to make it clear what is required for the immediate context, not just to assume it as the tacit Right Way that any decent student instinctively knows. This requires level 3 thinking: using a model of teaching to decide specifically what students are required to do, and how they are supposed to go about doing it.

Learning in context is simply aligned teaching: the TLAs encourage students to engage those cognitive processes most likely to achieve the objectives. And just to make sure, you use assessment tasks that will give them a healthy reminder that you mean business, as we see in the following two chapters.

If the level 3 position means anything at all, it is that all students benefit from good teaching. Conversely, under poor teaching, both local and international students face similar problems. In a comprehensive study across three universities, both local and international students nominated the following difficulties (Mullins *et al.* 1995):

- poor teaching;
- mismatch between student and staff expectations;
- lack of access to staff;
- heavy workload.

Differences between the two groups of students were not therefore in the nature of the problems they experienced. Although international students often experienced more difficulty in handling some of them, they cannot be nominated as being unable to adapt to our teaching, when other students already have the same problems. It is level 1 thinking again. The problem lies in the teaching, not in the students.

## Summary and conclusions

### Who are international students? What kinds of problem do they present?

In this chapter we address the problems perceived by many teachers, particularly pertinent in these days of selling our academic wares to overseas 'consumers', in teaching students of non-Anglo-Celtic ethnic backgrounds. Of course they experience problems of adjustment, homesickness and language, but our concern is with teaching method itself. Non-Anglo-Celtic students are perceived as not fitting well into our established ways of teaching. But how you perceive that depends on your vantage point; each of our three levels of teaching presents a different perspective on the teaching of ISs.

We have tended to concentrate here on ISs from Far Eastern countries. That is because the relevant research has been done on these students. The present argument, and the remedy, is, however, precisely the same whether the students are African, Asian or European.

### Level 1: teaching as assimilation

A level 1 view belongs in the pre-multicultural days of enforced assimilation. The more ISs are seen to differ from local students, the greater the expected problems in teaching them. So, they must become more like local students. Teachers with this view look for differences between ISs and locals, and find them. Many differences are real enough in themselves, but they lead to stereotyping, which in turn leads to self-fulfilling prophecies: 'They will only rote learn, so all I can do is lecture them and give recall tests. I'd prefer not to, of course!' Of course.

### Level 2: teaching as accommodation

Level 2 thinking asks that teachers accommodate to student differences. The extreme view of this is that we learn several packages of 'alien teaching technologies', as one writer suggested, so we can teach each alien group in their own alien-specific way – which is quite absurd. What we can do is to accommodate in our normal teaching by speaking more slowly, less colloquially, backing up verbal with non-verbal content. As Ballard and Clanchy (1997) say, 'Address the problems presented by ISs, and you'll teach better.'

### Level 3: teaching as educating

But I say, 'Teach better, and you'll address the problems presented by ISs.' You teach better by focusing not on how students differ, not even on what you are doing, but on what your students are doing. The level 1 view that Asians, for example, find difficulty with 'active' teaching methods is dangerously wrong. Active methods are the basis of good teaching with any students. Examples are given where Asian students do as well as westerners under innovative teaching methods, any differences lying in the tactics of implementation, not in the strategy of teaching.

### Approaches to teaching international students

Levels 1 and 2 lead to deficit approaches to teaching, which cannot be justified empirically or in principle. Level 3 leads to a contextual approach, which uses the context established to extract the appropriate learning behaviour from students – all students, whether Anglo-Celtic or not. Contextual teaching is inclusive, and it rests on three propositions:

1 Persistent teaching problems lie not in the student but in the teaching.
2 In our teaching, we should focus on the similarities between students rather than on the differences. Differences obviously exist, but to focus on them is counterproductive.
3 Accordingly, allowing for the needs of special groups, such as ISs, is best done within the whole teaching system.

Level 3 teaching is inclusive, addressing the needs of all students: Robert, Susan, Nirmala and Ah Hung.

### Further reading

Allen, A. and Higgins, T. (1994) *Higher Education: The International Student Experience*. London: Heist.
Ballard, B. and Clanchy, J. (1997) *Teaching International Students*. Deakin, ACT: IDP Education Australia.
McNamara, D. (ed.) (1997) *Overseas Students in Higher Education*. London: Routledge.
Watkins, D. and Biggs, J. (eds) (1996) *The Chinese Learner: Cultural, Psychological and Contextual Influences*. Hong Kong: Centre for Comparative Research in Education/Camberwell, Vic.: Australian Council for Educational Research.
Watkins, D. and Biggs, J. (eds) (2001) *Teaching the Chinese Learner: Psychological and Pedagogical Perspectives*. Hong Kong: Centre for Comparative Research in Education/Camberwell, Vic.: Australian Council for Educational Research.

The first three books give background on ISs in the UK and Australia. While the issues are the same, the specifics are different, in particular the cultural backgrounds of ISs in these two countries.

The last two books are on teaching students in the Chinese diaspora. The first focuses on the so-called paradox of the Chinese learner: given that the classroom teaching conditions seem by western criteria to be substandard, how is it that Chinese students do so very well in international comparisons? Addressing that 'paradox' raises many of the issues addressed in the present chapter. The second book delves into the kind of teaching that students receive in their own countries, and from which we in the West could gain much of value – and not only when teaching students from the Confucian heritage culture.

# 8

## Assessing for learning quality I: principles

What and how students learn depends to a major extent on how they think they will be assessed. Assessment practices must send the right signals to students about what they should be learning and how they should be learning it. Current practice, however, is distorted because two quite different models of summative assessment have, for historical reasons, been confused, and the wrong signals are often sent to students. In this chapter, these issues are clarified. We examine the purposes of assessment, the relation between assessment and the assumed nature of what is being assessed, assessing for desirable but unexpected learning outcomes, and who might usefully be involved in the assessing process. The underlying principle is that the assessment tasks should comprise a genuine representation of the objectives of the course or unit.

### Backwash: the effects of assessment on learning

We teachers might see the curriculum objectives as the central pillar of teaching in an aligned system, but our students see otherwise: 'From our students' point of view, assessment always defines the actual curriculum' (Ramsden 1992: 187). Students learn what they think they will be tested on. This is *backwash*, when the assessment determines what and how students learn more than the curriculum does. In a poorly aligned system, where the test does not reflect the objectives, this will result in inappropriate surface learning.

Backwash is almost invariably seen negatively (Crooks 1988a; Frederiksen and Collins 1989). Recall the 'forms of understanding' that Entwistle and Entwistle's (1997) students constructed: not to apply to problems but to meet presumed assessment requirements (see p. 35). But learning for the

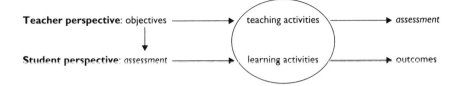

**Figure 8.1:** Teacher's and student's perspectives on assessment

assessment is inevitable; students would be foolish if they didn't. The trick is to align the assessment to what students should be learning (Figure 8.1). Backwash then becomes positive.

To the teacher, assessment is at the end of the teaching–learning sequence of events, but to the student it is at the beginning. If the curriculum is reflected in the assessment, as indicated by the downward arrow in Figure 8.1, the teaching activities of the teacher and the learner activities of the learner are both directed towards the same goal. In preparing for the assessments, students will be learning the curriculum.

It sounds easy, but there is a long tradition of thinking about assessment, and some time-honoured assessment practices, that complicate matters. In this chapter, we clarify some of the conceptual issues involved; in the next, we look at assessment practices that tell us what we want to know, which is how well our students are learning what we have taught them.

## Why assess?

### Formative and summative assessment

There are many good reasons why we should assess students, but two are outstandingly important:

1 *Formative* assessment, the results of which are used for *feedback* during learning. Students and teachers both need to know how learning is proceeding. Feedback may operate both to improve the learning of individual students, and to improve teaching.
2 *Summative* assessment, the results of which are used to *grade* students at the end of a unit, or to accredit at the end of a programme.

Other reasons for assessing include: selecting students, controlling or motivating students (the existence of assessment keeps class attendance high and set references read), and to satisfy public expectations as to standards and accountability. These and other aspects of assessment will be addressed as necessary.

Formative assessment is inseparable from teaching. Indeed, the effectiveness of different teaching methods is directly related to their ability to provide formative feedback. The lecture itself provides little. The improvements to the lecture mentioned in Chapter 6 were almost all formative in function, checking ongoing understandings. Admitting error leads to better understanding in future. Students need to learn to take over the formative role for themselves, monitoring themselves as they learn, and as we shall see, self- and peer assessment are particularly helpful for this.

Summative evaluation is carried out after the teaching episode has concluded. Its purpose is to see how well students have learned what they were supposed to have learned. That result, the grade, is final. Students fear this outcome, as futures hinge on it. They will be singularly unwilling to admit their mistakes. Error no longer is there to instruct, as in formative assessment; error now signals punishment. This difference between formative and summative is important in discussing progressive assessment (see below).

Nevertheless, both formative and summative assessment are similar in that in each we match performance as it is, with the performance as it should be; the difference between them is that at some point that judgement has to be final. 'When the chef tastes the sauce it is formative assessment; when the customer tastes it, it is summative' (Anon).

Figure 8.2 puts this another way. Say four topics are to be learned in a semester. The objectives of each are symbolized as O1, O2, O3 and O4. At

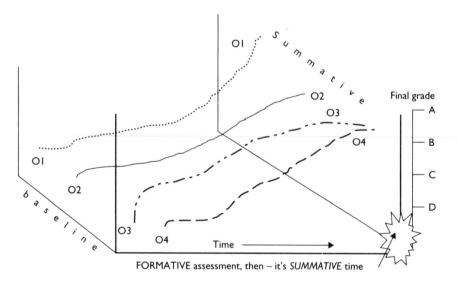

**Figure 8.2:** Learning in four topics and their formative and summative assessment

the start of the semester (labelled 'baseline'), students enter with little or some knowledge, which with teaching keeps on growing until the end of the semester. Formative assessment checks that growth and sees that it is on track. Then it is time to see where each student stands with respect to each of the four topics; this is the summative assessment task. Finally, there is the administrative matter of converting those four positions into a grade, taken here as A, B, C and D.

This model of topic-learning underlies most of the issues to be discussed in this and the next chapter. From now on, we are mostly concerned with the most problematical form of assessment, summative. It arouses passion, resistance and subterfuge. In this chapter we see that the waters have been muddied because two quite different models of assessment have become confused. When we have unconfused them, we look in the next chapter at putting the appropriate model of assessment to work.

## Norm-referenced and criterion-referenced assessment

The results of summative assessment can be expressed in two ways:

1 We can report a grade that tells us which students performed better than other students. The rank order is the simplest such grading, which tells who is better than whom. Such assessment is *norm-referenced* (NRA).
2 We can report a grade that tells us what a student has learned and how well. Here, each student's grade depends on the goodness of fit with the objectives and is independent of any other student's. Such assessment is *criterion-referenced* (CRA).

### Norm-referenced assessment

NRA is widespread, if not in the simplest form where a student's final grade is expressed as his or her position in class, in some other method based on comparisons between students. Universities, for example, frequently 'grade on the curve'; that is, the top 10 per cent of the class, say, are awarded high distinction, the next 15 per cent distinction, the next 25 per cent credit, and 45 per cent pass. The results will appear to be stable from year to year, and from department to department. If there is a query from the odd student about the grade awarded, it is easy to point to an unarguable figure: all objective, very precise. 'You didn't earn enough marks. The others were too good for you. Sorry.'

The very term 'high distinction' is comparative, applicable only to the few who are highly distinguished. This puts the brake on the number of high distinctions awarded. If one-third of a class obtained high distinctions, it would be seen as a contemptible fall in standards, not as a cause for congratulation. The more neutral 'A' for the top grade makes it easier to accept that a high proportion of students could reach the A standard – and that that would be a cause for celebration rather than for scorn.

### Criterion-referenced assessment

The logic of CRA is stunningly obvious: say what you want students to be able to do, teach them to do it, and then see if they can in fact do it. There is a corollary that is not often taken up: if they cannot do it, try again until they can, as in 'mastery learning' (Bloom *et al.* 1971). The Keller Plan is a mastery model for universities (Keller 1968). Students are allowed as many tries at the assessment as they (reasonably) need in order to pass the pre-set standard. Some students pass in short order, others take much longer, and that requires flexible organizing. The main problem with such mastery learning models historically was that the pre-set criteria tended to be quantitatively defined, which work well with surface-oriented students. Lai and Biggs (1994) found that surface-oriented biology students performed better and better under mastery learning, while deep-oriented, initially better, ended up performing worse than the surface students, which is an unusual finding.

Such objections do not apply to the principle of CRA, but to the criteria used. As a teaching strategy, CRA is used universally outside formal education. Parents don't lecture a toddler on shoe-tying, and give a multiple-choice test at the end. The objective, the teaching/learning activity, and the assessment are all the same: it is tying a shoe. In the case of driving instruction it is driving a car. The alignment is perfect. This is what we should be aiming for in university teaching.

Sometimes we seem to have it right, particularly at postgraduate levels. Despite the prevailing norm-referenced cast of mind at undergraduate level, the sheer logic of CRA is readily seen in assessing theses and dissertations (but not always readily enough, see Box 3.1). We expect a dissertation to display certain characteristics: coverage of the literature, definition of a clear and original research question, mastery of research methods, and so on. The categories of honours (first class, upper second, lower second) originally suggested qualities that students' work manifested: a first was qualitatively *different* from an upper second, it was not simply that the first got more sums right. Today, this approach might be in jeopardy, as these categories seem increasingly to be defined in terms of ranges of marks, which is unfortunate, as we will be examining.

An interesting twist on CRA is Cowan's (2001) 'sound system' or 'plus/minus marking', which is so obvious, he says, it 'surely must have emerged in umpteen schools of assessment'. Well, it apparently hasn't. In sound system the teacher writes a detailed benchmark statement about what a motivated student might reasonably be expected to do with respect to a set assignment or other assessment task. This would be about halfway between a bare pass and the border for first class honours. The teacher then awards a plus or double-plus each time the student work exceeds the benchmark, or minus when it falls short, with respect to the benchmark statements. Cowan uses a quantitative system, starting at 55 per cent (midway between 40 per cent pass and 70 per cent first class), but it could be used with a qualitative category system (see below) just as easily. The great virtue of the system is that it is transparent, both teacher and student use it, and follow up with 'informed debate'.

For CRA to work, we first need to be clear about what our students *should* be learning, either in terms of qualities or performances that define the grading categories (preferably A, B, C, D), or in Cowan's case that define a benchmark position, and then to devise assessment tasks that tell us how well they meet the criteria. The first task is a matter of setting objectives, which was the subject of Chapter 3. The second task of assessing against the criteria is the focus for this and the following chapter.

### Differences between NRA and CRA

Because of the universality of many NRA practices in teaching, and the educational logic of CRA, we should be quite clear about the differences. To recap briefly:

1 NRA results are expressed in terms of comparisons between students after teaching is over. CRA results are expressed in terms of how well a given student's performance matches criteria that have been already set.
2 CRA standards are usually set before teaching has taken place. Exceptionally, you might find after teaching that the criteria for CRA were inappropriately high or low and need changing before reporting the final grades. But any student's grade is still in terms of the final criteria. NRA grades can only be known after both teaching and assessing are completed.
3 NRA makes judgements about *people*, CRA makes judgements about *performance*.

Task 8.1 presents a quick, criterion-referenced test to sort the sheep from the goats (joke). Answers can be found at the end of this chapter.

A summary of the differences between CRA and NRA is captured in Table 8.1, which lists a lexicon of NRA and CRA words. The only term common to both? Summative assessment.

### Task 8.1:  NRA or CRA?

**Two common queries.** I am assessing two students in a CRA system, and note that I have awarded Robert a B and Susan an A. I then take a second look and decide that Robert's paper is as good as Susan's, so I give both an A. Is this now NRA (comparing students) or CRA (judging on standards)? Why?

_____

_____

I am intending to operate a CRA system, and in deciding what standards are reasonable to set for the grading categories, I look at last years' distributions of As, Bs, Cs, Ds and Fs, and adjust the difficulty of the tasks so that I am likely to obtain a similar result this year. Is this NRA or CRA? Why?

_____

_____

_____

_____

**Table 8.1:**   Two lexicons

| _Norm-referenced assessment_ | _Criterion-referenced assessment_ |
| --- | --- |
| mark, percentage, decile, rank order, summative assessment* | assess, authentic/performance assessment, contextualized, standards, formative assessment, summative assessment*, criteria |
| exam, multiple-choice test, short answer decontextualized assessment, standardization, 'fairness' | portfolio, concept map, reflective journal, individualization, optimal performance, student-centred qualitative, grading categories, curriculum objectives, alignment, judgement, distribution-free, non-parametric statistics |
| quantitative, average, grade-point average, normal/bell curve, normal distribution | |
| grading on the curve, a good spread of scores | |
| parametric statistics, test–retest reliability, internal consistency, discrimination | effort, skill, learning, competency, expertise, mastery |
| selection, competition, high flier, ability | |

*The one word in common.

## The measurement model of assessment

In Han Dynasty China, in the 4th century BC, the purpose of education was selective. Students were required to master a huge classical curriculum in order to put into effect Confucius' belief that 'those who excel in their study should become officials' (quoted in Zeng 1999: 21). The winners, however lowly their background, were motivated by a rich prize: a lifetime of wealth and prestige. This was norm-referenced assessment in the raw. The idea was to select the best individuals in terms of stable characteristics: 'not only intelligence, but also character, determination, and the will to succeed' (p. iv).

Twenty-three centuries later, psychologists in the nineteenth century also became interested in sorting people out. Sir Francis Galton (1889) found that physical and mental differences such as height, weight and performance on various mental tests, which he called traits, were distributed in 'an unsuspected and most beautiful form of regularity' (p. 66). He was of course referring to the normal curve, a distribution that occurs *inter alia* as a result of polygenetic inheritance of traits. Galton's assumptions, not only about statistical techniques but also about the inheritance of ability and of educability, were built into the burgeoning industry of mental testing in the early part of this century. Educability was assumed to be about how bright people were and, back to the Han Dynasty, education was seen as a device for sorting people out. Today, the so-called parametric statistical procedures, based on Galton's work, are used for constructing educational tests, establishing their reliability and validity, and interpreting test scores. Taylor (1994) refers to this individual differences model as 'the measurement model' of educational assessment. We turn to this now; there is some deconstructing to do.

The measurement model is designed to measure an underlying trait or ability, and express that measurement along a graduated scale so that individuals can be compared, either with each other or against population norms. This is fine for research, or for diagnosis when dealing with individuals – for example to say how atypical a person is on reading ability – but when applied to assessing educational outcomes, several problems arise. First we examine the assumptions underlying the model, then we look at some common procedures the model generates, and finally we examine the backwash on students' learning.

### Assumptions underlying the measurement model

Following are five assumptions underlying the model as it applies to education.

*1   The measurement model is based on a quantitative view of knowledge*
Assumptions about learning and its assessment may be quantitative or qualitative in nature (Cole 1990; Marton *et al.* 1993). In a quantitative framework, learning is evaluated according to how much correct material has been learned and can be displayed. Better learners are those who know more. The level 1 view of teaching makes essentially quantitative assumptions, as we noted briefly in Chapter 2: teaching involves transmitting the main points, assessment involves marking students on their ability to report them back accurately. The uni- and multistructural stages of the SOLO taxonomy are quantitative, where learning is a matter of finding out more and more about the topic.

The level 3 view of teaching and learning, on the other hand, makes qualitative assumptions: teaching involves helping the learner to construct more effective ways of viewing a section of the world. The relational and extended abstract SOLO levels are qualitative because both depend on the way data have been structured rather than on the amount of data present. We return to the qualitative framework later.

The present point is that the measurement model necessarily requires quantitative view of learning, because it projects individual performances as scores along a continuum so that individuals may be compared with each other. This quantitative basis gives rise to procedures that create problems, as examined below.

*2   Percentages are a universal currency*
One of the commonest forms of quantification is the percentage, derived either as the ratio of number right to maximum possible multiplied by 100, or as sets of ratings the maxima of which total 100. When this transformation is carried out, it is assumed that percentages are a universal currency, equivalent across subjects areas, and across students, so that different students' performances in different subjects can be directly compared. This is completely unsustainable, yet universities have long and earnest debates about one faculty using 75 per cent as the cut-off for an A grade, and another using 70 per cent as the cut-off. 'We must level the playing-field across faculties, otherwise it's not fair that it's easier to get an A in arts than it is in science!' These otherwise intelligent people are trying to extract certainty from the unknowable. There is simply no way of knowing if 75 per cent in physics is the same standard as 75 per cent in history; or even if a student's result of 75 per cent in psychology 2 this year represents an improvement over 70 per cent the same student obtained in psychology 1 the previous year.

*3   The test needs to spread students out, clearly sorting the high from the low performers*
This assumption is built into the construction of tests. Measurement experts have maintained that a good attainment test yields 'a good spread'

that follows the bell curve (back to Galton). However, this only applies if ability is the sole determinant of academic attainment, and if ability itself is normally distributed. But the ability of our students is not likely to be normally distributed, because students are not randomly selected (not quite yet, anyway). So, there is not only no reason to expect a bell curve distribution of ability in our classes, at university level there is every reason *not* to expect such a distribution.

In any event, ability is not the sole determinant of students' learning outcomes. Other factors are called 'teaching' and 'learning'. As argued in Chapter 1, good teaching tends to override individual differences, producing a *smaller* spread of final results than that predicted by the initial spread of ability. The gap between Robert and Susan is narrowed. The distribution of results after good teaching is not bell-shaped but skewed, with high scores more frequent than low scores. Forcing attainment scores to follow the curve prevents us from seeing the real picture of what standards are achieved.

*4 Quantitative approaches to assessment are scientific, precise and objective*

Numbers mislead. The measurement model yields an extended continuous scale that invites minute distinctions between students, but we have to be careful. The error of measurement in usual class sizes is bound to be rather more than one percentage point. Worse, the scales we are dealing with are not equal-interval scales where the difference between any two adjacent numbers is the same as between any other two. This is an *essential* property if we are to average and accumulate marks: that is, the difference between 73 and 74, say, must be the same as the difference between 79 and 80, if I am going to add marks or average them. But the difference between 79 and 80 becomes zero when first class honours is awarded to a dissertation of 79 marks when the cut-off is 80 (Box 3.1, see p. 52). Many times, teachers and boards of examiners are faced with the borderline case, and argue that as the scale is not accurate to one mark, we'll give the student the benefit of the doubt. Our scale is elastic, and distinctly more rubbery at some points along the scale than at others.

Do such decisions show how human we are, or are we just being sloppy? We are both and neither. We are being wonderfully inappropriate. We are cooking a gourmet dinner in the chemistry lab. The precision of the parametric measurement model is just as out of place in the classroom as is weighing sugar in milligrams. It is worse actually, because the procedure of quantifying qualitative data, such as shifts in students' understandings, requires arbitrary judgements as to what is a unit, what is 'worth' one mark, five marks, however many marks. These judgements are not only subjective, they often do not even have an explicit and examinable rationale, beyond a vague norm-referencing: 'I am marking out of five, this is the best so it gets five, this is above average so it gets four.' What it is that makes 'best' is not specifically examined.

What happens, then, is that a series of independent minor subjective judgements – a mark for this, a mark for that – accumulate. The big decision – pass or fail, first class or upper second class honours – is made on the aggregate of numbers, which includes the aggregate of error in all those minor judgements. That big decision should be made not on the accumulation of unknowably flawed minor judgements, but on a reasoned and publicly sustainable judgement about the performance itself.

The application of a precise and scientific model to an area where it does not apply cannot be scientific.

### 5  University education is selective
A traditional view of universities reflects that of Han Dynasty China. Universities are a selective device to find the intellectuals in the population. A related view is that because the purpose of the undergraduate years is to weed out the pass-level students from the potential postgraduate research students, assessment should be norm-referenced. A not uncommon practice is inserting trick questions in the exam that aren't in the curriculum 'to identify the high fliers'. The aim is clearly to search for an ability or quality inherent in the student – à la measurement model – not to see how well the curriculum has been learned.

The only place for selective assessment in the university context is for entry to university, or to graduate school. At entry, a convenient estimate of scholastic ability is obtained by summing a student's best three, or best five, HSC or A-level subjects, with or without adjustments for second attempt. What you get is a measure of scholastic ability, which is robust enough to allow direct comparisons between students in different subject areas. It is rough, but it works over large numbers. Once students have been selected, however, the aim of teaching is to get students to learn what is in the curriculum. And in that enterprise the measurement model has no place.

### Some procedures deriving from the measurement model

There are numerous examples where current practice is muddied with procedures deriving from the measurement model.

### 1  Grading on the curve
Many people, teachers, administrators and even students, feel that it is 'fitting' that a few should do extremely well, most should do middling well, and a few do poorly, some failing. This feeling comes straight from the assumptions that ability determines learning outcomes and that ability is normally distributed. Both assumptions are untenable as we have seen.

Then there are the practical reasons for grading on the curve. First, it is so easy. All you need to determine the grades is a test that will rank order the students – a quick and dirty multiple-choice test will do – and then you simply award an A to the first 15 per cent, B to the next 25 per cent and so on. Alignment is irrelevant. The second reason appeals to administrators. Grading on the curve conveys the impression that standards over all departments are 'right', not too slack, not too stringent, and we have got it right, year after year. This is an artefact: the distribution has been defined that way, whatever the actual results in any given year or department.

The worst thing that can be said about grading on the curve is that it precludes CRA and aligned teaching. It is a procedure that cannot be justified on educational grounds.

### 2 *Marking by counting bottom-up and averaging*

Marking is an assessment procedure that comes directly from quantitative assumptions. It is so widespread as to be universal, but it is a procedure that needs to be examined closely. By 'marking', I mean quantifying learning performances, either by transforming them into units (a word, an idea, a point), or by allocating ratings or 'marks' on a subjective if not arbitrary basis. One mark must be 'worth' the same as any other, so that they can be added and averaged. A grade is then awarded on the number of marks accumulated; it seems almost universally accepted that half the total available is the pass mark. Thus, it does not matter *what* is correct, as long as there are enough of them.

Multiple-choice tests enact these assumptions exactly. Learning is represented as the total of all items correct. Students quickly see that the score is the important thing, not how it is comprised, and that the ideas contained in any one item are of the same value as in any other item (Lohman 1993). We return to a more detailed consideration of this assessment format in the next chapter.

The essay format, technically open-ended, does not preclude quantitative means of assessment. When multiple markers use marking schemes, they give a mark or two as each 'correct' or 'acceptable' point is made, possibly with bonus points for argument, or style. This too sends misleading messages to students about the structure of knowledge and how to exploit its assessment (Biggs 1973; Crooks 1988a). A good example is the strategy in timed examinations of attempting all questions and finishing none, rather than writing a properly structured answer to fewer questions. The reasoning is that the law of diminishing returns applies: the time spent on the first half of an essay nets more marks than the same time spent on the second half. The more facts, the more marks – never mind the structure they make. The point is that students don't learn 'marks', they learn structures, concepts, theories, narratives, skills, performances of understanding. These are what should be assessed, not arbitrary quantifications of them. It is like examining architects on the number of bricks their designs use, never mind the structure, function or aesthetics of the building itself.

Analytic marking of essays or assignments is also common, and is often highly recommended for its reliability. Here, a complex performance, such as an essay, is reduced to independent components, such as content, style, referencing, argument, originality, format and so on, each of which is rated on a separate scale. The final performance is then assessed as the sum of the separate ratings. Of course it is helpful formatively to give students feedback on how well they are doing on component aspects of a task, but the final performance, such as treating a patient, or making a legal case, make sense only when seen as a whole. We return to this issue later in this chapter.

### 3 Assessment separated from teaching

In the measurement model, assessment is a stand-alone activity, unrelated to teaching as such. Accordingly, it attracts its own context and culture. One feature is the need for standardized conditions, a necessary condition when students are to be compared with each other. Guaranteeing standardized procedures leads to a theory X, bureaucratic assessment climate: emphasis on decontextualized assessment tasks that can be given under timed conditions and invigilated, strict deadlines for assignments that usually require deducting marks if they are not met, no revising or second attempts, and common assessment tasks that all students have to attempt ('choice of question' in an exam being the main concession to individuality).

In universities that work in this way, teaching occupies the greater part of the academic year, assessment a frantic couple of weeks at the end. I can recall, now with shame, not even thinking about the final examination until the papers were due to be sent to the central examinations section. You teach as it comes, you set an examination, the examination centre invigilates it for you, you allocate the marks. Alignment doesn't come into it.

### The effects of backwash from the measurement model

The messages sent to students from measurement model procedures have been alluded to in the above discussion. Let me recapitulate briefly:

1 The trees are more important than the wood. Maximizing marks is the important thing, not seeing the overall structure of what is being learned. Put another way, the measurement model encourages multistructural thinking, not relational or extended abstract.

2 Verbatim responses will gain marks. If we are marking 'units', then although a verbatim replay of a unit in the text or in the lecture may not be very noble, it has to be given some credit (if cheating is ruled out

under an invigilated testing context) in a multistructural marking scheme. This happens even when the teacher warns that verbatim responses will be penalized (Biggs 1973).

3 Attributions to uncontrollable factors such as ability, luck. An individual's result under NRA depends on the competition, who is more able. Thus, in the event of a poor result, the student can either blame bad luck or, more damagingly, come to the conclusion that he or she is simply not as able as other people. The individual can do nothing about luck or ability; their performance is out of their hands. The attribution under CRA is different: 'Here is what I am supposed to have achieved, I didn't, what went wrong?' The answer to that could be: 'I didn't put in enough effort', 'I didn't know how to do it', at worst, 'I am dumb.' Apart from the last, the other attributions under CRA are under the individual's control, where none of those under NRA are.

Given all this, why do measurement model procedures remain? Box 8.1 suggests some answers.

---

**Box 8.1: Why measurement model procedures remain**

**1 Tradition, habit**
- Why question what has worked well in the past, especially when administrative structures and procedures make change difficult?

**2 Bureaucratic convenience**
- Dealing with numbers gives the illusion of precision. Any appeal or disagreement is over trivial issues. Let the numbers make the big decisions.
- Grading on the curve gives the illusion of constant standards, no egregious departments or results.
- The language of percentages is generally understood (another illusion).
- Given the tight security of exams, assurances of authenticity can be given.
- Combining results from different departments needs a common framework: the percentage and normalized scores (both illusions, see above).

**3 Teaching convenience**
- You teach, the exam questions can be left until well into the teaching, exams section will see to the details. It is flexible on coverage, what questions you set.
- You can easily average and combine marks across tasks, and across courses.
- You can use marks for disciplinary purposes (deduct for late submission).
- It's easier to argue numbers with students in case of dispute than to argue 'subjective' structures.

**4 Genuine belief in the measurement model**
- My job *is* to sort the sheep from the goats.

Nevertheless, some academics realize the problems with marking and the measurement model, and try to avoid them. Box 8.2 represents a valiant attempt by an arts faculty at an unnamed university to move towards CRA. Previously, a marks system was used to define A+, A and A−, and so on, and the attempt was made at faculty board to devise a scheme

---

**Box 8.2:   How faculty office suggests final grades should be determined**

The following guidelines were issued to all staff in the faculty. They were to use these in arriving at their final grade distributions:

**A** (A+, A, A−)   Excellence, up to 10 per cent of students. The student must show evidence of original thought as well as having a secure grasp of the topic from background reading and analysis.

**B** (B+, B, B−)   Good to very good result, achieved by next 30 per cent of students who are critical and analytical but not necessarily original in their thinking and who have a secure grasp of the topic from background reading and analysis. Occasionally, a student who shows originality but is less secure might achieve this result.

**C** (C+, C, C−)   Satisfactory to reasonably good result. The students have shown a reasonably secure grasp of their subject but probably most of their information is derivative, with rather little evidence of critical thinking. Most students will fall into this category.

**D**                     Minimally acceptable. The students have put in effort but work is marred by some misunderstandings, but not so serious that the student should fail. Students falling into this category, and outright failures, would not normally comprise more than about 10 per cent.

*Source:* The Faculty of Arts Handbook, the University of . . .

What is the problem here?  _____

_____

_____

_____

An answer is given at the end of the chapter.

that defined the grading categories, avoiding marks. The new system was issued to all teachers in the faculty.

Now let us turn to what we should be doing.

## The standards model of assessment

The standards model of assessment is the model designed especially for assessing learning in a teaching situation. Unlike the measurement model, it is based on a qualitative view of learning, and has different implications for assessment. The standards model makes the following assumptions:

1 *We can set standards (criteria) as course or unit objectives.* This has been done in Chapter 3. Qualitative assessment does not directly address the question of how much the student knows, but *how well.* If the objectives are arranged in a letter-grade hierarchy, the assessment tasks indicate the level in the hierarchy at which a given student can perform. That level becomes the grade awarded.

2 *Most students should be able to reach these standards at an acceptable level.* This is what the grading system is about. What is 'acceptable'? Using SOLO, it seemed that a relational level of understanding – being able to integrate topics and use the knowledge – is probably the main aim on most units, which is fairly high compared with many requirements. Most students should therefore be achieving grade B or more? What will your colleagues on the board of examiners think of that? Clearly, we need to be both realistic and clear-thinking about what 'most students' should be able to achieve. As a matter of principle, most students *should* achieve a relational level (but see Box 8.2, where most students were expected to use derivative information). On the other hand, most students should pass, so there is a fine balance to achieve.

3 *Different performances can reflect the same standards.* While standardized conditions are required when individuals are to be compared, when we are seeking to find the optimum performance of individuals, the more standardized the conditions the less valid the test is likely to be for any given individual. Individuals learn and perform optimally in different conditions, and with different formats of assessment. Some work better under pressure, others need more time. As in professional work itself, there are often many ways of achieving a satisfactory outcome. Individual students demonstrate their best work in different ways, which is a major advantage of portfolio assessment.

4 *Teachers can judge performances against the criteria.* This is critical. In order to make these holistic judgements teachers need a theory of learning as it applies to their discipline. All this means is that teachers need to know what is poor quality performance, what is good quality, and why.

There are some aspects of such a theory that are quite general, such as constructivism itself, which states that as a result of learner activity, learning proceeds cumulatively and changes its structure as it evolves, in the way described in the SOLO taxonomy for example. However, the description of the growth of complexity in learning is also topic-specific. How does a student's understanding of cardiac problems occurring during oedema grow in complexity? How will I recognize when the student's understanding meets the requirements in the objectives? Comparing this student's understanding with that student's, and grading accordingly, is no answer. Thus, the theory of topic learning must be articulated enough so that the quality of a given student performance can be described in terms of that theory.

These points are elaborated in the rest of this chapter.

### Authentic or performance assessment

It follows that in the standards model the assessment tasks authentically represent the knowledge to be learned. Verbal retelling is not often authentic; for example, we do not teach psychology or any other subject just so that students can tell us in their own words what we have told them. We need some sort of 'performance of understanding' (see pp. 36–8) that reflects the kind of understanding of the discipline that we want. Obvious as this may seem, some considered it necessary to make a point of what has become known in the literature as 'authentic assessment' (Wiggins 1989; Torrance 1994). The assessment tasks should at some point require an *active demonstration* of the knowledge in question, as opposed to talking or writing about it. However, the term 'authentic' implied that all other forms of assessment were inauthentic, which was unacceptable, so now we speak of 'performance assessment' (Moss 1992). It reminds us of what we already know in aligned teaching, that the test or assessment task should require students to do more than just tell us what they know – unless of course that really is all that we require.

### Performative and decontextualized assessments

The question of performance assessment raises the related question of whether the assessment tasks should be decontextualized or should require students to perform in context. Where the objectives target declarative knowledge, it is quite appropriate to assess it using declarative methods such as conventional pencil-and-paper tests. We thus arrive at an important distinction in assessment formats:

- Decontextualized assessments such as a written exam, or a term paper, which are suitable for assessing declarative knowledge.

- Performative assessments, such as a practicum, problem-solving or diagnosing a case study, which are suitable for assessing functioning knowledge.

While both decontextualized and contextualized learning and assessment have a place, in practice decontextualized assessment has been greatly overemphasized in proportion to its place in the curriculum. As we saw in Figure 3.1, functioning knowledge is underwritten by declarative knowledge, and we need to assess both. A common mistake is to assess only the lead-in declarative knowledge, not the functioning knowledge that emerges from it. For example, take the following SOLO hierarchy of assessment, from declarative to functioning, in rehabilitation science:

1 Test knowledge of the bones and the muscles of the hand (multistructural, declarative).
2 Explain how the bone and muscle systems interact to produce functional movement of the hand, for example in picking up a small coin from the floor (relational, but still declarative).
3 Given a trauma to one muscle group rendering it out of action, design a functional prosthesis to allow the hand to be used for picking up a coin (relational, functioning).

**Holistic and analytic assessment**

We return to the issue of holistic assessment which is so neglected in the measurement model. A valid or authentic assessment must be of the total performance, not just aspects of it. Example 3 above refers to a total performance. Consider this example from surgery. You want to be sure that the student can carry out the whole operation with high and reliable competency. An analytic assessment would test and mark knowledge of anatomy, anaesthesia, asepsis and the performance skills needed for making clean incisions, and then add the marks to see if they reach the requisite 50 (or in this case perhaps 80) per cent. Say a student accrues more than the number of marks needed to pass but removes the wrong part. On the analytic model a pass it must be.

Absurd this example may be, but in an analytic marking scheme inevitably some aspects of knowledge are traded off against others. The solution is not to blur the issue by spreading marks around to fill the cracks, but to require different levels of understanding or performance according to the importance of the sub-topic. Here, knowledge of anatomy was insufficient to allow the correct performance, hence the proper judgement is 'fail'. This is not to say that assessment of components should not be undertaken as formative assessment – in which case it is particularly useful (Lejk and Wyvill 2001a) – but, in the end, assessment should address the whole.

### Judging performances against the criteria

In making holistic assessments, however, the details are not ignored. The question is whether, like the bricks of a building or the characters in a novel, the specifics are tuned to create an overall structure or impact. We arrive at such a 'hermeneutic' judgement by understanding the whole in light of the parts. For example, an essay requiring reasoned argument involves making a case, just as a barrister has to make a case that stands or falls on its inherent plausibility. The judge does not rate individual aspects of the barrister's case – uses legal terms correctly (+10 marks), makes eye contacts with the jury (+5 marks), for too long (–3 marks) . . . – and then aggregates the counsel with most marks winning the suit. The argument as a whole has to be judged. It is the whole dissertation that passes, the complete argument that persuades, the comprehensive but concise proposal that gets funded, the applicant's case that wins promotion. Holistic assessment addresses that integral act.

Critics argue that because holistic assessment involves judgement, it is subjective. But as we have seen, awarding marks is a matter of judgement too, a series of mini-judgements, each one small enough to be handled without qualm. The numbers make the big decisions: if they add up to 50 or more, then it is a pass. At no point does one have to consider *what the nature* of a passing grade is as opposed to a fail, or of a distinction level of performance as opposed to a credit. One of the major dangers of quantitative assessment schemes is that teachers can shelter under them and avoid the responsibility of making the judgements that really matter: What is a good assessment task? Why is this a good performance? (Moss 1992).

The strategy of reducing a complex issue to isolated segments, rating each independently, and then aggregating to get a final score in order to make decisions, seems peculiar to schools and universities. It is not the way things work in real life. Moss (1994) gives the example of a journal editor judging whether to accept or reject a manuscript on the basis of informed advice from referees. The referees don't give marks, but argue on the intrinsic merits of the paper as a whole, and the editor has to incorporate their advice, resolve conflicting advice, and make a judgement about the whole paper: reject it, revise it, accept it. Moss reports that one of her own papers, which argued for a hermeneutic approach to educational assessment, was rejected by the editor of an educational journal on the grounds that a hermeneutic approach was not the model of assessment accepted in the educational fraternity. She then pointed out that the editor had used a hermeneutic approach to arrive at that conclusion. Her paper was accepted.

In order to assess learning outcomes holistically, it is necessary to have a conceptual framework that enables you to see the relationship between the parts and the whole. Teachers, like journal editors, need to develop their own framework. The SOLO taxonomy can be useful in assisting that process (see Figure 3.2, p. 48; also Boulton-Lewis 1998; Hattie and Purdie 1998; Lake 1999).

### Convergent and divergent assessment

We used the terms convergent and divergent in Chapter 5 in connection with student questioning. These terms were used originally by Guilford (1967) to describe two different forms of ability, but it is more useful to think of them as processes:

* *Convergent* – solving problems that have a particular, unique answer, as in most intelligence and ability test items. Convergent thinking is focused, or 'closed'.
* *Divergent* – generating alternatives, where the notion of being correct gives way to other assessments of value, such as aesthetic appeal, originality, usefulness, self-expression, creativity and so on. Divergent thinking is 'open'.

Sciences are seen as requiring convergent thinking, with bodies of knowledge to be mastered, and literary criticism as requiring divergent thinking, to generate a point of view. Hudson (1966) showed that undergraduate students with a convergent bias in their thinking did better at science, while those with a divergent bias did better in arts. This is, however, misleading because scientific research requires a dose of divergent thinking. Researchers and research students need to think generatively: 'What is wrong with this experiment?' 'How can I test this hypothesis?' Likewise, literary critics need to get their facts straight.

Both processes are involved in most high-level thinking and in professional work. Although the extended abstract end of the SOLO taxonomy is replete with open-ended verbs, such as 'generate', 'hypothesize', 'theorize', 'reflect', they cannot be effectively activated without prior content mastery. Creativity and originality need a solid knowledge base.

Teaching and assessment should therefore address both convergent and divergent processes, but convergent ones receive far more emphasis in the event. It is much easier to teach, and especially to assess, convergently. A right answer is easy to tell from a wrong answer. A creative answer is much more challenging:

*Teacher*: Can anyone tell me what infinity means? (*silence*). What is infinity?
*Billy*: Uh. I think it's like a box of Creamed Wheat.
*Teacher*: Don't be silly!

(Jones 1968: 72)

Creamed Wheat boxes had a picture of a man holding up a box of Creamed Wheat that had a picture of a man . . . *ad infinitum.*

A homely little example, but you can see why highly divergent students, even those who achieve well, tend to be disliked by teachers (Getzels and Jackson 1962). In our convergent focus, we can too easily dismiss an insight that at first glance seems irrelevant. But that flexibility of perspective is what sparks research ideas: what-would-happen-if. Fortunately, divergent thinking can be encouraged; I found plenty of divergent surprises in my student portfolios that conventional assessment would have missed, as reported in Chapter 11.

A level 1 view of teaching sees all assessment as convergent: 'Get right what I have just taught you.' When essays are marked with a checklist, marks are awarded only for matching the prescribed points, none for other points just as good or better. This is not what assessment should be about. Virtually all university-level subjects require at least some divergent assessment. Setting only closed questions is like trying to shoot fish in murky water, as we see in the next aspect of qualitative assessment.

**Unintended outcomes**

Now consider another metaphor for assessment, provided by a student teacher:

> When I stand in front of a class, I don't see stupid or unteachable learners, but boxes of treasures waiting for us to open.
>
> (In-service teacher education student,
> University of Hong Kong)

What 'treasures' students find in their educational experience is something that can surprise, delight, and of course disappoint too. When we assess using closed questions something like this occurs:

> *Teacher*: How many diamonds have you got?
> *Student*: I don't have any diamonds.
> *Teacher*: Then you fail!
> *Student*: But you didn't ask me about my jade.

Students' treasures need not be just in diamonds. If you only ask a limited range of questions, then you will probably miss the jade: the treasure that you didn't know existed because you didn't ask. Of course, if the objectives are expressed only in diamonds that is one thing, but frequently they are not, or ought not to be.

Any rich teaching context is likely to produce learning that is productive and relevant, but unanticipated. The value of many formal activities lies precisely in the surprises they generate, such as field trips, practica or lab sessions, while informal activities bring about unanticipated learning in infinite ways. The student talks to someone, reads a book not on the reading list, watches a television programme, browses the Net, does a host of things that sparks a train of thought, a new construction. Such learnings probably will not fit the questions being asked in the exam, but they could nevertheless be highly relevant to the unit objectives. Probably most scientific discoveries came about as a result of paying attention to unintended outcomes.

Assessment practices should allow for such rich learning experiences, but rarely do. In my undergraduate days, my psychology professor occasionally included the following in the final exam paper: 'Based on the first year syllabus, set and answer your own question on a topic not addressed in this paper.' Another was: 'Psychology. Discuss.' You had to answer these questions extremely well. He also used the rubric: 'Answer about five questions.' The conservative or insecure students answered exactly five. The more daring answered three, even two. They were, of course, the deep learners. Other ways of assessing unintended outcomes are reflective journals, critical incidents and the portfolio. We look at these in the next chapter.

Some may see a problem of 'fairness' here. Shouldn't all students be assessed on the same criteria? This complaint has weight only in a norm-referenced context, when you are comparing students with each other. Then, yes, you have to standardize so that all have a fair crack at however many grade As or higher distinctions have been allocated. In a criterion-referenced system, however, the complaint is irrelevant. The aim is to see what students have learned. If student A has learned X, and student B has learned Y, and X and Y are both interesting and valuable things to learn, where is the problem? Where the top level of objectives specifies creativity and originality, what is unfair is when the system does *not* allow for their assessment.

## Who takes part in the assessing? Self- and peer-assessment

Three stages are involved in assessment:

1 *Setting the criteria* for assessing the work.
2 *Selecting the evidence* that would be relevant to submit to judgement against those criteria.
3 *Making a judgement* about the extent to which these criteria have been met.

Traditionally, the teacher is the agent in all three assessment issues. As just noted, level 1 teaching sees assessment through convergent eyes. The teacher decides in advance that the evidence for learning comprises correct answers to a set of questions that again in the teacher's opinion addresses and represents the core content of the course, and the teacher does the marking.

*Self-assessment* (SA) and *peer-assessment* (PA) usually refer to student involvement in stage 3 above, but students can and often should be involved in stages 1 and 2 as well. Arguments can be made for all or any of these combinations (Harris and Bell 1986; Boud 1995). Students can be involved in discussing with the teacher what the criteria might be, which need not be the same for all students, as happens in a contract system. Students can also be involved in stage 2, that is, as the ones responsible for selecting the evidence to be put up against the criteria, as happens with assessment by portfolio. Finally, students can be involved in making the summative judgement (stage 3), but whether their involvement is for the value of the experience or is so their judgement can be included in the final grade, is another matter we look at in the next chapter.

Probably the strongest argument for SA and PA is that it provides a teaching/learning activity (TLA) that engages crucial and otherwise neglected aspects of student learning:

1 First-hand knowledge of the criteria for good learning. Students should be quite clear about what the criteria for good learning are, but when the teacher sets the criteria, selects the evidence and makes the judgement of the student's performance against the criteria, it is too easy for the students just to accept the teacher's judgement. They should be more actively involved in knowing what the criteria really mean. They should learn how to apply the criteria, to themselves and to others.

2 What is good evidence to submit to the criteria, and what is not? Telling students may not engage them. They need to learn what is good evidence being themselves actively involved in selecting it.

3 Making judgements about whether a performance or product meets the given criteria is vital for effective professional action in any field. Professionals need to make these judgements about their own performance (SA) and that of others (PA). It is the learning experience professionals say is most lacking in their undergraduate education (Boud 1986). Brew (1999) argues that students need to distinguish good from poor information now they are faced with an incredible overload of information from the web. A more general argument along these lines is that conventional assessment disempowers learners, whereas education is about empowering learners, and assessment can be made to play an empowering role (Leach *et al.* 2001).

4 The above three arguments are all about *learning*, not assessment in the traditional sense of checking after the learning event. Thus, SA and PA underline the essential unity of learning and assessment, as in Figure 8.2.

This is not to say that SA and PA cannot be used for summative assessment as well. The techniques of doing that are discussed in the next chapter.

## Reliability and validity

A frequent criticism of qualitative assessment is that it is subjective and unreliable. The measurement model is talking. Let us rephrase to apply to both models of assessment: Can we rely on the assessment results? Are they assessing what they should be assessing?

### Can we rely on the assessment results?

In the measurement model, reliability means:

* *Stability* – a test needs to come up with the same result on different occasions, independently of who was giving and marking it. Hence, test–retest reliability: give the same test to the same group again and you get the same result.
* *Dimensionality* – the test items need to measure the same characteristic, hence the usual measures of reliability: split-half, internal consistency (Cronbach $\alpha$).
* *Conditions of testing* – each testing occasion needs to be conducted under standardized conditions.

Here reliability is seen as a property of the test. Such tests are conceived, constructed and used within a sophisticated framework of parametric statistics, which requires that certain assumptions be met, for example that the score distributions need to be normal or bell-shaped.

In the standards model reliability means:

* *Intra-judge reliability* – does the same person make the same judgement about the same performance on two different occasions?
* *Inter-judge reliability* – do different judges make the same judgement about the same performance on the same occasion?

Here reliability is not a property of the test but of the ability of teachers/judges to make consistent judgements. This requires that they know what their framework of judgement is, and how to use it. It is not a matter of statistical operations but of being clear about what we are doing, what learning outcomes we want and why. In other words, reliable assessments are part and parcel of good teaching. We have been explicating the framework and the specific criteria for making informed and reliable judgements about students' learning from Chapter 3 onwards.

**Do the test scores assess what they should be assessing?**

In the measurement model, the test needs to be validated against some external criterion to show that the trait being measured behaves as it should if it were being measured accurately. Thus, the scores could be correlated with another benchmark test, or used as a variable in an experimental intervention, or in predicting an independent outcome.

In the case of the standards model, validity resides in the *interpretations and uses* to which test scores are put (Messick 1989), that is, in the test's alignment with the total teaching context. For example, if an exam results in students rote-learning model answers, then that is a consequence that invalidates the test. An aligned, or properly criterion-referenced assessment task is valid; a non-aligned one is invalid. The glue that holds the objectives, the teaching/learning environment, and the assessment tasks and their interpretation together is, again, *judgement.* There is now quite a good deal of agreement about reliability and validity in qualitative assessment (Frederiksen and Collins 1989; Moss 1992, 1994; Shepard 1993; Taylor 1994).

Table 8.2 draws all these points together, contrasting the measurement and standard models.

## Summary and conclusions

**Backwash: the effects of assessment on learning**

The effects of assessment on learning are usually deleterious. This is largely because assessment is treated as a necessary evil, the bad news of teaching and learning, to be conducted at the end of all the good stuff. Students second-guess the assessment and make that their syllabus, and will underestimate requirements if the assessments tasks let them, so they get by with low-level learning strategies. In aligned teaching, on the other hand, the assessment reinforces learning. Assessment is the senior partner in learning and teaching. Get it wrong, and the rest collapses. This and the following chapter aim to help you get it right.

**Why assess?**

The first thing to get right is the reason for assessing. There are two paramount reasons why we should assess: formative, to provide feedback during learning; and summative, to provide an index of how successfully the student has learned when teaching has been completed. Formative assessment is basic to good teaching, and has been addressed in earlier chapters. Our main concern in this chapter is with summative.

**Table 8.2:** Comparing the measurement and standards models

|  | *Measurement model* | *Standards model* |
|---|---|---|
| **Theory** | Quantitative. Classic test theory, using assumptions of parametric statistics | Qualitative. A theory of learning enabling consistent judgements. No assumptions about distributions |
| **Stability** | Scores remains stable over testing occasions | Scores after teaching should be higher than before teaching |
| **Dimensionality** | The test is unidimensional. All items measure the same construct | Test multidimensional (unless there is only one objective). The items address all of the course objectives |
| **Testing conditions** | Conditions need to be standardized | Conditions reflect an individual's optimal learning in the intended application of the learning |
| **Validity** | External: how well the test correlates with outside performances | Internal: how well scores relate to the teaching objectives and to the target performance domain |
| **Use** | Selecting students. Comparing individuals, population norms. Individual diagnosis | Assessing the effectiveness of learning, usually after instruction |

### Norm-referenced and criterion-referenced assessment

For a long time there has been a tradition that students should be graded according to how they compare against each other, as in ranking. Such assessments are norm-referenced (NRA), but they don't tell us what we as teachers really need to know: have the students learned what we set out to teach them? Have they, in other words, reached the criteria for learning that we set in our objectives (CRA)? NRA may be used for selecting students for university, but when teaching begins, CRA should be used to assess and report the progress of students in terms of the standards of performance reached. In practice, the thinking and practices of NRA have muddied the waters, in undergraduate education particularly.

### The measurement model of assessment

Norm-referenced thinking about educational assessment led to the easy hijacking of a model from individual differences psychology: the measurement model, designed to measure stable characteristics of individuals, so that they can be compared with each other or with population norms. The quantitative assumptions on which this model is based send all the wrong messages about what is to be learned and how it should be learned. The backwash tells students that they need to grub for marks, which requires them to atomize academic tasks rather than see the meaning of the whole. Unfortunately, many procedures deriving from the measurement model, such as marking, averaging and determining cut-off points for passing and higher grades, are very common.

### The standards model of assessment

The appropriate model for educational assessment is the standards model, which is based on CRA in a qualitative framework. It defines forms of knowledge to be reached at the end of teaching, expressed as various levels of acceptability in the objectives and grading system. This framework requires higher levels of judgement on the part of the teacher as to how well the students' performances match the objectives than does quantitative assessment. The assessment tasks need to be 'authentic' to the objectives, stipulating a quality of performance that the assessment tasks demand. The backwash tells students they need to match the target performances as well as they are able. In matching assessment tasks to the objectives, we need to consider the context of assessment, its holistic nature, whether the tasks are divergent or convergent, and to allow for unintended outcomes of teaching. Students will always learn relevant content in ways or forms that the teacher cannot anticipate – and cannot discover if only closed questions are asked.

### Who takes part in the assessing? Self- and peer-assessment

Traditionally, the teacher is the one who sets the assessment tasks, selects the evidence and makes the summative judgements. There are, however, many reasons why students should be brought into these assessment processes; knowing and being able to use the criteria for assessing how good one's learning is, is an intrinsic part of the learning process itself.

### Reliability and validity

Most of the prevailing wisdom about the reliability and validity of assessment is based on the measurement model. As that model goes out the window, so too do many of our assumptions about what is a 'good' test. As the quantitative scaffolding is dismantled, we find that notions of reliability and validity depended more and more upon the teacher's basic professional responsibility, which is to make judgements about the quality of learning.

## A choice to be made

To conclude this rather complex chapter, we are faced with a choice: a commitment to either the measurement or the standards model (Task 8.2). It is counterproductive to select aspects from each, as they are designed to perform different functions, they speak different languages (Table 8.1). Much common practice suffers from confusion between the two models. We must be clear about what we are doing.

Having made our choice between package 1 and package 2, there is the practical matter of carrying out summative assessment in line with the chosen package. We need to decide what particular modes of assessment might best suit our objectives, how to evaluate using these tasks, and to form summative statements of performance, and then to report the results. These practical matters are concern of the next chapter.

---

### Task 8.2:  Choose your assessment package

Assessment package 1 (norm-referenced)

- Knowledge is conceived as aggregated from units.
- Assessment tasks are decontextualized.
- Assessed analytically, processed and reported in quantitative terms.
- The teacher controls all aspects of assessment.

This model has a sophisticated technology, very effective for comparing students and for making actuarial decisions about students. It is not about knowledge, but about measuring characteristics of people. When used for assessing learning, it does violence to the structure of knowledge, creating negative backwash.

Assessment package 2 (criterion-referenced)

- Knowledge conceived as expressed in the objectives.
- Usually assessed qualitatively (but could be quantitative where appropriate.
- Assessment tasks are contextualized for assessing functioning knowledge and decontextualized for assessing declarative knowledge.
- Summative assessment is holistic but formative, may be analytic for determining ongoing progress.
- Reporting in qualitative categories (maybe later convertible to quantitative scales).
- Aspects of assessment can be teacher-controlled, peer-controlled or self-controlled as suits the task to be learned.

In this model, assessment is integral to teaching, the intention being to represent the objectives authentically.

### Choose your package!

---

## Further reading

Crooks, T.J. (1988) *Assessing Student Performance*, Green Guide No. 8. Sydney: Higher Education Research and Development Society of Australasia.

Dart, B. and Boulton-Lewis, G. (1998) *Teaching and Learning in Higher Education*. Camberwell, Vic.: Australian Council for Educational Research.

Entwistle, N. (1999) Approaches to studying and levels of understanding: the influences of teaching and assessment, in J.C. Smart (ed.) *Higher Education: Handbook of Theory and Research*, Vol. XV. New York: Agathon Press.

Moss, P.A. (1994) Can there be validity without reliability? *Educational Researcher*, 23(2): 5–12.

Taylor, C. (1994) Assessment for measurement or standards: the peril and promise of large scale assessment reform, *American Educational Research Journal*, 31: 231–62.

Torrance, H. (ed.) (1994) *Evaluating Authentic Assessment: Problems and Possibilities in New Approaches to Assessment.* Buckingham: Open University Press.

I have included two of the seminal review articles that outline the principles of the rethink on assessment, where the criteria are qualitatively defined. Taylor traces the historical and conceptual roots of NRA and CRA, clearly outlining where the confusions in current practice have crept in. Moss brings this up to date conceptually, while Torrance's book contains some commentaries on the new approach. Crooks gives a useful outline of some basic principles as they apply to tertiary education. Dart and Boulton-Lewis contains chapters by Boulton-Lewis, Dart, and Hattie and Purdie which deal specifically with SOLO as a conceptual structure for holistic assessment.

Entwistle's chapter is a comprehensive review of student learning research, with an emphasis on the implications for assessment. It is recommended for the reader who wants to go in deep on the theory side.

**Answers to the NRA/CRA problem (Task 8.1)**

Both are examples of CRA. Despite the fact that Susan's and Robert's performances were compared, the purpose was not to award the grades but to check the consistency of making the judgement. Essentially in CRA, a student's performance is matched with the predetermined standards to see which grading category applies. What happened here was my initial judgement of Robert's performance was inaccurate, possibly because of a halo effect ('Ah, here's Robert's little effort. That won't be an A!' I murmured to myself, and promptly fulfilled my own prophecy). It took a direct comparison with Susan's effort to see the mistake. The standards themselves were unaltered.

In the second case the standards were set up before grading began. The fact that they were in part defined from norm-referenced data is irrelevant. At the end of teaching, each student's performance would be compared with those pre-set standards, not with each other: hence, CRA.

---

**What I believe is the problem in Box 8.2**

The intention is to assess according to quality, but the boundaries of quality are relative, and, where there is a conflict, it seems that the NRA guidelines would be expected to prevail. For instance, if 30 per cent of students 'showed evidence of original thought as well as having a secure grasp, (etc.)' that would be seen here to be anomalous, but as a teacher I would be very happy if this is what I found. And I would be very disappointed if most students displayed 'derivative information' (grade C), as I would consider I hadn't taught them properly. Here, however, I am told that that is what I should expect to find. In other words, the definitions of learning outcome appear to be based on expected distributions of ability. Major departures from that distribution suggest either that something is wrong with one's teaching, or that one is too soft in assessing.

# 9

## Assessing for learning quality II: practice

**In this chapter we look at implementing assessment package 2 from Task 8.2. What assessment tasks are available, and for what purpose is each best used? How can large classes be assessed effectively? How can students be quickly provided with feedback, particularly in large classes? How should self/peer assessment be used? How can qualitative assessments be combined across several tasks, or across units, to yield a single final grade? How can students' performance be graded qualitatively when results have to be reported in percentages? These and other fundamental questions are addressed in this chapter.**

### What are the best formats for summative assessment?

Let us say you chose assessment package 2 (if you didn't, you might as well skip the rest of this chapter). You are now faced with assessing a large class. I will put it to you in the form of a multiple-choice (MC) test item:

> *My question.* What format will you use to assess your class of 400 first-year biology students?

> 1 An individual research project (maximum 4000 words).
> 2 A multiple-choice test.
> 3 An 2000 word assignment during the term, and a final three-hour examination.
> 4 A portfolio, comprising a reflective journal and three lab reports.

> *Your reply.* Not (1), it takes too long to mark; same for (3). In (4) is Biggs trying to be funny, or is he serious but hopelessly unrealistic? Should be (2), which is what most people use, but it's clear what

the prejudices of He Who Set The Question are. But I'll risk it and say (2).

Well, you could be right, but the question is unanswerable as it stands. A crucial consideration has been omitted: *What are your objectives?* The 'best' assessment method is the one that best realizes your objectives. In your first-year class, are you targeting declarative knowledge or functioning knowledge, or both? What levels of understanding do you require, and for what topics: knowledge of terminology, description, application to new problems . . . ? As you rightly said in response to the MC question, multiple choice *is* widely used, and yes it is convenient, but will it assess what you are after?

We need to clarify further. Although you chose package 2, some issues are not entirely clear-cut. Let me again think aloud on your behalf:

- *NRA or CRA?* CRA. I want the grades to reflect learning, not relativities between students. (However, there's no room in second year for all of them, we may have to cull somehow . . . )
- *Quantitative or qualitative?* Hopefully qualitative, but aren't there certain basic facts and skills I want students to get correct?
- *Holistic or analytic?* Holistic, but how do I combine holistic assessments of several tasks to make one final grade?
- *Convergent or divergent?* Do I want students to get it right, or to show some lateral thinking? Probably both.
- *Performative or decontextualized?* Both. Students must understand the literature, but they need to show they can use their knowledge.
- *Teacher assessed or self/peer assessed?* I intend to be the final arbiter, but self/peer assessment has educational and workload advantages.
- *Backwash?* What effect will my assessment tasks have on students' learning?
- *Time-constrained? Invigilated?* In part, if my institution requires formal examinations conditions.

There are no right answers, only better or worse ones, and the range of assessment formats to choose from is large. We have to strike a balance between practicality and validity. Chapter 8 set a stern example to live up to, but we have to be realistic. There are 400 students to assess, and their results have to be sent to the board of examiners the week following the examination. I wouldn't have time to assess 400 portfolios even if I wanted to.

Throughout this chapter, we will be reviewing many different modes of assessment. You should read reflectively as before, with a particular problem class in mind. Ask yourself: how might this help in developing my own assessment practices? At the end of the chapter, we return to the problem posed by the first-year class.

## How important is the format of assessment?

First, let us see if it matters, apart from convenience, whether you use multiple choice, essay exam or assignment. This depends on the activities an assessment format usually elicits. Are they ones that match your teaching objectives? If they do match your objectives, the backwash is positive, but if they do not, the backwash will encourage students to use surface approaches to learning.

The evidence is very clear that different formats do produce typical forms of backwash. Different formats get students doing different things in preparing for them, some being much more aligned to the unit objectives than others. Tang (1991) used questionnaire and interview to determine how physiotherapy students typically prepared for short-essay examinations and for assignment (see Box 9.1).

Exams tended to elicit memorization-related activities, assignments application-related activities. The assignment required deep learning from the students with respect to one topic; the exam required acquaintance with a range of topics. The teachers concerned realized the assignment better addressed the desired course objectives, but only with respect to one topic. They accordingly adopted a policy to use both: short-answer exams to ensure coverage, the assignment to ensure depth. A not unusual compromise.

Scouller (1996, 1998) found that students saw MC tests as requiring low cognitive level processes; indeed, using deep approaches was *negatively* related to MC test performance. The opposite occurred with essays, which students saw as requiring higher-level processes, and were more likely to use them; this time those using surface approaches did poorly. Students

---

**Box 9.1: Learning activities reported by students in preparing for (a) short-essay question examination and (b) assignment**

*(a) Short-essay examination*
rote learning, question-spotting, going through past papers, underlining, organizing study time and materials, memorizing in meaningful context, relating information, visualizing patients' conditions, discussing with other students

*(b) Assignment*
choosing easy questions/interesting questions/what lecturers expect, copying sources, reading widely/ searching for information sources, relating question to own knowledge, relating to patients' conditions and clinical application, organizing, revising text to improve relevance, discussing with other students.

*Source:* Tang 1991

---

**Box 9.2: Two examples of students' views on multiple-choice tests**

I preferred MCQ ... It was just a matter of learning facts ... and no real analysis or critique was required which I find tedious if I am not wrapped in the topic. I also dislike structuring and writing and would prefer to have the answer to a question there in front of me somewhere.

A multiple choice exam tends to examine too briefly a topic, or provide overly complex situations which leave a student confused and faced with an 'eenie, meenie, minie, mo' situation. It is cheap, and in my opinion ineffectual in assessing a student's academic abilities in the related subject area.

*Source:* Scouller 1997

---

who preferred MC to essay assignment gave surface-type reasons: you can rely on memory, you can play the game (see Box 9.2). Yet these were the same reasons that other students disliked the MC; these students were angry at being assessed in a way that they felt did not do justice to their learning. When doing assignments, they felt they were able to show higher levels of learning. Short-answer examinations assessed similar levels of cognitive activities as multiple choice, but did not attract the anger.

Assessment by portfolio leads students to see it as 'a powerful learning tool', and as requiring them to be divergent: 'it led me to think of many questions that I never think of' (see p. 135). Wong (1994) used SOLO to structure a secondary 5 (year 11) mathematics test in the ordered outcome format (see below), and compared students' problem-solving methods on that with those they used on the traditional format. The difference was not on items correct, but on how they went about the problems. They behaved on the SOLO test like experts do, solving items from first principles, while on the traditional test they behaved like novices, applying the standard algorithms.

In sum, then, format is important. MCs and short-answer tend to elicit low-level verbs, while portfolios and SOLO encourage high-level verbs. Unfortunately, there appears to be little further research on backwash from other assessment modes. Tang's study suggests how one might go about this: matching verbs denoted as desirable in the objectives with the verbs students say the assessment tasks encouraged them to use.

We now review particular assessment formats in detail, under four headings: extended prose, objective, performance and rapid assessments, which are particularly suitable for large classes.

## Extended prose (essay-type) formats of assessment

The essay, as a continuous piece of prose written in response to a question or problem, is commonly intended to assess higher cognitive levels. There are many variants:

1 The timed examination, students having no prior knowledge of the question.
2 The open-book examination, students usually having some prior knowledge and are allowed to bring reference material into the exam room.
3 The take-home, where students are given notice of the questions and several days to prepare their answers in their own time.
4 The assignment, which is an extended version of the take-home, comprises the most common of all methods of evaluating by essay.
5 The dissertation, which is an extended report of independent research.

### Timed essay examinations

Essay exams are best suited for assessing declarative knowledge. They are usually decontextualized, students writing under time-pressure to demonstrate the level of their understanding of core content. The format is open-ended, so theoretically students can express their own constructions and views, supporting them with evidence and original arguments. The reality is often different.

The time constraint for writing exams may exist for several reasons:

1 *Convenience.* A time and a place are nominated for the final assessment, which teachers, students and administration can work around. We all know where we stand.
2 *Invigilation.* Having a specified time and place makes it easier for the timekeeper to prevent cheating. This enables the institution to guarantee the authenticity of the results.
3 *Conditions are standardized.* Nobody has an 'unfair advantage'. But do you allow question choice in a formal examination? If you do, you violate the standardization condition, because all candidates are not then sitting the 'same' examination (Brown and Knight 1994). Standardization is in fact a hangover from the measurement model; it is irrelevant in a criterion-referenced situation.
4 *Models real life.* The time constraint reflects 'the need in life to work swiftly, under pressure and well' (Brown and Knight 1994: 69). This is unconvincing. In real-life situations where functioning knowledge is time-stressed – the operating theatre, the bar (in the courts, that is), or the classroom – this point is better accommodated by performance assessment than by pressurizing the assessment of declarative knowledge

in the exam room. Alignment suggests that time constraints be applied only when the target performance is itself time constrained.

Time constraint creates its own backwash. Positively, it creates a target for students to work towards. They are forced to review what they have learned throughout the unit, and possibly for the first time see it as a whole: a tendency greatly enhanced if they think the exam will require them to demonstrate their holistic view. Students' views of examinations suggest that this rarely happens.

The more likely backwash is negative, with students memorizing specific points to be recalled at speed (Tang 1991). Students go about memorization differently. Learners who prefer a deep approach to learning create a structure first, then memorize the key access words ('deep-memorizing'), while surface learners simply memorize unconnected facts (Tang 1991). So while timed exams encourage memorizing, this is not necessarily *rote* memorizing or surface learning. Whether it is or not depends on the students' typical approaches to learning and on what they expect the exam questions to require.

Does the time constraint impede divergent responses? Originality is a temperamental horse, unlikely to gallop under the stopwatch or to flourish in the climate of a stern regimented silence. A couple of years ago I was in a situation where university regulations required me to set a final examination in addition to a term assignment. The difference between the quality of the assignment and the examination was sobering. Except for a couple of Susans, the exam texts were dull, crabbed and cloned; most focused on the same content to memorize. Qualitatively, there was little between them. The assignments of these same students, on the other hand, were fresh, frequently telling me something I didn't know before, and sometimes even appeared to have been written with pleasure.

Yet it is possible for students to display originality in examinations, if they can prepare their original answers at leisure. But then they need to know the questions, at least in general outline. You can encourage this high-level off-track preparation by making it known you intend asking open questions ('What is the most important topic discussed in the unit this semester? Why?'), or by telling the students at the beginning of the semester what the exam questions will be. Assessing divergent responses must be done holistically. The use of a model-answer checklist does not allow for the well-argued surprise. Students should be told how the papers are to be marked, analytically or holistically, then they can calculate their own risks.

In sum, time constraints in the exam room cannot easily be justified educationally. The most probable effect is to encourage memorization, with or without higher-level processing. In fact, time constraints exist for administrative not educational reasons. They are convenient, and they make cheating more difficult. Whether these gains are worth the educational costs is a good question.

**Open-book examinations**

Open-book examinations remove the premium on memorization of detail but retain the time constraint. In theory, students should be able to think about higher-level things than getting the facts down. In practice, they need to be very well organized otherwise they waste time tracking down too many sources. Baillie and Toohey (1997) moved from a traditional examination in a materials science course to a 'power test' – an open-book exam with opportunities for collegial interaction – with positive results on students' approaches to learning.

Exams are almost always teacher-assessed, but need not be. The questions can be set in consultation with students, while the assessing and awarding of grades can be done by the students themselves and/or their peers. Boud (1986) describes a conventional mid-session examination, where students in an electrical engineering course were, after the examination, provided with a paper of an unnamed fellow student and a detailed model answer, and asked to mark it. They then did the same to their own paper, without knowing what marks someone else might have given it. If the self- and peer-assessed marks were within 10 per cent, the self-mark was given. If the discrepancy was greater than 10 per cent, the lecturer re-marked the script. Spot-checking was needed to discourage collusion ('Let's all agree to mark high'). Student learning was greatly enhanced, and teacher marking time slashed by nearly one-third.

**The assignment and, the take-home**

The assignment, or term paper, deals with declarative knowledge, the project (see below) with 'hands-on' research-type activities. The assignment is not distorted by immediate time limitations, or by the need to rely on memory. In principle, it allows for deeper learning; the student can consult more sources, and with that deeper knowledge base, synthesize more effectively. However, plagiarism is easier, which is why some universities require that a proportion of the assessments in a unit is invigilated. The take-home, with shorter time limits, makes plagiarism a little more difficult.

*Self/peer assessment* can be used to assess assignments. Given the criteria, the students award a grade (to themselves, to a peer's paper, or both), and justify the grade awarded. That in itself is a useful learning experience. But whether the self/peer grading(s) stand as the official result, or part of it, are matters that can be negotiated. In my experience, students like the peer- and self-assessing processes, but tend to be coy about their being a significant part of the final result.

## Assessing extended prose

Years ago, Starch and Elliott (1912; Starch 1913a,b) originated a devastating series of investigations into the reliability of assessing essays. Marks for the same essay ranged from bare pass to nearly full marks. Sixty years later, Diederich (1974) found things just as bad. Out of the 300 papers he received in one project, 101 received every grade from 1 to 9 on his 9-point marking scale.

The problem was that judges were using different criteria. Diederich isolated four families of criteria, but different judges disagreed about their relative importance, some applying all, others applying one or few. The criteria were:

1 *Ideas*: originality, relevance, logic.
2 *Skills*: the mechanics of writing, spelling, punctuation, grammar.
3 *Organization*: format, presentation, literature review.
4 *Personal style*: flair.

These criteria were for English essay writing but they have their counterparts in other subjects. It would be very valuable if staff in a department collectively clarified what they really are looking for under these, or other, headings.

## Back to the holistic/analytic question

When reading an essay, do you rate separately for particular qualities, such as those mentioned by Diederich, and then combine the ratings in some kind of weighted fashion? Or do you read and rate the essay as a whole, and give an overall assessment?

We dealt with the general argument in the previous chapter. The analytic method of rating the essay on components, and adding the marks up, is appealing. It leads to better agreement between markers. But it is slow. Worse, it does not address the essay as a whole. The unique benefit of the essay is to see if students can construct their response to a question or issue within the framework set by the question. They create a 'discourse structure', which is the point of the essay. Analytic marking is ill-attuned to appraise discourse structure.

Assessing discourse structure requires a framework within which that holistic judgement can be made. SOLO helps you to judge if the required structure is present or not. Listing, describing, narrating are multistructural structures. Compare-and-contrast, causal explanation, interpretation and so on are relational. Inventive students create their own structures which, when they work, can make original contributions: these are extended abstract.

The facts and details play their role in these structures in like manner to the characters in a play. And the play's the thing. You do not ignore details, but ask of them:

- Do they make a coherent structure (not necessarily the one you had in mind)? If yes, the essay is at least relational.
- Is the structure the writer uses appropriate or not? If yes, then the question has been properly addressed (relational). If no, you will have to decide how far short of satisfactory it is.
- Does the writer's structure open out new ways of looking at the issue? If yes, the essay is extended abstract.

If the answer is no to all of the above, the essay is multistructural or less, and should not be rated highly, no matter how rich the detail. If you want students to list points, the short-answer or even the MC are the appropriate formats. These are easier for the student to complete and for you to assess.

This distinction recalls that between 'knowledge-telling' and 'reflective writing' (Bereiter and Scardamalia 1987). Knowledge-telling is a multistructural strategy that can all too easily mislead assessors. Students focus only on the topic content and tell all they know about it, often in a listing or point-by-point form. Using an analytic marking scheme, it is very hard not to award high marks when in fact the student hasn't even addressed the question. Take this example of an ancient history compare-and-contrast question: 'In what ways were the reigns of Tutenkhamen and Akhnaton alike, and in what ways were they different?' The highest-scoring student gave the life histories of both pharoahs, and was commended by the teacher for her effort and depth of research, yet her discourse structure was irrelevant to the question (Biggs 1987b).

Reflective writing transforms the writer's thinking. E.M. Forster put it thus: 'How can I know what I think until I see what I say?' The act of writing externalizes thought, making it a learning process. By reflecting on what you see, you can revise it in so many ways, creating something quite new, even to yourself. That is what the best academic writing should be doing.

The essay is obviously the medium for reflective writing, not knowledge-telling. Tynjala (1998) suggests that writing tasks should require students:

1 actively to transform their knowledge, not simply to repeat it;
2 to undertake open-ended activities that make use of existing knowledge and beliefs, and that lead to questioning and reflecting on that knowledge;
3 to theorize about their experiences;
4 to apply theory to practical situations, and/or to solve practical problems or problems of understanding.

Put otherwise, the question should seek to elicit higher relational and extended abstract verbs. Tynjala gave students such writing tasks, which they discussed in groups. They were later found to have the same level of knowledge as a control group, but greatly exceeded the latter in the *use* to which they could put their thinking. The difference was in their functioning, not in their declarative, knowledge.

## Maximizing stable essay assessment

The horrendous results reported by Starch and Elliott and by Diederich occurred because the criteria were unclear, unrecognized or not agreed upon. The criteria must be aligned to the objectives from the outset, and be consciously applied.

Halo effects are a common source of unreliability. Regrettable it may be, but we tend to judge the performance of students we like more favourably than those we don't like. Attractive female students receive significantly higher grades than unattractive ones (Hore 1971). Halo effects also occur in the order in which essays are assessed. The first half-dozen scripts tend to set the standard for the next half-dozen, which in turn reset the standard for the next. A moderately good essay following a run of poor ones tends to be assessed more highly than it deserves, but if it follows a run of very good ones, it is marked down (Hales and Tokar 1975).

Halo and other distortions can be greatly minimized by discussion; judgements are social constructions (Moss 1994). There is some really strange thinking on this. A common belief is that it is more 'objective' if judges rate students' work without discussing it. In one fine arts department I visited, a panel of judges independently awarded grades without discussion, the student's final grade being the undiscussed average. The rationale for this bizarre procedure was the postmodern argument that the works of an artist cannot be judged against outside standards. Where this left the examining process itself I was unable to discover.

Out of the dozens of universities where I have acted as an external examiner for research dissertations, only one invites examiners to resolve disagreement by discussion before the higher degrees committee adjudicates. Consensus is usually the result. Disagreements between examiners are more commonly resolved quantitatively, for example by counting heads, or by hauling in additional examiners until the required majority is obtained. In another university such conflicts are resolved by a vote in senate. The fact that the great majority of senate members haven't even seen the thesis aids their detachment. Their objectivity remains unclouded by mere knowledge.

Given all the above, the following precautions suggest themselves:

1 All assessment should be blind, the identity of the student concealed.
2 All rechecking should likewise be blind, the original assessment concealed.
3 Each question should be assessed across students, so that a standard for each *question* is set. Assessing by the student rather than by the question

allows more room for halo effects, a high or low assessment on one question influencing your judgement on the student's answers to other questions. In the standards model, we assess performances, not students.

4 Between questions, the papers should be shuffled to prevent systematic order effects.

5 Grade coarsely (qualitatively) at first, say into excellent, pass and fail, or A, B/C and D/F, depending on your grading categories. It is then much easier to discriminate more finely within these categories, whether assessing quantitatively (awarding marks) or qualitatively.

6 Teachers within a given department should discuss standards, hopefully to seek agreement on what constitutes excellent performances, pass performances and so on, with respect to commonly used assessment tasks.

7 Spot-check, particularly borderline cases, using an independent assessor. Agree on criteria first.

8 The wording of the questions should be checked for ambiguity and clarity by a colleague.

## Objective formats of assessment

The objective test is a closed or convergent format requiring one-correct answer. It is said, misleadingly, to relieve the marker of 'subjectivity' in judgement. But judgement is ubiquitous. In this case, it is shifted from scoring items to choosing items, and to designating which choices are correct. Objective testing is not more 'scientific', nor is it less prone to error. The potential for error is pushed to the front end, where the hard work is: designing and constructing a good test. The advantage is that the financial benefits rapidly increase the more students you test at a time. With machine scoring, it is as easy to test 1020 students as it is to test 20: a seductive option.

There are many forms of the objective test: true–false, multiple-choice, matching items from two lists, cloze and ordered outcome. We now consider the MC and the ordered outcome. The cloze is considered later, under 'rapid assessment'.

### Multiple-choice tests

The MC is the most widely used objective test. In theory, MCs can assess high-level verbs. In practice they rarely do, and some students, the Susans rather than the Roberts, look back in anger at the MC for not doing so (Scouller 1997). MCs assess declarative knowledge, usually in terms of the least demanding process, recognition. Probably the worst feature of MCs, though, is that they encourage the use of game-playing strategies, by both student and teacher. Some examples:

*Student strategies*
- In a four-alternative MC format, never choose the facetious or the jargon-ridden alternatives.
- By elimination, you can create a binary choice, with the ignorant having a 50 per cent chance of being correct.
- Does one alternative stimulate a faint glow of recognition in an otherwise unrelieved darkness? Go for it.
- Longer alternatives are not a bad bet.

*Teacher strategies*
- Student strategies are discouraged by a guessing penalty: that is, deducting wrong responses from the total score. (Question: Why should this be counterproductive?)
- The use of facetious alternatives is patronizing if not offensive.
- Rewording existing items when you run out of ideas. Anyway, it increases reliability.

MC tests allow enormous coverage, that 'enemy of understanding' (Gardner 1993). One hundred items can cover a huge range of topics. Exclusive use of the MC greatly misleads as to the nature of knowledge because the method of scoring makes the idea contained in any one item the same value as that in any other item. Consider this example (Lohman 1993). An MC test was given to fifth-grade children on the two-hundredth anniversary of the signing of the US Constitution. The only item on the test referring to Thomas Jefferson was: 'Who was the signer of the Constitution who had six children?' A year later, Lohman asked a child in this class what she remembered of Thomas Jefferson. She remembered that he was the one with six children, nothing of his role in the Constitution. Students, including tertiary students, quickly learn that

> there is no need to separate main ideas from details; all are worth one point. And there is no need to assemble these ideas into a coherent summary or to integrate them with anything else because that is not required.
>
> (Lohman 1993: 19)

The message is clear. Get a nodding acquaintance with as many details as you can, but do not be so foolish as to waste your time by attempting to learn anything in depth.

MC tests can be useful if they supplement other forms of assessment, but when used exclusively they send all the wrong signals. Unfortunately, they *are* convenient.

### Ordered-outcome items

An ordered-outcome item looks like an MC, but instead of opting for the one correct alternative out of the four or so provided, the student is required to attempt all sub-items (Masters 1987). The sub-items are ordered into a hierarchy of complexity that reflects successive stages of learning that concept or skill. The students ascend the sequence as far as they can, thus indicating their level of competency in that topic.

The stem provides sufficient information for a range of questions of increasing complexity to be asked. How those questions are derived depends on your working theory of learning. SOLO can be used as a guide for working a sequence out. A SOLO sequence would look like this:

1 *Unistructural.* Use one obvious piece of information coming directly from the stem.
2 *Multistructural.* Use two or more discrete and separate pieces of information contained in the stem.
3 *Relational.* Use two or more pieces of information each directly related to an integrated understanding of the information in the stem.
4 *Extended abstract.* Use an abstract general principle or hypothesis which can be derived from, or suggested by, the information in the stem.

The student's score is the highest correct level. If the response to the first question is inadequate, the student's understanding is assumed to be prestructural.

The levels do not, however, need to correspond to each SOLO level, or to SOLO levels at all. In a physiotherapy course (Tang, private communication), an extended abstract option was inappropriate for first year, and so two levels of relational were used, as in (c) and (d) of Box 9.3, where (c) refers to conceptual integration (declarative) and (d) to application (functioning).

Sub-item (a) in Box 9.3 is unistructural because it requires only a correct reading of the diagram: a simple but essential first skill. Sub-item (b) is a multistructural response, requiring the comparison of two different readings. Sub-item (c) requires interpretation at a simple relational level response, while (d) is relational but more complex, requiring a complete interpretation integrated with functioning knowledge of caring skills.

Key situations can be displayed in this format, and a (d) or (c) level of performance required (in this case, anything less would not be of much help to patients). It is sometimes possible to use a one-correct-answer format for extended abstract items: 'Formulate the general case of which the preceding (relational) item is an instance.' Often, however, extended abstract items use open-ended verbs, so we have in effect a divergent short-answer sub-item: 'Give an example where (c) – the preceding item – does *not* occur. Why doesn't it?'

**Box 9.3:    An ordered-outcome item for physiotherapy students**

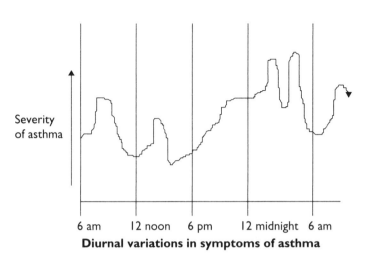

Severity
of asthma

6 am       12 noon     6 pm      12 midnight   6 am
**Diurnal variations in symptoms of asthma**

(a)  When is the asthma attack most severe during the day?
(b)  Is an asthmatic patient physically fitter at 1 pm or 8 pm?
(c)  Do you expect an asthmatic patient to sleep well at night? Give your
     reasons.
(d)  Advise an asthmatic patient how to cope with diurnal variation in
     symptoms.

The ordered-outcome format sends a strong message to students that higher is better: recognition and simple algorithms won't do. This was the format in which Wong (1994) found students operating from theory rather than applying algorithms. Lake (1999) used SOLO to provide a 'four-step template' of generalized questions, rather like ordered outcome, that led students from the basic skills of data retrieval to the advanced skills of critical analysis.

Constructing ordered outcome items is the difficult part. The items need to form a staircase: unistructural items must be easier than multi-, and multi- than relational, and relational than extended abstract. This can be tested with trial runs, preferably using the Guttman (1941) scalogram model, or software is available (Masters 1988). Hattie and Purdie (1998) discuss a range of measurement issues involved in the construction and interpretation of ordered-outcome SOLO items. Basically, it is, as always, a matter of judgement.

Scoring ordered-outcome items makes most sense on a profile basis, that is you have nominated key situations or concepts, about which the students need to achieve a minimal level of understanding. In the physiotherapy item (Box 9.3), (c) is possibly adequate in the first year, but by the second year students really should be responding at an applied treatment (d) level. The profile sets minimum standards for each skill or component.

It is tempting to say that sub-item (a) gets 1 mark, (b) 2 marks, (c) 3 marks and (d) (let's be generous) 5 marks. We then throw the marks into the pot with all the other test results. While this is convenient, it misleads as to a student's level of understanding. If the score is less than perfect, a nominal understanding of one topic could be averaged with a performative understanding of another, yielding moderate understanding across all topics, which was not the case at all.

## Performance assessment

Performance assessment requires students to perform tasks that mirror the objectives of the unit. Students should be required to demonstrate that they *see and do things differently* as a result of their understanding.

The problems or tasks set are, as in real life, often divergent or ill-formed, in the sense that there are no single correct answers. For example, there are many acceptable ways a software program could be written for use in a real estate office. What is important is that the student shows a 'real-life' understanding of the situation: how the problem may reasonably be approached, how resources and data are used, how previously taught material is used, how effectively the solutions meet likely contingencies, and so on. Clearly, this needs an open-ended assessment format and assessment process. Almost any scenario from the professions can be used: designing a structure, teaching a new topic, dealing with a patient with an unusual combination of symptoms. Various formats reflect this authentic intention with varying fidelity.

### The practicum

The practicum, if properly designed, should call out all the important verbs needed to demonstrate competency in a real-life situation, such as practice teaching, interviewing a patient, any clinical session, handling an experiment in the laboratory, producing an artistic product. It goes without saying that CRA is the most appropriate way of evaluation. An assessment checklist should *not* look like this:

A   Definitely superior, amongst the best in the year
B   Above average
C   Average

D   Below average, but meets minimal standards
E   Not up to standard

It should be quite clear that the student has to perform certain behaviours to a specified standard. It then remains to find if the learner can perform them, and if not, why not. Videotaping is useful, as then students can rate their own performance against the checklist of desired behaviours before discussing the supervisor's rating.

The closer the practicum is to the real thing, the greater its validity. The one feature that distorts reality is that it *is* an assessment situation, and some students are likely to behave differently from the way they would if they were not being assessed. This may be minimized by making observation of performance a continuing fact of life. With plenty of formative assessment before the final summative assessment, the student might nominate when he or she is 'ready' for final assessment. This might seem labour intensive, but recording devices can stand in for *in vivo* observation, as can other students.

In fact, the situation is ideal for peer assessment. Students become accustomed to being observed by each other, and they can receive peer feedback. Whether student evaluations are then used, in whole or in part, in the summative assessment is a separate question, and worth considering.

## Presentations and interviews

The class presentation is evaluated in terms of what content is conveyed, and how well. Where the focus is on declarative understanding, the students declaring to their peers, we have the traditional *seminar*, which is not necessarily meant to reproduce a situation in which students will later find themselves. The seminar, if used carefully, offers good opportunities for formative discussion, and peer assessment both formative and summative. However, it can easily become a poor substitute for proper teaching (see p. 89).

Student presentations are best for functioning rather than declarative knowledge. Peer input can be highly appropriate in this case. In one fine arts department, the examining panel comprises teachers, a prominent local artist and a student (rotating), who view all the student productions, have a plenary discussion with all staff and students about each, and then submit a final, public, examiners' report. This is not only a very close approximation to real life in the gallery world, but actively involves staff and students in a way that it is rich with learning opportunities.

The *poster presentation* follows the well-known conference format. A student or group of students displays their work according to an arranged format during a poster session. This provides excellent opportunities for peer assessment and for fast feedback of results. However, Brown and Knight (1994: 78) warn that the poster 'must be meticulously prepared'. The specifications need to be very clear, down to the size of the display, and how to use back-up materials: diagrams, flowcharts, photographs. Text needs to be clear and highly condensed. Assessment criteria can be placed on an assessment sheet, which all students receive to rate all other posters. Criteria would include substance, originality, impact and so on.

The *interview* is used most commonly in the examination of dissertations and theses. In the latter case, the student constructs a 'thesis' that has to be 'defended' against expert criticism. Almost always, these oral defences are evaluated qualitatively. The student makes a case, and is successful, conditionally successful, unsuccessful but is given another try (with or without formal re-examination), or irredeemably unsuccessful. Here again the criteria are usually clearly spelled out: the required structure of the dissertation, what constitutes good procedure, what is acceptable and what unacceptable evidence, clarity of writing, format and so on. These criteria are usually seen as hurdles, in that they have to be cleared before the assessment itself proceeds, which addresses the holistic issues of the *substance* and *originality* of the thesis itself.

In undergraduate teaching, the interview is not used as widely as it might be, probably on the ground that it takes too long. However, a properly constructed interview schedule could see a fruitful interview through in 20 minutes, possibly 30, while carefully run group interviews could deal with four or five students at a time. How long does it take to properly assess each written product of a three-hour examination, or a 2500 word assignment? Thirty minutes? Interviews are not as time-consuming as they appear to be.

Unstructured interviews can be unreliable, but bear in mind that the point of interviewing – that it is interactive – is lost if the interview is too tightly structured. Teachers have a chance to follow up and probe, and students have a chance to display their jade, pearls and opals – their unanticipated but valuable learning treasures. Oral assessments should be tape-recorded, both in case of dispute (when student and an adjudicator can hear the replay), and so that you may assess under less pressure, or subsequently check your original assessment.

Self-assessment is an interesting option here, with the teacher- and self-assessments themselves being the subject of the interview.

### Critical incidents

Students can be asked to report on 'critical incidents' that seem to them powerful examples of unit content or that stimulate them to think deeply about the content. They then explain why these incidents are critical, how they arose and what might be done about it. This gives rich information about how students (1) have interpreted what they have been taught, and (2) can make use of the information.

Such incidents might be the focus of an assessment interview, or of a reflective journal, or be used as portfolio items (see below).

## Individual and group projects

Whereas an assignment usually focuses on declarative knowledge, the project focuses on functioning knowledge applied to a hands-on piece of research. Projects can vary from simple to sophisticated, or carried out individually or by a group of students.

Group projects are becoming increasingly common for two major reasons: they aim to teach students cooperative skills, in preparation for many workplace situations, and the teacher's assessment load is markedly decreased. They are not, however, popular with students, for several reasons: students from different programmes often find it difficult to coordinate times, the assessment does not usually take into account individual contribution, or group processes, and workplace cooperation involves individuals with distinct roles, who are frequently assessed individually for their contribution (Morris 2001). The common practice of simply awarding an overall grade for the outcome, which each student receives, fails on all counts.

Group projects need to be used carefully. Peer evaluation of contribution is certainly one way to make them more acceptable, but giving that a typical 5 per cent towards the final grade is not enough to overcome the problem (a student quoted in Morris 2001). Lejk and Wyvill (2001a,b) have carried out a series of studies on assessing group projects, this question of assessing contribution of members being one aspect. They found that self-assessment was not effective and suggest that the fairest way is to use peer assessment conducted in secret, not openly, but following an open discussion between students about relative contributions.

Most attempts to assess relative contribution use quantification. A simple example would be to award an overall 60 per cent to the assignment. If there are four participants, this means that 240 marks need to be allocated. You may make this allocation on the basis of interviews with the students, or get them to do it. One problem is that they may go uncontroversial and divide the marks equally – some hating themselves as they do so. Lejk and Wyvill (2001a) use an elaborate matrix where students rate each other on aspects of the task, and derive an index for each student, which is used to weight the calculation of the grade of each. The reliability of peer assessment in assessing group projects is an interesting and neglected issue that is handled by Magin (2001).

A problem with collaborative projects is that individual students too easily focus on their own task, not really understanding the other components or how they contribute to the project as a whole. The idea of a group project is that a complex and worthwhile task can be made manageable, each student taking a section they can handle. However, the tasks should not be divided according to what students are already good at: Mario will prepare the literature review, Sheila will do the stats. In that case, little *learning* may take place. We want students to learn things other than what they already know, so a better allocation is that Sheila does the literature review and Mario the stats. This is likely to end up with each helping the other, and everyone learns a lot more.

Most important, we want them to know what the whole project is about, and how each contribution fits in, so an additional holistic assessment is necessary. Students might be required to explain where and how their contribution fits into the project as a whole, either verbally or using a concept map for example. If a student fails that, the project is failed. The backwash: make sure you know what your colleagues are doing and why.

### Contracts

Contracts replicate a common everyday situation. A contract would take into account where an individual is at the beginning of the course, what relevant attainments are possessed already, what work or other experience, and then within the context of the course objectives, he or she is to produce a needs analysis from which a programme is negotiated: what is to be done and how it is proposed to do it, and within what timescale. Individuals, or homogeneous groups of students, would have a tutor to consult throughout, and with whom they would have to agree that the contract is met in due course. The assessment problem hasn't gone away, but the advantage is that the assessments are tied down firmly from the start and the students know where they stand (Stephenson and Laycock 1993).

A more conventional and less complicated contract is little different from clear criterion-referencing: 'This is what an A requires. If you can prove to me that you can demonstrate those qualities in your learning, then an A is what you will get.' This is basically what is involved in portfolio assessment (see below).

### Reflective journal

In professional programmes in particular, it is useful if students keep a reflective journal in which they record any incidents or thoughts that help them reflect on the content of the unit. Such reflection is basic to proper professional functioning. The reflective journal is especially useful for assessing: content knowledge, reflection, professional judgement and application. One teacher told me she had tried journals but found them useless because the students wrote what was in effect a diary of routine events that were mostly irrelevant to the course. One needs to be clear about what course objectives the journals are meant to be addressing.

Assessment can be delicate, as journals are often very personal; and boring, as they are often very lengthy. It is a good idea to ask students to submit selections, possibly focusing on critical incidents. Journals should not be marked, but taken as evidence of quality in thinking, particularly the students' ability to realistically evaluate their own learning and thinking in terms of course content.

## Case study

In some disciplines, a case study is an ideal way of seeing how students can apply their knowledge and professional skills. It could be written up as a project, or as an item for a portfolio. Case studies might need to be highly formal and carried out under supervision, or be carried out independently by the student. Possibilities are endless.

Assessing the case study is essentially holistic, but aspects can be used both for formative feedback and for summative assessment. For example, there are essential skills in some cases that must be got right, otherwise the patient dies, the bridge collapses, or other mayhem ensues. The component skills here could be pass–fail; fail one, fail the lot (with latitude according to the skill and case study in question). Having passed the components, however, the student then has to handle the case itself appropriately, and that should be assessed holistically.

## Portfolio assessment

In a portfolio, the student presents and explains his or her best 'learning treasures'. Students have to reflect and use judgement in assessing their own work, and explain its match with the unit objectives. When students give their creativity free rein, portfolios are full of complex and divergent surprises, aligned to the unit aims in ways that are simply not anticipated by the teacher.

In their explanations for their selection of items, students explain how the evidence they have in their portfolios addresses their own or the official unit aims. One danger with portfolios is that students may go overboard, creating excessive workload both for themselves and for the teacher. Limits must be set (see below).

Assessing portfolio items can be deeply interesting. It may be time consuming, but that depends on the nature and number of items. Many items, such as concept maps, can be assessed in a minute or so. In any event, a morning spent assessing portfolios feels like 30 minutes assessing look-alike assignments.

Following are some suggestions for implementing portfolio assessment:

1 *Make it quite clear in the teaching objectives what the evidence for good learning may be.* The objectives should be available to students at the beginning of the semester.
2 *State the requirements for the portfolio.* These need to be made very clear:
    (a) *Number of items.* In a semester-long unit, four items is about the limit.
    (b) *Approximate size of each item.* The total portfolio should not be much longer than a project or assignment you would normally set. I suggest no more than 1500 words for any one item, but that depends on the nature of the item. Some items, such as concept maps or other diagrams require less than a page.
    (c) *A list of sample items,* but emphasize that students should show some creativity by going outside that list, as long as the items are relevant.
    (d) *Each item should address a different objective.* Items should not be repetitive, making the same point in different ways.
    (e) *Any compulsory items?* In my courses (in teacher education) I usually prescribe a journal, leaving the other items to student choice.
    (f) *Source of items.* Items may be specific to a unit or drawn from other units in the case of evaluating at the end of a course/programme. In some problem-based courses, students will be continually providing inputs, often on a pass/fail basis, over a year or two years. The final evaluation could then comprise – *in toto* or in part – samples of the best work students think they have done to date.
    (g) *What are the items supposed to be getting at?* Are your teaching objectives, best addressed as a package, or as a list of separate items?
3 *Decide how the portfolio is to be graded.* There are two alternatives:
    (a) Assessing individual items, and then combining.
    (b) Assessing the portfolio as a whole (the 'package').

In 3(a), the situation is the same as combining several assessments within a unit to arrive at a final grade (see pp. 197–201 below). It is tempting to mark each item separately, and then total, but that misses the point of the portfolio, which is embedded in 3(b) above. Each item should address some aspect of learning, so that the whole addresses the thrust of the unit. This really gets back to *your* conception of your unit: do you see yourself teaching a collection of topics, or do those topics constitute a *thrust*? If the latter, the students' portfolios should address that thrust. In the last case, the student is in effect saying: 'This is what I got out of your class. I have learned these things, and as a result my *thinking* has changed in the following ways.' If their package can show that, they have learned well indeed.

You might include other assessment tasks apart from the portfolio, for example a conventional assessment to establish 'coverage' of basics. You will then need to decide how to combine the two sets of results.

Portfolios have been used for years in the fine arts, but they can be used to assess almost any course content. Portfolios are very appropriate for 'capstone' projects, which assess programme goals, not individual modules, but the items could come from key modules in the programme. A case study of portfolio assessment is given in Chapter 11.

## Self- and peer assessment

Self-assessment (SA) and peer assessment (PA) can be fitted into quite conventional examination situations, as we have seen, or be more radical self- and peer-assessing on student-generated criteria, on student-selected tasks (Boud 1986). SA and PA are particularly well suited for performance assessment, because such assessments are what are required in real life, and they can easily be made 'public'. As we see in the next chapter, they fit easily into online learning.

Let us recap the advantages:

1 SA and PA give the students first-hand, active involvement with the criteria for good learning.
2 Students learn how to select good evidence.
3 Judging whether a performance or product meets given criteria is vital for effective professional action.

It is important that these educational justifications are made clear to the students, not only because the rationale for all teaching and assessing decisions should be transparent, but also because it is necessary to get the students on side; a common belief is that assessment is the teacher's responsibility, and some students resent being required to do the teacher's dirty work (Brew 1999). Other findings are that PA can be stressful (Pope 2001), and that when comparing PA with SA, good students under-assess themselves, compared with how their peers would rate them, while poor students over-assess themselves (Lejk and Wyvill 2001b).

How well do SA and PA agree with teacher assessments? Falchikov and Boud (1989), reviewing 57 studies, found that agreement was greatest with advanced students, least in introductory courses and in convergent content subjects, such as science, medicine and engineering, rather than in arts and social science. Good agreement requires explicit criteria of assessment, and discussion and training in using them (Fox 1989).

## The timing and organizing of assessment

### Programme assessment

One serious case of non-alignment is the assessment of programme aims. Many programmes – by this I mean a degree programme comprising, say,

24 semester-length modules – have high-sounding aims about the sort of graduate who will emerge, for example one having certain generic skills, and professional skills including professional ethics and attitudes, none of which are directly assessed. When I have asked this at validation panels, the reply has been that they are subsumed under module objectives, but all too frequently a detailed analysis of modules shows they are not. In any event, the sum total of module outcomes does not necessarily make up the broad outcomes claimed at the programme level. It's the analytic/holistic argument all over again.

One way of addressing this is to have programme-level assessment, independently of particular module assessment. The American notion of a 'capstone' project is concerned with seeing how programme goals or intended outcomes themselves have been met. This could be a final-year dissertation or it could be a portfolio comprising work (assignments, projects) completed within particular modules, with a reflective statement explaining how the student thinks this selection of items, plus any others deemed appropriate, might meet programme goals. Such a procedure might tone the programme-level rhetoric down a little.

### Progressive assessment

Progressive, or continuous, assessment uses results taken during the course for grading purposes while learning is proceeding. While this seems to take the heat off a final summative assessment, it must not conflate the formative and summative roles. For formative to work, students must feel free to reveal their ignorance and the errors in their thinking, but if the results are to be used for grading, they will be highly motivated to conceal those same errors.

Summative assessments may be collected while a unit is ongoing, but the formative and summative functions should be separated. Working on the kinds of problem that will make up the final exam throughout the semester is an excellent formative learning experience. But if some are to count in the final grade, students should know which ones, and they can adjust their strategies accordingly. For example, a trial go at the final assessment tasks can be used both formatively, the mistakes being used to correct misunderstandings, and summatively, but only if an individual is happy with the result. If they are not happy, they should be allowed another go at the task later on.

There is another problem with progressive assessment when it is used during the learning of a topic. Figure 8.2 explains. Say we have two students who at the end of the semester achieve similar levels of learning on topic 2. Student 1 entered the unit knowing little about topic 2, whereas student 2 knew a lot; student 1's learning curve was steep, student 2's almost flat. A summative assessment result at the end of the unit says that both achieved the same *level* of learning in topic 2, which is true, but student 1 actually learned more. However, as grades are a statement of final levels of learning, this is logical, even if a little unfair on student 1. But if you now use progressive assessments, given in week 4 and week 8 say, and combine them with the final summative assessment, you get an unacceptable result: the grade of student 1, who learned most, would now be *lower* than the grade of student 2, who learned least.

Unless the teaching of a topic has completely finished, progressive assessment penalizes the better learners.

### Deadlines

Part of the felt pressure summative assessments put on both staff and students is due as much to poor timing as to the amount of work itself. In large classes particularly, you have to be ruthless about deadlines. One value of multiple assessments is that some can be collected earlier in the seminar if the topics have been completed – but be careful not to confuse the formative and summative roles of assessment discussed above.

It is important to discuss your deadlines with colleagues to make sure they are evened out, for the benefit of both students and assessors.

### Feedback, open information

Following are some suggestions to cut time considerably:

- Make sure the students know exactly what is expected of them.
- Place the assessment criteria on a pro-forma, which is returned to the students with specific evaluations of their work against the criteria. It saves a lot of writing, particularly if you keep a library of comments on computer for each assignment you set. They can be ordered according to the grade or performance level in which they occur. In the next chapter we discuss how educational technology can be used for this.
- Assess the work holistically, but provide a quick rating along such dimensions as may be seen as desirable. You could rate them on a quantified scale, but that encourages averaging. Better to put an X along each line, which just as clearly lets the students know where they are:

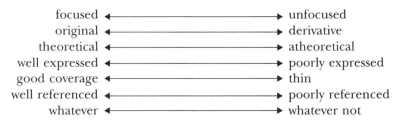

focused ←——————————→ unfocused
original ←——————————→ derivative
theoretical ←——————————→ atheoretical
well expressed ←——————————→ poorly expressed
good coverage ←——————————→ thin
well referenced ←——————————→ poorly referenced
whatever ←——————————→ whatever not

You are letting the student know that these individual qualities are important, whether or not they make a quantifiable difference to the final grade. You could do as is done in dissertations and treat them as hurdles which have to be cleared satisfactorily before the real assessment begins.

Put multiple copies in the library of previous student assignments (anonymous, but nevertheless better get permission), representing all grades, and annotated with comments. Students can then see exactly what you want, that you mean it, and what the differences are between different grades. This is also likely to save time on post-mortems.

## Assessing in large classes

If lecturing is the default for large-class teaching, MCs and timed exams are the default for large-class assessment. Exams take a lot of time to assess, but with tutor assistance and the clear timeslots in which things have to be done and reported, we can come to terms with them. Unfortunately, as we have seen, exams are not the best modes of assessment. We now look at alternatives for large-class assessment that are:

1 rapidly administered, completed and assessed;
2 access higher-order learnings than the two default modes do.

First, some strategic decisions need to be made:

1 You may be able to justify postponing time-consuming qualitative assessments in first year, such as individual practica or portfolios, to later years. At least students will have had the experience of these assessments before they graduate.
2 Cut down on massive, mind-numbing, single-mode assessments such as the final exam. Assess more often, with more varying assessments (Brown and Knight 1994; Davis and McLeod 1996b).

Let us see, then, what further assessment tasks we might use.

### Concept maps

Concept maps, introduced as a TLA (see pp. 84–5), can also be used for assessment. We can tell at a glance if a student has an impoverished knowledge structure relating to the topic, or a rich one (see Figure 5.1).

### Venn diagrams

Venn diagrams are a simple form of concept map, where the boundary of a concept is expressed in a circle or ellipse, and interrelations between concepts expressed by the intersection or overlap of the circles. Venn diagrams, like concept maps, are economical ways of expressing relationships. They can be used for teaching purposes, in conveying relationships to learners, and for assessment purposes, so that learners may convey their ways of seeing relationships between concepts. Getting students to draw and briefly explain their own Venn diagrams, or to interpret those presented, can be done quickly, where the target of understanding is relationships between ideas. Venn diagrams make good gobbets (see below).

### Three-minute essay

We met the three-minute essay in Chapter 6 as a method of introducing activity into large-class teaching, by asking such questions as:

- What do I most want to find out in the next class?
- What is the main point I learned today?

These questions provide useful information for the teacher. Formatively, they tell us how the content is interpreted by students. Summatively, this information can be used for grading purposes (but let them know first – see above). The three-minute essay can be answered in minutes in a large class.

### Short-answer examinations

In short-answer assessments the student answers in note form. This format is useful for getting at factual material, such as interpreting diagrams, charts and tables, but is limited in addressing main ideas and themes. The examiner is usually after something quite specific, and in practice operates more like the objective format than the essay (Biggs 1973; Scouller 1996). However, it has advantages over the standard MC in that it is less susceptible to test-taking strategies: the answer can't be worked out by elimination, it requires active recall rather than just recognition, and it is easier for you to construct, but not as easy to score.

### Gobbets

Gobbets are significant chunks of content with which the student should be familiar and to which the student has to respond (Brown and Knight 1994). They could be a paragraph from a novel or of a standard text, a brief passage of music, a Venn diagram, an archaeological artefact, a photograph (a building, an engine part), and so on. The student's task is to identify the gobbet, explain its context, say why it is important, what it reminds them of, or whatever else you would like them to comment on.

Gobbets should access a bigger picture, unlike short answers that are sufficient unto themselves. That big picture is the target, not the gobbet itself. Brown and Knight point out that three gobbets can be completed in the time it takes one essay exam question, so that to an extent you can assess both coverage and depth.

## Letter to a friend

In the 'letter-to-a-friend', the student tells an imaginary or real friend, who is thinking of enrolling in the unit next year, about their own experience of the unit (Trigwell and Prosser 1990). These letters are about a page in length and are written and assessed in a few minutes. The student should reflect on the unit and report on it as it affects them. Letters tend to be either multistructural or relational, occasionally extended abstract. Multistructural letters are simply lists of unit content, a rehash of the course outline. Good responses provide integrated accounts of how the topics fit together and form a useful whole (relational), while the best describe a change in personal perspective as a result of doing the unit (extended abstract). Letters to a friend also provide a useful source of feedback to the teacher on aspects of the unit.

Like the concept map, letters supplement more fine-grained tasks with an overview of the unit. They also make good portfolio items.

## Cloze tests

Cloze tests were originally designed to assess reading comprehension. Every seventh (or so) word in a passage is deleted, and the reader has to fill in the space with the correct word (flexible versions allowed a synonym). A text is chosen that can only be understood if the topic under discussion is understood, rather like the gobbet. The omitted words are essential for making sense of the passage.

## Procedures for rapid assessing

The following procedures speed up assessment, particularly valuable in large classes.

### Self/peer assessment

Self/peer assessment can fractionate the teacher's assessment load, even when conventional assessments such as exam or assignment are used. When posters are used, the assessment can be over in one session. But as noted above, the criteria have to be absolutely clear. If self/peer assessments agree within a specified range, whether expressed as a qualitative grade or as a number of marks, the higher grade is best awarded (collusion can be mitigated by spot-checking). Boud (1986) estimates that self/peer assessment can cut the teacher's load by at least one-third. Gibbs (1999) in his 'Case of the Pharmacist', cut marking time for the teacher by 18 hours a week by using peer assessment, while summative marks increased by 20 per cent.

*Group assessment*
When teaching large classes, group assessment is appealing. With four students per assessment task, you get to assess one-quarter the number you would otherwise. But there are problems (pp. 187–8).

*Random assessment*
In Gibbs's (1999) 'Case of the Mechanical Engineer', 25 reports through the year were required, but as each was worth only a trivial 1 per cent, the quality was poor. When the requirements were changed so that students still submitted 25 reports as a condition for sitting the final exam, but only 4 reports were marked at random, two benefits resulted: the students worked consistently throughout the term and submitted 25 good reports, and the teacher's marking load was one-sixth of what it had previously been.

## Final grades and reporting assessment results

The final stage of assessing involves converting judgements of the student's performance into a final summative statement, in the form required by administration. This raises several issues:

1 Combining results in several assessment task to arrive at a final grade.
2 Reporting in categories or along a continuous scale.
3 Is there any distribution characteristic to be imposed on the results?

### Combining assessment results within a unit to arrive at a final grade

As the grade awarded for a unit usually depends on performances assessed in a number of topics, and those topics will be passed at various levels of understanding, we need to decide how to combine these separate estimates to yield one final grade. Our commitment to holistic assessment makes this an important issue.

Say we have four assessment tasks: AT1, AT2, AT3 and AT4. (These could be separate tasks or portfolio items.) Determining the final grade from these components is conventionally achieved by *weighting* so that important tasks count more, and then averaging. But on what basis can you calculate that AT3 is worth twice as much (or however much) as AT1? Expected time taken is the only logical currency I can think of, but that is more a matter of the nature of the task than of its educational value. In holistic and qualitative assessment, we must weight tasks in other ways.

In selecting these tasks, presumably we wanted each to assess a particular quality. Let us say AT1 is to assess basic knowledge, the task being main ideas taken throughout the course; AT2 problem-solving (a case study, group assessed); AT3 an overview of the unit (a concept map); AT4 to assess the quality of the student's reflections on course content (a journal). Now we have a logical package which makes a statement about what we want students to learn, and how well. The logic is that all aspects being assessed are important, and must all be passed at *some* level of competency. Otherwise, why teach them?

There are two main strategies for handling the problem of weighting and combining assessment results: working qualitatively throughout, and using numerical conversions for achieving the combinations.

*Work qualitatively throughout*
There are several ways of preserving your holistic purity:

1 *The dissertation model.* Look upon the sub-tasks as hurdles to be cleared before grading on the key task. In our example, you might decide that the case study, AT2, is the key task. The qualitative grading of AT2 thus determines the final grade for the whole unit, as long as all the others tasks are satisfactory. If they are not, they should be redone and resubmitted (with due care about the submission and resubmission deadlines).
2 *The profile.* Where all tasks are of equal importance, each is graded qualitatively. Then look at the pattern. Is the modal (most typical) response B? If so, the student is mostly working at B level, so B it is. In the case of an uneven profile, you might take the highest level as the student's final grade, on the grounds that the student has demonstrated this level of performance in at least one task. A student who got the same grade on all tasks would, however, see this as unfair. Alternatively, you can devise a conversion: A = maximum performance on all tasks; B = maximum on two tasks, very good on remaining ones; C = one maximum, two very good, rest pass, and so on.
3 *Implied contract.* Different tasks are tied to different grades. If a student only wants a C, they do AT1 alone, say, which will show they have attended classes, done the reading and got the general drift of the main ideas dealt with. To obtain a B, they add AT3 to AT1, showing they can hang all the ideas together. Grade A requires all for the B plus AT4, to show in addition they have some reflective insights into how it all works. A+ or high distinction needs all the rest plus AT3, the key test of high-level functioning, the case study.

4 *Weighted profile.* Different levels of performance are required in different tasks. Some require a high-level of understanding (e.g. relational in SOLO terms), others might only require 'knowledge about' (multistructural), others only knowledge of terms (unistructural). All have to be passed at the specified level. This is a form of pass/fail but the standards of pass vary for different tasks. Weighting in this case is not an arbitrary juggling of numbers but a profile determined by the structure of the curriculum objectives. The only problem is in the event of one or more fails. Logically, you should require a resubmission until the task is passed. Practically, you might have to allow some failure and adjust the final grade accordingly. A version of the weighted profile is given in Boxes 9.4 and 9.5.

*Convert categories into numbers*
First, let us distinguish absolutely clearly between assessing the performance, which is done qualitatively, and dealing with the results of that

---

**Box 9.4:  Objectives and grade criteria for a unit for educational psychologists**

**Curriculum and instruction**

**Course objectives and grade criteria**

Grading will be based on your attaining the following objectives:
1 Demonstrate that you correctly understand and can apply the principles of good teaching and assessment to chosen contexts.
2 Demonstrate a knowledge of selected aspects of curriculum design and management and how they relate to the educational system in Hong Kong.
3 Show how the content and experiences in this course may enhance your effectiveness as an educational psychologist.
4 Show evidence of reflective decision-making.

Final grades will depend on how well you can demonstrate that you have met all objectives:
**A (70+):** awarded if you have clearly met all the objectives, displaying deep knowledge of the base content, original and creative thinking, perhaps going beyond established practice.
**B (60–69):** awarded when all objectives have been met very well and effectively.
**C (50–59):** awarded when the objectives have been addressed satisfactorily, or where the evidence is strong for some objectives, weaker but acceptable in others.
**F:** less than C, work plagiarised, not submitted.

Learning outcomes are graded qualitatively in the first instance.

---

**Box 9.5: Assessing and grading the Curriculum and Instruction portfolio**

Name

**Items**

*Paper*
Comments on teacher ed before and after teaching for real very insightful. Cure: mind-set, personal social and academic goals, all very relevant, but the catalyst I think is reflective practice (you say this later, but isn't quite clear at this point). Backwash from traditional assessment also insightful. Teacher ed reflects methods of school practice, not vice versa. Yes, you've got it right here, very critical; in the right way. More on objective I than 2, but OK I now read your self-assessment and see what you mean.

*Report*
Alignment: the report of the Chinese History activity sound very familiar both in process and outcome. Your diagnosis is sharp and correct. Likewise homework policy. Your analysis reminds me that alignment need not only be formal and upfront, but every activity the teacher endorse needs to show alignment, otherwise it leads to surface learning. I'm sure I needed to be reminded of this at times during our class. The discussion on assessment is very frank, especially as you point out to me that my timing was wrong in the peer/teacher assessment task. I agree with that. However, I don't regret the episode, as I think it was very ripe for reflective practice on all our parts. Objectives 3 and 4 addressed very well indeed

*Rationale of your group presentation*
Very good indeed on objective I, with some reflective application to induction of new teachers.

*Self-evaluation* showing how you have addressed each of the objectives. Your clarification here is exemplary – very helpful to me as assessor.

*Grading*
I Understand and can apply the principles of good teaching and assessment.
2 Curriculum design, management re Hong Kong educational system.
3 This course and effectiveness as an EP.
4 Reflective decision-making.

**Final grade**. Covered all objectives, penetrating criticisms and high reflection – do they amount to creativity, originality? I think so.          **A– (73)**

---

assessment, which is done quantitatively. Quantifying performances that have been assessed holistically is simply an administrative device; there is no educational problem as long as it follows after the assessment process itself has been completed.

Quantifying can be used for two related tasks:

1 Combining results of different tasks in the same unit to obtain a final grade.
2 Combining the results of different units to obtain a year result, as for example does the familiar grade-point average (GPA).

The GPA is the simplest way of quantifying the results of a qualitative assessment: A = 4, B = 3, C = 2 and D = 1. You weight and combine the results as you like. Crude, but simple.

You may want finer discrimination within categories. There are two issues to decide:

1 Qualitative: what *sort* of performance the student's product is.
2 Relative: how *well* it represents that sort of performance.

The latter is often done in three levels: really excellent As (A+), solid, middle-of-the-road As (A), and As but only just (A−). Here, the original assessment of each task is first done qualitatively, then quantitatively. The final result using a four-category system is a number on a 13-point scale (A+ = 12, . . . , D− = 1, F = 0). Note, however, that this is not really a linear 13-point scale (12 + 0), but a two-dimensional structure (4 × 3 + 0) that we have opened out for practical reasons.

The results can now be combined in the usual way, but the conceptual difficulty is that we are back to arbitrarily assigning numerical weights: even taking an average is using a weighting system of one, which is just as arbitrary as saying that a task should be given a weighting of 2, or 5.7. Nevertheless, it is what is usually done, and it is at least convenient. When the results of different subjects have been combined, the final report can be either along the same scale or converted to the nearest category grade. For example, if the weighted outcome score is 9.7, the nearest grade equivalent is 10, which becomes A−.

### Reporting in categories or along a continuous scale

Having combined the results from several assessment tasks, we now have the job of reporting the results. This is a matter of institutional procedure, and obviously we need to fit in with that. There is no problem for us level 3 teachers where the policy is to report in categories (high distinction, distinction, . . . or A, B, C . . .), but what if your institution requires you to report in percentages? Or as some do, report in percentages so that they can then convert back to categories: high distinction = 85+, distinction = 75–84, credit = 60–74, pass = 50–64? This last case is exasperating. Why not report in categories in the first place?

All is not lost. We simply extend the principle of the 13-point scale.

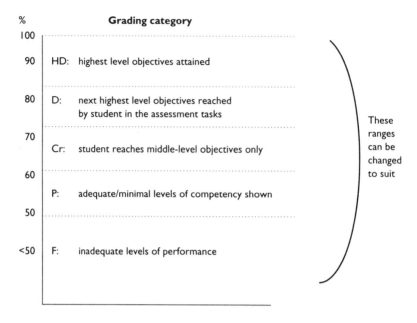

**Figure 9.1:** Assessing qualitatively and reporting as a percentage

1 The first step is the same. The assessment tasks are criterion-referenced to the objectives, which tells you whether the performance is high distinction (or A) quality, distinction (or B) quality, and so on through the category system you use.
2 Allocate percent ranges within each category according to your institutionally endorsed procedures (see Figure 9.1).
3 Locate the individual student's performance along that within-category scale.

Step 3 now uses a much finer scale than the previous three-level scale, something like 15 points within each category, and the student performance is quantified accordingly. You can do that by using a global or holistic rating scale. This procedure was used to obtain the 73 per cent in Box 9.5.

Although we have ended up with a precise number, the *backwash* for students is still positive: aim for quality, because a category shift means a disproportionately large increase in final score. That score also tells them something about the quality of their performance, because it falls within a range that is tied to a category. So they know the quality of their performance, and how well they did within the quality of performance. They will also be clearer about what they would need to do to obtain a better score in future.

Boxes 9.4 and 9.5 give an example of assessing holistically, then report-ing in percentages because that was required. The course was one I taught: a unit in Curriculum and Instruction for educational psychologists at masters level. The objectives and grading categories were included in the handout to the students at the beginning of the semester, and assessment was by portfolio, each item chosen to best address one objective (although in the event there was overlap). Administration required a percentage grade, so I told the students I would be grading qualitatively, but would convert to numbers for reporting purposes using the administration's own scale (A– = 70–75, A = 76–85, A+ = 86 and above, and using the midpoints).

As can be seen, grades A and B required all objectives to be addressed well and effectively, but A demanded evidence of originality, going beyond established practice (extended abstract). The students were given the proforma in Box 9.5, which discussed how well their portfolio items met the grade criteria, and their overall grade fell out easily. This report is authentic. Grading was simplicity itself, while the students had the oppor-tunity to discuss if they disagreed; it was a matter of looking for the grad-ing criteria in the students' work and explaining to them. Converting to numbers was easy once I had fine-graded within each category (B–, B, B+), and then read off what B+, say, would be on the official scale. No counting, averaging, trading failures for good work elsewhere.

In sum, then, qualitative and holistic assessment can meet the logistic and administrative demands of (1) combining assessment tasks to achieve a final grade for the unit, and (2) reporting in percentages, or any other quantitative scale, if that is what is required.

### Is there any distribution characteristic to be imposed on the results?

If the answer to the above is yes, we cannot be so accommodating. Requir-ing results to fit some predetermined distribution, normal, rectangular or whatever, *cannot be justified on educational grounds*. The problem is illus-trated in Box 8.2: it is illogical to 'ration' criterion-reference assessments. If your results are required to fit a curve, you cannot use CRA.

In discussing this issue at staff workshops, teachers frequently tell me that, for them, CRA is pie in the sky because they *must* grade on the curve. Few institutions are in the event rigid on this point. Many 'suggest' that grades follow a distribution – 'It would usually be expected that in large classes no more than 10 per cent of high distinctions be awarded' – but I have found that the operative word is 'usually'. In most cases, it is accepted that in 'special' circumstances, for example a criterion-referenced system, the grades of a particular class might depart from the suggested guidelines. Calling CRA 'a special circumstance' is galling, but if a special circumstance is the Trojan horse that makes the aligned teaching possible, so be it.

If a teacher is employed in an institution where summative results really are required to adhere closely to some predetermined curve, then there is a problem. The solution now can only be political: lobby to get the policy changed. Step 1: photocopy Chapter 8 of this book and send it to the teaching quality committee and to the appropriate pro-vice-chancellor.

## Implementing assessment package 2

Let us return to the problem we faced at the beginning of the chapter: implementing assessment package 2 in a class of 400 first-year students in biology, a laboratory-based course. You might remember that practicalities suggested MC as the preferred mode of assessment. We now know that there are many better options. How might we now address that problem?

First, let us make the scene, a common one, more specific.

*Class*: 400 first-year students.

*Teaching structure*: Two plenary lectures, one tutorial of 20 groups of 20 students, and one 2–3 hour lab a week, again 20 groups of 20 students. There are eight major topics introduced and variously elaborated in the lectures and tutorials over the 12 week semester.

*Staff*: One lecturer in charge, who delivers all the lectures and takes a couple of tutorials. Three teaching assistants between them take the remaining tutorials and help with the assessment. Twenty student demonstrators conduct the labs and assess the lab reports for their own groups.

*Existing assessment*: The following assessment procedures exist, and there are rules: percentage reporting of results, and at least 60 per cent of the final grade is by invigilated exam.

|  |  | *Percentage of final* |
|---|---|---|
| Mid-semester: | 1 hour MC | 30% |
| Final exam 2 hours: | 1 hour MC | 30% |
|  | 2 essay questions | 30% |
| Lab reports: |  | 10% |

The mid-semester is used to alleviate the pressure at the end of the semester and to provide feedback to students. The MCs are all machine scored, so the main assessment load is provided by the two essay questions, which are marked by checklist by the lecturer and three tutors, and by spot-checking the lab reports. Say that the final occurs at the end of the examination weeks, and there is only a weekend and five working days in which to mark, collate and report the assessment results.

In previous years, there was pressure to cull the first years by about 50 per cent, in order to ease pressures in second year and to focus on promising research students. This pressure led to grading on a curve designed so that the bottom half received no more than a pass. Credit and above thus became the *de facto* prerequisite for second year. However, with the current realization that more students means more money, that pressure has largely disappeared, and with it the pressure for norm-referencing using predetermined grade proportions.

### Problems with existing assessment

The major problem is that the assessment tasks are overwhelmingly quantitative, and address declarative knowledge. An attempt was made to offset the MCs with the essay questions, but the gesture is nullified by checklist marking. Students are not in practice encouraged to look for relating ideas, broad principles or functioning knowledge. The only non-declarative knowledge is assessed in the lab reports, but they contribute 10 per cent only and are in the event assessed by student demonstrators, not content experts. An attempt is made to provide formative feedback, apart from informal feedback in tutorials and labs, with the mid-semester, but it is in the form of marks only.

### A suggested rescue package

Our present task is to design a package that would work for the given teaching structure. Let us say that resource and other limitations prevent any drastic change in the number of plenaries, labs and tutorials, and that the average assessment time per student for the final exam cannot exceed much more than 15 minutes per student (which rules out portfolios and other extended qualitative assessment tasks).

We do not immediately consult Table 9.2 under 'rapid assessment' and start throwing in concept maps, cloze tests, gobbets and so on. We first should specify what we want to assess, what our objectives are, then we might look at the most practical ways of assessing that, given the present constraints. Given the number of component assessments, the need to weight and combine them, and traditional practice, one advisable constraint would be to collate and report the assessment results quantitatively, even though we shall be using qualitative tasks for the assessments proper (see above pp. 199–201).

Table 9.1 suggests some of the levels or kinds of understandings that we should want from the students, and what kinds of assessment tasks, practical within our constraints, might be used.

1 Basic factual knowledge and terminology is suitably assessed by MC or short-answer, as long as we are clear that that is all they are doing, and

**Table 9.1:** Required levels and kinds of understanding, and suitable assessment tasks

| Objectives | Kinds and levels of understanding | Suitable assessment tasks |
|---|---|---|
| 1 Basic facts, terminology | recall, recognition | MC or short-answer |
| 2 Topic knowledge | individual topics, relational, some multistructural relations between topics | gobbets, critical incidents gobbets, critical incidents |
| 3 Discipline knowledge | conception of unit as a whole | letter to a friend, concept map |
| 4 Functioning knowledge | topic or discipline knowledge put to work | problem-solving, research project |
| 5 Laboratory skills | procedural knowledge | laboratory behaviour, lab reports |
| 6 Monitoring and evaluation skills | meta-cognitive knowledge, self-directed learning | self- and peer assessment |

that these modes do not dominate the assessment package. Let us use short-answer for the mid-term, which being open-ended might also show more revealing misunderstandings than an MC, and when marking time is not so pressing. MC will then be used in the final exam when time is more pressing.

2 Topics ideally should be understood at least at relational level, but 'knowing about' will do as long as the most important topics are understood relationally, and as functioning knowledge. The topics could then be embedded in gobbets, at the individual topic level in the mid-semester, and gobbets requiring integration of topics in the final. A critical incident or case study in the final would also be useful. For example, the student knows a newspaper clipping of an eco-problem will be presented, and they have to suggest solutions in the light of topics dealt with. They don't know, however, what the problem is, rather like Gibbs's (1999: 231) video on educational philosophy.

3 By 'discipline knowledge' I mean the picture of the whole: having studied a list of topics that make up a first-year biology course, what is the student's view of biology itself? Letter-to-a-friend is a good way of ascertaining this (Trigwell and Prosser 1990). A description or list of topics studied (multistructural) is not good enough; a working view of an integrated subject called biology is very good (relational); a changed perspective of the biological world would be marvellous (extended abstract), if rather unlikely at this level.

4 Functioning knowledge. It is reasonable to expect that students can solve a real-world problem. It is suggested that six such problems are given throughout the semester as the subject of peer assessment, much

as described by Gibbs (1999), two such problems being self- and peer-assessed for inclusion in the final grade (Boud 1995).

5 Laboratory skills are mainly assessed *in situ* by student demonstrators, and probably do not go much more than the procedural level, i.e. correct performance of laboratory procedures and writing them up appropriately. Laboratory work ultimately involves functioning knowledge, but it is doubtful if it would be validly assessable in first year under these conditions. This can be better addressed in labs in higher years.

6 Monitoring and evaluation skills, as argued elsewhere (p. 162), are essential learnings for students if they are to become autonomous and self-directed in their tertiary learning, and later in their professional lives. Internalized standards of competency, which enable reflective thinking and self-direction, can be developed by self- and by peer assessment (Boud 1995; Gibbs 1999). In essence, four of the six problems are assessed by a peer according to a marking sheet, and then each is returned to the owner. The last two problems become part of the final grade: students self-assess first on a separate sheet of paper, which is handed in, then the peer assessment is made. If these agree within specified limits, the higher grade is taken; if they disagree, the lecturer adjudicates and also spot-checks some of the others at random.

A range of assessment tasks has emerged here: quantitative (MC and short-answer), qualitative (three gobbets, critical incident, letter-to-a-friend, problem-solving), and procedural (lab report). For logistical reasons, we need to turn all these into numbers while retaining the qualitative nature of the majority of the assessment tasks. The qualitative tasks, with the possible exception of the problems (see below), may be assessed with SOLO, using a five-point scale within each:

| SOLO level | Range |
|---|---|
| unistructural: | 1–5 |
| multistructural: | 6–10 |
| relational: | 11–15 |
| extended abstract: | 16–20 |

In other words, top of the multistructural range is in conventional terms a bare pass (10 out of a possible 20) in six of the main assessment tasks. This sends a strong message to the students that 'knowing more' just will not do; you have to structure and use your knowledge.

How this applies to the problems is held in abeyance at this stage. It depends on the individual problem, but as we are also using these problems for self- and peer assessment, the assessment procedures need to be particularly clear. The lecturer needs to devise a 20-point marking scheme that students can use, but there is no reason why it too shouldn't be structured along similar lines: four categories (SOLO or other), five points within each.

The SOLO scale arbitrarily but conveniently yields a maximum of 20 'marks' per task, which can be combined with the results from other tasks, including the MC. This may sound complicated but in fact it is not, as may be seen from the following assessment schedule:

| Mid-semester exam | Max. points | Final exam | Max. points |
|---|---|---|---|
| 2 Gobbets, 20 each | 40 | 1 Gobbet | 20 |
| Short-answer | 20 | 1 Critical incident | 20 |
| | | 1 Letter-to-a-friend | 20 |
| | | 2 Problems (SA/PA) | 40 |
| | | MC | 20 |
| Total | 60 | Total | 120 |

With 20 points for the lab report, the total number of points becomes 200: divide by 2 to report in percentages.

The weightings here for mid-semester, final and labs are identical to those for the previous, traditional, assessment. However, these can easily be changed if you think, say, the lab reports ought to get more and the problems less (being self- and peer-assessed); maybe you would prefer to leave the self- and peer assessments out of the final grade.

Let us now take a look at the marking load. Let us say that each of the qualitative assessments, problems aside, is written on no more than one page. You read this, and then first decide on its category (multistructural, relational), and then you rate how well it exemplifies that category on a five-point scale. This takes no more than five minutes, with practice rather less. (It will however be necessary for the lecturer and the teaching assistants to have a training session, and to reach a criterion of at least 90 per cent agreement allowing one category difference, which is better than the usual agreement on essay ratings using the Bloom taxonomy (Hattie and Purdie 1998).)

The time needed for assessing individual students now becomes:

| *For the mid-term short-answer test:* | 5 minutes |
|---|---|
| 2 Gobbets | 10 minutes |
| Total | 15 minutes |

| *For the final:* | |
|---|---|
| MC | minimal, clerical work |
| 3 Qualitative assessments | 15 minutes maximum |
| Spot-checking problems | 5 minutes? |
| Total | 20 minutes maximum |

In addition, you will probably want to spot-check the demonstrators' marking of the lab reports. If this is too much, perhaps you could cut out the critical incident or a gobbet.

As to formative assessment, that synonym for good teaching (see p. 142 above), the previous scheme did very little apart from reporting relative progress in marks. The changes suggested here for the summative assessment tasks also suggest ways in which the plenary and tutorials can be used more effectively (see Chapters 5, 6 above). One would be to use pauses and the three-minute essay to provide feedback: what students thought to be the main point of a particular lecture could become the focus of tutorial discussion. Like the four peer-assessed problems, also carried out in the plenaries, these essays could be required but not formally assessed before the student is allowed to sit the final exam.

We now have an assessment package that takes only a little more time, but it is manageable within the resources allowed. The assessments specifically address the higher-level objectives of the unit so that they will encourage better quality learning from the students, will equally certainly be more interesting for both you and the students, and they provide much more effective formative feedback to students.

None of these suggestions are, however, cast in stone. We have not yet come to Chapter 10, which deals with educational technology and how that might help. If we didn't operate with the restriction of 60 per cent final exam, we might have had fewer plenaries (lectures), more out-of-class group tasks that would save assessment time, more online work. The important thing is the intention and conceptualization, not the specific techniques you use. Note that when you do rethink what you are doing to one aspect, assessment, adaptive changes occur throughout the system: objectives become clearer, teaching methods themselves improve, and of course the assessment tasks get at what they should be assessing.

## Summary and conclusions

This has been an encyclopaedic chapter. Table 9.2 is a better way of summarizing the major points on assessment tasks than section summaries.

### Expressing and reporting the results of assessment

We then addressed administrative issues: how to combine results to give a single summative statement, how to report in numerical form such as percentages when assessing holistically, and how to avoid grading on the curve.

When the final grade depends on performances assessed in a number of topics, passed at various levels of understanding, the different results need to be combined. Two general ways of combining results were described: consistently holistic, and doing the major assessments holistically then converting into numbers for ease of administrative handling. The latter is a compromise but the important point is that grades are defined qualitatively in the first instance, and the result tells students something meaningful. The

**Table 9.2:**  Some different assessment tasks and the kinds of learning assessed

| Assessment mode | Most likely kind of learning assessed |
| --- | --- |
| *Extended prose, essay-type* | |
| essay exam | rote, question-spotting, speed structuring |
| open-book | as for exam but less memory, coverage |
| assignment, take-home | read widely, interrelate, organize apply, copy |
| *Objective test* | |
| multiple choice | recognition, strategy, comprehension, coverage |
| ordered outcome | hierarchies of understanding |
| *Performance assessment* | |
| practicum | skills needed in real life |
| seminar, presentation | communication skills |
| posters | concentrating on relevance, application |
| interviewing | responding interactively |
| critical incidents | reflection, application, sense of relevance |
| project | application, research skills |
| reflective journal | reflection, application, sense of relevance |
| case study, problems | application, professional skills |
| portfolio | reflection, creativity, unintended outcomes |
| *Rapid assessments (large class)* | |
| concept maps | coverage, relationships |
| Venn diagrams | relationships |
| three-minute essay | level of understanding, sense of relevance |
| gobbets | realizing the importance of significant detail |
| short-answer | recall units of information, coverage |
| letter to a friend | holistic understanding, application, reflection |
| cloze | comprehension of main ideas |

one problem we couldn't solve was an uncompromising insistence on reporting grades along a curve, which makes criterion-referencing impossible.

The major thrust of both chapters on assessment is really quite simple. You can't beat backwash, so join it. Students will always second-guess the assessment task and then learn what they think will meet those requirements. But if those assessment requirements mirror the curriculum, there is no problem. Students will be learning what they are supposed to be learning.

### Implementing assessment package 2

Finally, we returned to the difficulty facing first-year teachers in particular: how to assess qualitatively under the usual conditions of large student numbers and poor resources.

Has this helped you with your own assessment problems? Turn to Task 9.1.

---

**Task 9.1: Choosing appropriate modes of assessment**

What key topics do you want to assess?

Turn to your objectives (Chapter 3, Task 3.1):
• What less important topics do you want to assess?
• What levels of understanding of each: Use the appropriate verbs to operationalize this.
• Do the topics refer to declarative knowledge? Functioning knowledge? Both?
• Are there any basic facts, skills, you want to check?
• What physical constraints do you have to accommodate to?
  – Large-class assessment methods?
  – Final exam. If so, is it invigilated?

Now choose from Table 9.2 those assessment modes that seem most suitable.

---

How do you propose to combine the results from each assessment task to produce a student's final grade for the unit?

Holistic throughout? _____

Holistic then convert to numbers? _____

Other? _____

Comments _____

_____

---

## Further reading

Angelo, T. and Cross, K.P. (1993) *Classroom Assessment Techniques: A Handbook for College Teachers.* San Francisco: Jossey-Bass.

Boud, D. (1995) *Enhancing Learning through Self-assessment.* London: Kogan Page.

Brown, S. and Glasner, A. (eds) (1999) *Assessment Matters in Higher Education*. Buckingham: Society for Research into Higher Education/Open University Press.

Brown, S. and Knight, P. (1994) *Assessing Learners in Higher Education*. London: Kogan Page.

Gibbs, G., Habeshaw, S. and Habeshaw, T. (1989) *53 Interesting Ways to Assess Your Students*. Bristol: Technical and Educational Services.

Gibbs, G., Jenkins, A. and Wisker, G. (1992) *Assessing More Students*. Oxford: PCFC/Rewley Press.

Harris, D. and Bell, C. (1986) *Evaluating and Assessing for Learning*. London: Kogan Page.

Nightingale, P., Te Wiata, I., Toohey, S. *et al.* (eds) (1996) *Assessing Learning in Universities*. Kensington, NSW: Committee for the Advancement of University Teaching/Professional Development Centre, UNSW.

Stephenson, J. and Laycock, M. (1993) *Using Contracts in Higher Education*. London: Kogan Page.

There are many books of practical suggestions on assessment; the above is a good sample. Some are obviously one-topic: Boud on self-assessment, Stephenson on contracts. Angelo and Cross contains over fifty classroom assessment techniques (CATs), grouped according to the purpose. Their American perspective is a useful contrast to the otherwise Austro-British line-up. Nightingale *et al.* collate 'best practice' from 100 university teachers, grouped under 'verb' headings, such as thinking critically, solving problems, reflecting, and so on. The chapters by Gibbs and Brew in Brown and Glasner are particularly useful for ideas on SA and PA, and 'using assessment strategically', as Gibbs puts it.

# 10

## Using educational technology: ET not IT

**The globalization of education has coincided with the development of information technology, so that there are enormous pressures on teachers to get with it and harness this technology, not only to improve their teaching but also to enable their universities to sell their educational wares on the other side of the world. The commercial and political implications of this are not the concern of this chapter; the implications for quality teaching and learning are. Let us first make it clear that we are concerned with *educational* technology (ET) not *information* technology (IT). ET has great potential in helping us reach our educational aims and objectives: in managing learning, in engaging students in appropriate learning activities, in assessing learning and in enabling off-campus learning. This chapter explores where ET can contribute in these areas.**

### 'Harnessing technology for more effective teaching'

The section title comes from the mission statement of a tertiary education institution, and that is the only reference made to enhancing teaching. No reference to reflective practice, not even to teaching development: just using information technology will do the trick. This institution – ironically, a single-purpose institution dedicated to teacher education – is not alone in this belief. Many tertiary institutions in Australia and Hong Kong, and to a lesser extent in the UK, are downsizing their teaching development units and restructuring them with educational technology units, often under the aegis of a director with IT, not learning and teaching, credentials. The message is as clear: use IT, and teaching problems will disappear as we join the globalized, online, knowledge economy.

This is dangerously misleading, the more so as this message is linked to another dubious position, discussed in Chapter 13, that of quality assurance, as opposed to quality enhancement. At worst, this trust in IT assumes the transmission model. If teaching is the transfer of knowledge from teacher to student, then the World Wide Web, with virtually unlimited information a mouse-click away, has to be a top quality teaching device. This view is also implied in the phrase 'surfing the Net': surface indeed, with cut-and-paste here, cut-and-paste there, link up with a few connecting sentences, rewrite some sentences in your very own personalized style, and bingo . . . an assignment that looks terrific but contains no original or deep thinking. This surface approach to learning has its counterpart in those teachers who believe that by putting their lecture notes on the Web they have joined the information revolution. If this is all they do, it is rather like filming a book, page by page, and then telling the students to go to the cinema to read it. It not only underuses the medium, it reinforces the idea that presenting and accessing information is what teaching and learning are about. It is no advance at all on lecturing itself.

It is important to get away from the notion that the use of technology is about presenting more and more information. The word 'information' before 'technology' may easily imply that. Efficient information-handling is certainly most useful and convenient in managing learning and administering programmes, but in teaching itself, we should not limit ourselves just to the information-handling facility of electronic technology. Hence the title of this chapter: 'Using educational technology: ET not IT'.

The message now could be: use ET and all will be well. This time the model of teaching is at level 2: good teaching is what the teacher does. But readers already know that any teaching approach is as good as its ability to fulfil a particular purpose. If your intention in a particular teaching session is to teach students to solve problems, you do not lecture them; if it is to present a large amount of information, you do not use problem-based learning.

Box 10.1 tells of a journey undertaken by a teacher in which he moved from a level 2 conception of using ET to level 3. He saw that it was what the students did that mattered, not what he did. This shows us clearly that ET is as good as the use to which it is put.

What, then, are the uses of ET? I distinguish the following, which shall be dealt with in turn:

1 *Managing learning.* ET, or rather IT in this case, can greatly facilitate administrative and management issues. Web pages can be used to allow access to all the relevant information to do with the department, programmes, courses, regulations and so on. IT can also be used to communicate with students or other enquirers, and receive information back from students.

---

**Box 10.1:   A level 3 approach to using ET**

*Problem.* Ninety per cent of nursing students experience difficulty in under-standing the topic: oedema associated with cardiac failure.

*Hypothesis.* A visual approach is more suited to the subject, and to students' learning styles.

*Solution.* Develop 'a multisensorial approach from which there could be no escape'. It has to have visual appeal, and movement: hence multimedia, an animated slide show.

*Result.* Only a 'slight' improvement in students' understanding.

*Reflection.* I had wasted my time.

*But then.* Tyler read the first edition of this book and learned:

1 Don't blame the students.
2 Don't blame the teacher.
3 Don't blame the teaching tool.
4 Do blame the lack of alignment.
5 Do blame the lack of assessment.

*On further reflection.* 'The multimedia program was worthwhile . . . what it lacked was lack of alignment and assessment.'

*Students now:*

1 complete an assessable worksheet at home (marked and assessed by peers);
2 complete a similar worksheet in class (again marked by peers).

*Result.* Pass rates in clinical studies increased from 80 per cent to 99.5 per cent.

*Source:* Tyler 2001.

---

2 *Engaging learners in appropriate learning activity,* both non-interactive, such as receiving information from diverse sources, and interactive. ET enables learners to be engaged in a variety of relevant learning activities, sometimes more easily than conventional teaching, sometimes in activities that are not practicable under conventional teaching.

3 *Assessing learning.* ET can be used for designing assessment tasks for both summative and particularly formative assessment. Again, ET can be used in ways that are not practicable with conventional assessment formats.

4 *Distance or off-campus teaching.* Many aspects of ET work the same on- or off-campus, but their off-campus use has a potential for changing the nature not only of university teaching, but also of universities them-selves. This is a very broad issue and can be only briefly discussed here.

## Managing learning

Before we start looking at the educational uses of ET, let me start with how the information-handling facility of IT may aid in managing learning and administering programmes. The great value of IT's word processing, spreadsheets and databases is that any amount of data, say on courses, staff and students, can be conveniently stored and accessed, and selections combined and placed on the website, or distributed by email or hypermail.

The web page, which is available to anyone on the internet, can be used to provide information at any level in a hierarchy, and to integrate access to many different types of media. A web page is like the front door to a house that provides entry, perhaps with a password, to a succession of opening doors, each allowing access to more and more specialized information. The front door might be that of the department or the university, which can provide access to all the information at departmental level; the next door might deal with programmes, the next with units, courses or modules. It is with the level of individual units or modules that I am mainly concerned here.

The programme and module web pages can provide students with everything they need to know: the course outlines, regulations and procedures, staff and student lists, and then the detail of the module itself, such as the teaching methods, readings, assignments, assessment deadlines and so on. The TLAs themselves, and the assessment tasks, will be dealt with in the appropriate section below. The sheer power of the website can be seen by visiting www.WebCT.com which gives a better description of what the programme offers than I can give here. WebCT provides a widely used format for structuring an instructional web page, allowing all sorts of information, including when and for how long the pages have been visited, and by whom.

WebCT, Blackboard, or any like tools, not only present information but also receive it. Thus they can be used for online enrolment, answering questions from students or the public, submitting assignments, and so on.

The great benefit of online teaching is two-way communication. Students can be emailed individually or in groups about teaching or administrative matters, and the originals and records of replies are kept automatically. A nice example of this is given by Mazur (1998), who kept the photographs of the 160 students in his physics class in his address file. His concern was to give students regular feedback about small weekly learning tasks. The tasks were such that errors fell into few categories, say four or five, so that there were in essence only five generic emails to be sent, to groups of thirty or students. By clicking on the student's address, up would come the face to remind him whom he was talking to, and then he could tune the opening and the close to the individual: 'Hi there, Jenny. You slipped up a bit here, after last week's great effort. Here seems to be the problem . . . (then the appropriate generic email). Let me know if it's not clear now. Best, . . .'

This example, which is described in substantive detail below, is a mixture of managing and teaching roles of ET, but it gives an idea of how ET can handle a simple information-giving task much more effectively than traditional methods.

In sum, online management of student records and data is immensely convenient and time-saving, making the educational use of technology so much easier.

## Engaging learners in appropriate learning activity

### Information presentation

The power of ET in storing and accessing information is impressive and well understood: probably too well because, as we have seen, some people do not go beyond that and see the 'educational' value of electronic technology beginning and ending with its ability to access information from the World Wide Web. It only needs a key word to be typed into a search engine, such as Google, and all the up-to-date information a student could ever need is there for the downloading. Web-based information sourcing also includes: readings and lecture notes the teacher puts on the site, e-books and e-journals, and information from other supplied web addresses. The databanks are so enormous that students need to be trained to be selective, to use key words that cross-classify so that the data can be gleaned to be as relevant as possible, and to 'surf' fruitfully, so that it is not mind-boggling or a waste of time. Brew (1999) suggests that self- and peer assessment provide good training in sorting out good from poor information.

Non-web sources include: commercial and teacher-prepared CDs and videos, and Microsoft® Office applications, including PowerPoint. Power-Point is now rapidly becoming a standard tool inside the classroom and needs some discussion here.

A couple of years ago, I gave a workshop on encouraging active learning in the classroom, followed by the usual evaluation. A comment on one evaluation form was negative, concluding: 'And he didn't even use PowerPoint.' I had not used PowerPoint precisely because I wanted the audience to be relevantly active. But I had failed, with at least one member of the group, because the very point I was trying to make had not been taken on board.

PowerPoint has most of the disadvantages of the lecture (see Chapter 6), except that the notes and diagrams in PowerPoint are usually much clearer and more appealing, and a conveniently compressed version of the frames can be printed and circulated. However, PowerPoint is best used sparingly. Sitting in semi-darkness, watching frame after frame, each accompanied by whizzing diagonal inputs with sound effects, is either soporific or distracting. To be sure, we can have a few diagrams and points, but when a few key frames have been presented, it is better to change the activity from receiving information to using it: have a discussion, say (see Chapter 6). The laptop can then be used to record the discussion, and project it onto a screen for all to see. This is equivalent to writing on a black/whiteboard, but (1) it is much clearer and faster than handwriting, and (2) the discussion, as well as the frames themselves, can be printed and circulated to the class. A similar function is performed by whiteboards that copy what is written onto a paper roll, which can then be photocopied and distributed, but the laptop is clearer, more flexible and – in my experience – more reliable.

Excessive use of devices like PowerPoint reinforces the view that good teaching is a one-way transfer of information. This is not to say that PowerPoint is not effective and economical for conference presentations, that is, for telling my peers what I have to say when they really do want to know what I have to say. Typical large-class teaching is not like this. Many, perhaps most, students do not come to each class genuinely wanting to know what I have to say, while none come with the background knowledge of my fellow professionals.

There is no doubt, then, that ET, either web-based or otherwise, can bring large amounts of up-to-the-minute information to students. However, care needs to be taken to see that students also learn the skills of discriminating useful from useless information, and indeed factual from misleading information, for there is plenty of the latter on the web. But even that is only the beginning.

### Interactive use of education technology

Woodley (2001) makes an essential point about using online teaching: it is *not* about one-way delivery, putting your notes on the web.

> The desire to tell students stuff is very strong. It takes a huge amount of reconfiguring to actually develop curriculum that begins steering towards a problem-based or even activity-focused approach . . . Not only must the content be interactive, but with the course being, at least in part, delivered online, we must also ensure that students are not working in isolation – just being interactive with a screen. Classroom interaction is vital to learning and we will need to explore the ways in which the type of interaction that takes place in the classroom can be emulated online. For that, we need to examine the

communication tools of WebCT and how students use or can be encouraged to use them.

(p. 68)

Woodley is making two very important points. The first is the same as that made above: ET can be used simply to translate the lecture into another one-way transmission medium, a temptation that must be resisted.

To get around that, we need to exploit the interactive potential of ET, and that is her second point. The real value of ET is that it can be used to encourage relevant learning activities.

There are two dimensions to the interactive use of ET that literally dissolve the boundaries of time and space, allowing many different kinds of interaction between people:

1 *Synchronous and asynchronous use.* Synchronous use is when teacher, or learning package, interacts with the student in the same timeframe. This is the case when teacher and student are online at the same time, as in tele- or video-conferencing. Students attending a PowerPoint lecture is also a synchronous use. With asynchronous use, participants make their communication in their own time, such as happens when using email or a bulletin board. For example, the teacher may post questions on the board and the students respond with answers or comments, as is convenient to them, prior to the stated deadline. Asynchronous use is particularly valuable in off-campus teaching, so that individuals with full-time jobs can enter their learning space at a time that suits them.

2 *Individual and social use.* We normally think of online teaching as involving a lonely individual at a keyboard responding asynchronously to a distant information source. This is only one, limited, use. When used synchronously, the student and teacher may 'chat' one-to-one, or one teacher may chat to many individuals, each at their own keyboards; likewise, many students may interact with each other at the same time, as they do with ICQ ('I seek you'). All these examples are of one person per keyboard, but pairs or larger numbers can use the same keyboard and discuss their comments, questions or responses before sending them. These groupings can be used synchronously or asynchronously.

Thus, the combinations of individual and group, and synchronous and asynchronous use, are many. Each combination has its own advantages and disadvantages; as always, it depends entirely on what and how you want your students to learn. A disadvantage of asynchronous online discussion is that those who are quickest to place their views online in a discussion can frustrate others who wanted to make the same points. This might be obviated by requiring students to post to a closed address, which would then be opened on a specified date. It helps considerably if groups can meet face to face first, so that when online discussion begins, people can put a face to the name and feel that they are genuinely conversing.

Many of the common group structures discussed in Chapters 5 and 6 can be replicated online. Some groups work better online, some worse. For example, going the rounds from student to student, seeking the opinion of each on the discussion topic, works much better asynchronously online than synchronously, either online or face to face. In the asynchronous use, students are not under pressure to say something when it is their turn, but rather they can take their time to think out their view, and then post it on the bulletin board. Buzz groups, on the other hand, work better face to face, where oral spontaneity is an important feature (Maier and Warren 2000). Syndicates also work well online, which can work synchronously at first, then subgroups may confer and report back, which can be synchronously for some phases and asynchronously for others. Battacharya (2002) reports a successful design where lectures videotaped by excellent teachers are circulated with supplementary readings, quizzes and assignments. These become stimulus material for small-group collaborative learning, with up to eight participants in study centres across India. The groups could stop the video at any time to raise questions and share views. Results were very satisfactory.

ICQ is used by many students informally for chat lines. That is, they sign up with a group and when they log on, the server can search for others in that group who happen to be online and inform them that a conversation is there for the having. Alternatively, members can agree to log on at a given time. ICQ is primarily used for non-academic purposes, but many students use it in Tang's (1993) sense of spontaneous collaboration over set work such as assignments. It can also be used as for tutorials if a tutor signs on with the tutorial group.

A few examples of interactive use follow. We saw Mazur's (1998) use of email, but that was only a small part of a bigger scenario. Mazur was adamant that he would not lecture on what the students could read more cost-effectively. Accordingly, he set readings that must be read before the class, and two or three simple questions had to be answered by the previous night, by email: 'Please tell us what you found difficult and confusing. If you found nothing difficult or confusing, please tell us what you found most interesting.' He would then go through these emails the night before the class, and form a database of generic comments. Each student would then receive the appropriate comment, duly personalized. The students felt they were getting personal attention, despite the large class, and although it took more time than not giving students feedback, it took much less time than providing feedback by writing the same comments on the original scripts.

In class the next day, the students were presented every ten minutes with an MC question based on the readings. Each student seat had an electronic voting device, so that students' responses could be tallied immediately. The question was usually about a 'trick' physical phenomenon:

for example, 'A flat plate of cast-iron, two feet square and one inch thick, has a large circular hole, diameter four inches, drilled in the center. The plate is then heated. Does the hole in the center increase in diameter, decrease, or remain the same, as the plate expands with heating?' While all the relevant physical principles were known by this stage, a wide diversity of opinion as to the outcome of heating was likely. The students were asked to find someone nearby who voted differently, and then to convince their neighbour that their own response was the correct one.

After discussion, another vote was taken and this time there was usually much more consensus, in the direction of the correct answer. Mazur reports that the learning was powerful and the students enjoyed it. He was consistently voted best teacher of the year. Mazur's design – pre-reading, answer questions, provide feedback, come to class for quizzes and discussion – could be put to work conventionally, but not nearly so easily or with such enjoyment as when using ET.

An example of enlightened bulletin board use with teachers attending a postgraduate educational psychology course is given by Chan (2001), who integrated computer-supported collaborative learning with regular teaching. The students were asked to post their learning notes and responses to questions on a bulletin board, and to comment on the notes and responses of others. The distinctive feature of her use of the bulletin board was the way she posted reflective prompts, such as:

- Is there anything interesting or useful you have learned?
- What are some things that are difficult to understand?
- How did reading these notes help you think about X and Y?
- Have the comments on your ideas made you rethink the issue?

Students did not have to address each as an assignment question, but as reminders to guide their thinking. Students were also asked about their conceptions of teaching and learning at the beginning and at the end of the course; the difference became a measure of the growth of their complexity of thinking about teaching and learning.

Chan found that the frequency of contribution to the bulletin board in itself was unrelated to a gain in complexity of thinking, but when the comments were divided into those that were derived collaboratively, or were simply posted as individual contributions, those who entered into collaborative engagement gained most in complexity of thinking.

A powerful software program encouraging collaborative knowledge construction is Knowledge Forum (originally called CSILE) by Scardamalia *et al.* (1994). Knowledge Forum involves students contributing to a bulletin board by generating their own problems, posing their own questions, and commenting on each other's work, rather like Chan's usage. The computer helps search all comments written by a student at different periods, which can then be rated in terms of the quality of the comments. The software comes with a program called Analytical Toolkit that can generate quantitative indices, such as how much each student has written, how often the individual has read others' notes, how often their comments are revised or elaborated, how are one student's notes related to others' notes, who is writing to whom, and so on. However, the program cannot recognize the quality of the comments written, and so analyses still need to be done by teachers; in some respects these analyses are not unlike SOLO. The main difference between Knowledge Forum and other discussion platforms is that the former includes thinking prompts and other devices to help students reflect deeply as they contribute, and it provides continual formative assessment of students' ideas as they are posted on the platform. One can also make a summative statement about students' growth and learning outputs at the end of the course. Knowledge Forum has mostly been applied to junior school science (Scardamalia and Bereiter 1999), but Chan *et al.* (2001) used the program with A-level geography in a Hong Kong school with great success.

It would be inappropriate here to attempt to catalogue the other many, and increasing, uses ET has in engaging students in appropriate learning activities. One very powerful and flexible use is the creation of 'virtual' environments, many available commercially on CD-ROM, that provide interesting interactive environments for students to explore. For example, Virtual Dig can take archaeology students through excavating a site; they can alter factors such as time of dig, method, whether to screen dirt for relics, and so on. There are many science lab virtual environments where students can try expensive or dangerous experiments at a fraction of the real cost.

In essence, ET is like any other medium: it is part of a general instructional design that is good only in so far as it enables one's objectives to be achieved. What it does do, however, is open out the options for engaging students in relevant activity.

## Assessing learning

There are several ways in which ET can be used to assess students. The most common is computer-assisted assessment (CAA), which uses the power of the computer to assess conventionally but more efficiently. CAA is most appropriate using objective format or closed question-types. There are commercial MCQ banks, or the teacher can design and use them through WebCT or Blackboard.

CAA has several advantages over pencil-and-paper format (Maier *et al.* 1998):

- Allows more than one attempt.
- Can supply hints.
- Provides immediate feedback.
- Can guide reading as a result of the test.
- May be either formative or summative.
- Can present questions in random or standard order.

Thus, there can be a databank of several questions on a topic and, when a student logs on, a different sample of questions can be presented each time. The difficulty level each student is getting correct can be recorded, diagnoses made and suggestions provided as to how learning may be improved. Given such a system, it would not be unreasonable to require near-perfect responses.

There are two main concerns about using CAA summatively. The first is that, in time, students can rote learn the correct responses, bypassing the mental process required to work out the correct response. This can be mitigated by randomizing the options at each presentation, and, on the principle of alignment, using the system precisely for items that require rote learning, such as terminology, rules and so on. When used on a pass–fail basis, 'pass' requiring 90 per cent correct responding, it is identical with mastery learning (see Chapter 8). And that is the problem. It is too easy to equate good learning with 'knowing more' if that is all CAA is used for.

The second problem with using ET for summative evaluation is that one needs to be sure that the person at the keyboard is the student who should be there. One way around this, as with conventional assessment, is to use personalized and contextualized material, such as reflections on work-based experience. Such material is either difficult or meaningless when done by someone else. Thus ET can and should be used for much more than the typical closed-format CAA situation.

Complex real-life situations can be given in multimedia presentations and students asked to respond. A video clip, with multiple-choice alternatives, could show a professional scenario, say a psychologist interviewing a client, and the student is required to choose from the options what type of situation is represented (Maier and Warren 2000). Even more revealing would be to change this into an open-ended assessment task by asking the student to comment on what is going on, give a critical analysis of the exchange, what steps the psychologist might take next, and so on. It is possible to get the best of the open-ended format, and some of the convenience of multiple choice, by the teacher inserting comments from a bank of comments in appropriate parts of the essay.

Students may be required to set up their own web pages and to post their learnings as they would in a learning portfolio. The advantage here is that all the other students in the course could access it, and post their own evaluative comments. This then leads naturally to self- and peer assessment much more readily than when assessments are made in hard copy. The UK Open University uses a student-created website in place of a traditional exam; details, and discussion of the issues involved, such as plagiarism, are discussed in Weller (2002).

In sum, ET may handle both quantitative and qualitative modes of assessment with considerable logistical and managerial advantages. There is always the problem of plagiarism, but that exists in both conventional and ET modes when conducted outside an invigilated environment. The potential of ET in assessment is most valuable in open-ended responding, in rich and contextualized situations, particularly with the advent of software like Knowledge Forum that facilitates both formative and summative assessment at either individual or group level.

## Distance or off-campus teaching

There is a confusion of terminology around the concept of off-campus teaching. At first referred to as 'external studies', then the term 'open learning' was used (see the first edition of this book, pp. 113–14). Whereas the latter term originally referred to open access to mature learners, Maier *et al.* (1998) now refer to open learning as relying on the use of learning packages on- or off-campus, while flexible learning refers to access to learning resources at a wide range of time and location. Off-campus teaching may be synchronous, as in tele- or video-conferencing, or asynchronous; it is in principle little different from on-campus teaching using ET. In fact, some on-campus degree programmes have online units without face-to-face teaching, while other programmes are distance learning in the full sense, where the students can be anywhere in the world.

International distance learning is seen by many as a fundamental quantum leap not only in teaching and learning modes, but also in the purpose and functioning of universities (Taylor 1995; Bourner and Flowers 1997; Laurillard and Margetson 1997). The implications for higher education can be immense, both educationally and politically. The competition provided by flexible delivery from prestigious overseas universities could even eliminate off-campus teaching at local universities, and seriously damage on-campus teaching. As one Australian vice-chancellor put it, 'most countries (apart from Britain, China and the USA) would be lucky to have one or two institutions that could be termed "world class"' (Niland 2000).

There is a view popular amongst politicians and others that online teaching is the answer to large classes; the 'classroom' may be infinitely large, as it were. I hope it is clear by now that this is a mistaken view, depending as it does on a one-way transmission view of teaching. If teaching is merely providing information to be downloaded, then yes, that is true. But as soon as it is realized that teaching involves engaging students in relevant activity, and that assessments need to be aligned to the course objectives, then there are obvious limits to the numbers that can be handled appropriately in interactive online teaching and assessment, whether synchronous or asynchronous. The difference between a teacher responding to 30 students using a bulletin board, and 3000, is obvious. As student enrolments in a course increase, it becomes correspondingly necessary to engage online teaching assistants who are both computer-wise and content-expert enough to help with assessing, classifying and collating student outputs, and assisting in communicating with students, as it was necessary in the old days to appoint tutors, demonstrators and teaching assistants. Getting search engines to 'trigger a personalized response', thereby reducing the cost of supporting students (Taylor, reported in Moodie 2001), is a solution fraught with the 'sought of problem wee no from spell cheques'. The human touch is needed, even for programs as sophisticated as Knowledge Forum.

## Summary and conclusions

### 'Harnessing technology for more effective teaching'

Too many people see ET as a fool-proof delivery system that obviates the need for expert, reflective teaching and that can be run by technocrats rather than educators. What ET does in fact is to provide some convenient alternatives to conventional methods of teaching and assessing. And, like any educational medium, it is only as good as it helps achieve our educational aims and objectives. The temptation to see ET as a means of transmitting masses of information is counterproductive to good learning. Unfortunately, it is precisely that function that tends to impress the most.

### Managing learning

One useful function of technology is its ability to manage learning and administer programmes. There are two complementary features of ET that reinforce each other: the ability to handle large databases, for example information about the university, the department, different programmes and modules, staff and student records; and the ability to handle two-way communications with students, individually or in groups.

### Engaging learners in appropriate learning activity

The educational strength of ET is its ability to engage numbers of students – in your time or in theirs – in learning activities that might be difficult or impossible to activate in the conventional classroom. Some activities are unique to ET in the sense that it is impractical to carry them out conventionally, such as engaging in public discussion asynchronously, while others are simply more convenient or interesting when mounted by ET, such as sampling student opinion on a contentious issue.

ET, however, is not a panacea. If not used in a properly aligned instructional design, matching objectives on the one hand and assessment tasks on the other, it is as ineffectual as any way of poor teaching.

### Assessing learning

The commonest use of ET is in computer-assisted assessment (CAA), born of multiple-choice testing, but much more efficient than hard-format MC testing, but open to the same problems as closed questions and, too frequently, low-level responding. Again, the strength of ET in the assessment process is in its open-ended use. It can be used to publicly display student products – cumulative discussion records, web pages as portfolios, any online task in fact – and so opens out the possibilities of self- and peer assessment much more easily than conventional modes. An interesting feature of this approach is that the distinction between formative and summative assessment is simply a matter of who does what and when: whether the chef tastes the casserole before serving, or the customer afterwards.

### Distance or off-campus teaching

As far as ET itself is concerned, off-campus teaching is little different in principle from on-campus. The same principles of synchronous and asynchronous use, with some on-campus options not being available off-campus, but the principles of good design of the delivery system apply always. The issues alluded to here were more sociological and political.

Table 10.1 summarizes the above uses of ET, with some typical examples of each.

## Further reading

### On the ET revolution

Maier, P. and Warren, A. (2000) *Integrating Technology in Learning and Teaching*. London: Kogan Page.

Oliver, R. and Herrington, J. (2001) *Teaching and Learning On-line: A Beginners Guide to E-learning and E-teaching in Higher Education*. Perth,

**Table 10.1:**  Uses of ET and some typical examples of each use

| Function | Examples of ET |
| --- | --- |
| Managing learning | WebCT, Blackboard, web pages presenting access to university/department/programme information; online enrolment; communications, bulletin boards |
| Information storage and presentation | *Web-based*: WebCT, Blackboard, e-books, e-journals, search engines, Library/Cybrary, web pages presenting access to university/department/programme information; online enrolment; communications, bulletin boards<br>*Non web-based*: PowerPoint and other Microsoft® Office applications, videos, CDs |
| Interactive tools, TLAs | Simulations, virtual environments, bulletin boards, Knowledge Forum, electronic voting<br>Can be used synchronously/asynchronously, and individually or in groups |
| Assessment tools | *CAA*: MCQ item banks, either commercial or teacher-produced<br>*Open-ended*: Knowledge Forum and bulletin boards generally, web pages, ideal for self-, peer as well as teacher assessment |
| Off-campus | *Synchronous*: telephone, tele- and video-conferencing<br>*Asynchronous*: all web-based, as above |

WA: Centre for Research in Information Technology and Communications, Edith Cowan University.

Khan, B.H. (ed.) (1997) *Web-based Instruction*. Englewood Cliffs, NJ: Educational Technology Publications.

Maier and Warren contains many website addresses for teaching development in ET, and for particular issues such as course design, collaborative learning, using videos, quality assurance. Oliver and Herrington is an excellent book for applying constructivism to teaching online. It describes successful strategies to guide the development of learning units that support knowledge construction and higher-order learning, including problem-based learning, case-based learning, role-playing and simulations. Khan provides a good collection of chapters addressing all aspects of web-based teaching, including the evolution of the web for teaching purposes, incorporating instructional design into web activities, formative evaluation, use of hypertext, and so on.

### On not becoming a dinosaur: some websites

Are you anxious about the terrible prospect of going online or becoming a dinosaur? Then visit what Gwenda Lavender and colleagues think is the best and worst of online teaching resources, and the product they developed: 'Where in the www is it and anyway is it any good?' located at www.staff.vu.edu.au/olp/courseeval.

For details of WebCT visit www.WebCT.com.

For the minimal skills and competencies needed by students to operate in an online learning environment, go to the ANTA Toolbox (provided by Tracey-ann Reynolds, Victoria University, Melbourne) at www.toolboxcentral.com.

One program, SyncStream (which may be downloaded for free), incorporates PowerPoint or other slide shows into the video of a lecture. This was developed by Samuel Shiffman of Seton Hall, University of South Grange, New Jersey, who says: 'If you want faculty to embrace technology, you have to make it attractive and easy to use.' Visit at http://tltc.shu.edu/initiatives/streaming/syncstream.htm.

# 11

## Some examples
## of aligned teaching

**In this chapter we look at some examples of teaching
that illustrate how alignment may work. The first
embodies an apparently minor and low-cost change
in an otherwise conventional teaching programme,
in which peer assessment became the major TLA.
The second is problem-based learning (PBL), which
is becoming increasingly popular, particularly in
professional education. In essence, the objectives
are compiled from professional problems, the major
TLAs involve solving them, and the assessment is
concerned with how well. The final example uses
the learning portfolio, the alignment here arising
bottom-up as the students negotiated how they
could provide examples of their learning that
would meet the objectives.**

### Peer assessment as a teaching/learning activity

Gibbs (1999) reports a case study of a compulsory second-year engineering programme where what seems to be a fairly minor change in assessment procedures produced a dramatic change in performance. Teaching
and assessment had been quite traditional: two lectures and one problem-
solving tutorial session a week, and an end-of-session final examination.
In the tutorials, students worked on problem sheets handed out at the
lectures, similar to the problems in the final exam. When the tutorials
comprised only ten students, the system worked reasonably well, but when
they became drastically larger – 20 and over – students could 'hide', not
ask questions, avoid eye contact and get away with little preparation.
Marking the weekly problem sheets created a crippling workload on the
tutors, and was dropped. The failure rate increased, the average mark
dropped to 45 per cent.

To improve matters, an innovation was adapted from Boud's (1986) work on peer assessment. Everything remained as before, except that six times during the unit the students met in a plenary session, bringing problem sheets they had completed since the previous plenary. They handed these in, with their names written on them, and the sheets were redistributed at random, with a how-to-mark sheet. They then marked the problem sheets they were given, with written comments, in the knowledge of whose work they were marking. No further instruction in marking was given, and no monitoring of their marking took place. The sheets were then handed back to their owners, who could not tell who had marked and commented on their work. The marks were not recorded, and did not contribute to the final grade, but students had to complete a specified number of problem sheets, otherwise they were failed. With just this change in procedure of the six plenary peer assessment sessions, the average in the final exam increased from 45 per cent to 75 per cent, with no failures.

In accounting for these dramatic results, Gibbs refers to five principles of learning that were invoked by the peer assessments:

1 The students not only had to spend more time (out of class) on problem-solving, their time was distributed evenly rather than concentrated on the last week or so in preparation for the final exam.
2 The activities generated were those required by the course. Students didn't spend out-of-class time on instrumental activities such as reading lecture notes. 'The best way to learn how to tackle problems is to tackle lots of problems,' as Gibbs puts it. Marking other students' problem-solving is itself a rich learning experience; students see how others might do the task, some using better problem-solving strategies than they themselves used, some using worse strategies thus signalling errors to avoid. The model answers provided them with standards to monitor their own future problem-solving.
3 Students received feedback on their own work by the end of each session, not weeks later when the tutor had managed to mark them all.
4 The feedback they received is socially amplified. Bad work is marked and commented on by their own peers, which Gibbs claims hits home much more effectively than negative feedback from a tutor they hardly know.
5 They learned to judge when a performance was good or not; they had internalized appropriate standards of quality control.

The motivation for handing in good work on a constant basis is social, so that the problems are willingly attempted although they do not form part of the final assessment, except in so far as they must be handed in. Gibbs comments that it hardly matters if the feedback is unfair or inexpert, the important thing is that it focuses the students' attention on appropriate learning activities.

Here, the six peer assessment sessions produced alignment in a system that was thrown out of alignment by the problem of increased student numbers. The course objectives addressed problem-solving, and the final exam likewise, but the problem sessions, which were the main TLA after the lecture, had become ineffectual. The peer assessments became TLAs that directly addressed the final assessment. Peer assessment was not so much an assessment device as a teaching/learning device.

This strategy of using peer assessment as a TLA may not work in all subjects. It would probably require conditions where peer assessment itself works best, that is where the assessment tasks are clearly defined, and mirror the course objectives (see p. 191). Under those conditions, alignment can be achieved at little extra cost – the supervision of the six extra plenary sessions – while the academic gains are considerable.

Another case Gibbs (1999) cites, where aligning the assessment produced dramatically improved results, was in a philosophy of education course for trainee teachers. The standard exam question was: 'Compare and contrast the philosophies of X and Y in relation to classroom practice Z'. It was possible to pass by memorizing what philosophers said, and then writing about X and Y as required. A new teacher on the course replaced the question with a 10 minute video of a teaching episode, and the instruction: 'Comment on what is going on in this class from a philosophical point of view.' The video changed each year but not the question. As Gibbs comments, 'There was no way students could prepare for such an exam by memorizing facts about philosophers' (p. 51). Students instead learned the ideas expressed, and borrowed videos of classrooms and discussed them with other students. As teachers, they did not need to know who said what, but needed functioning knowledge of the philosophy of education, which is what the new assessment – easily carried under examination conditions – demanded.

You can now tackle Task 11.1.

## Problem-based learning

Problem-based learning was first used in the 1960s at Case Western Reserve and at McMaster Medical School, in the United States and Canada, respectively, and was adopted by several medical schools during the 1970s before being applied to other areas of educating for the professions. PBL is not a method so much as a total approach to teaching, which could embody several possible TLAs and assessment methods. It can be implemented in a single unit or across a whole course/programme, and applied to basic academic subjects as well as to professional education (Poliquin and Maufette 1997), but is particularly common in medical and paramedical education.

---

**Task 11.1: Tracking down and fixing poor alignment**

The Gibbs examples in the first section of this chapter are simple but powerful examples where things were going wrong because the assessment or the teaching/learning activities were not aligned to objectives.

Now think of an example occurring in your own teaching or in the department. What seems to be the problem? Get together with a colleague and think up ways in which you can try something different that would seem to realign the teaching or the assessment the way it should be. For ideas, read Gibbs's chapter in Brown and Glasner (1999).

---

PBL reflects the way people learn in real life; they simply get on with solving the problems life puts before them with whatever resources are to hand. They do not stop to wonder at the relevance of what they are doing, or at their motivation for doing it. Formal schooling, on the contrary, operates on a fill-up-the-tanks model of knowledge acquisition. Young people are taught the sorts of thing they are likely to need to know one day, and some skills for finding out more, before they are let loose on the world.

Education for the professions for years followed this proactive model, and much of it still does. The disciplines are taught first, independently of each other, and armed with all that declarative knowledge, and with some skills, the student is accredited as ready to practise as a professional. Professional practice, however, requires functioning knowledge that can be put to work immediately, not just declarative knowledge (see Chapter 3). If the objectives nominate professional competency on graduation, but declarative knowledge is the output, something has been missed. Curriculum, teaching and assessment are not aligned.

PBL is alignment itself. If the aim is to become a doctor, then the best way of doing so is being a doctor – under appropriate guidance and safeguards. If the aim is to apply biology to solving biological problems, then solving biological problems is the main TLA. The objectives stipulate the problems to be solved, the main TLA is solving them, and the assessment is seeing how well they have been solved. If we return to Figure 3.1, we see that PBL works backwards from functioning knowledge to the underlying conditional, procedural and declarative knowledge.

Savin-Baden (2000) argues that PBL is commonly confused with problem-solving learning. The latter simply means setting problems for students to solve after they have been taught conventionally, and then discussing them later, as in the case of the mechanical engineering discussed above. In PBL, on the other hand, 'the starting point for learning should be a problem, query or a puzzle that the learner wishes to solve' (Boud 1985:

13). The problem, or a series of problems, is where learning starts, and in going about solving those problems the learner seeks out the necessary knowledge of disciplines, facts and procedures. The traditional disciplines do not define what is to be learned, the problems do. However, the aim is not only to solve those particular problems, but also in the course of doing so, to acquire knowledge, content-related skills, self-management skills, attitudes, know-how: in a word, professional wisdom.

In a fully blown PBL prgramme, the problems are selected so that by the end of the programme the learner is ready to move directly into the workforce. Less content may well be covered than in a traditional programme, but the *nature* of the knowledge so gained is different. It is acquired in a working context and is put back to use in that context. Coverage, so dominant in discipline-centred teaching, is considered less important. Instead, students learn the *skills* for seeking out the required knowledge as the occasion demands.

A typical PBL sequence goes like this:

1 The *context* is pressing. In a typical medical programme, students in their first week of first year are faced with the responsibility of a real patient with, say, a broken leg. The felt need to learn is strong.
2 Learners become *active* very quickly. They are assigned to small problem-solving groups and begin *interacting* with teachers, peers and clients (who present the problem).
3 Learners start from what they already know, and *build a knowledge* base on that. They learn where to go to check what they know, and to seek out more. They are variously guided towards resource materials, including films, videos, the library and lecture room. Knowledge is *elaborated and consolidated*. Students meet with a tutor and discuss the case in relation to the knowledge they have obtained.
4 The knowledge is functioning: it is *applied* to the problem in hand.
5 The problem is reviewed, and learners develop *self-management and self-monitoring skills*, which they review throughout the programme.

The italicized words may remind you of the characteristics of a rich learning context described in Chapter 5. PBL makes use of them all.

### Goals of PBL

There are several modifications and versions of what is called PBL, but all should address the four goals distinguished by Barrows (1986):

1 *Structuring knowledge for use in working contexts.* Professional education is concerned with functioning knowledge. PBL is concerned with constructing knowledge that is to be put to work.
2 *Developing effective reasoning processes.* Such processes refer to the cognitive activities required in the professional area concerned, and include:

problem-solving, decision-making, hypothesizing, etc. Each professional area has its own specific processes to be developed as relevant problems are solved.

3 *Developing self-directed learning skills.* Included here are the three levels of skill mentioned in Chapter 5: generic study skills, content-specific study skills and, especially, the meta-cognitive or self-management skills focused on what the learner does in new contexts. The latter should be the ultimate aim of all university teaching. They are frequently mentioned in mission statements under 'lifelong learning', and are specifically addressed in PBL, where they are learned in context, as they should be.

4 *Increased motivation for learning.* Students are placed in a context that requires their immediate and committed involvement. Thus, in terms of motivational theory (Chapter 4), the value is high, the expectation of success is high, as problems and cases are selected in which students are likely to be successful, so motivation is high.

To these four may be added a fifth:

5 *Developing group skills, working with colleagues.* Many professions require teamwork, so this becomes a goal in many PBL programmes. It might be noted that such teamwork takes place in a workplace-like context, unlike much group project work (see pp. 187–8).

Various forms of PBL may address these goals. Two major variables determine different kinds of PBL (Barrows 1986):

1 *The degree to which the problem is structured.* Some problems are tightly structured; the case study is given in detail, with all the information needed to solve it. Such problems can only be considered a lead-in to PBL. Others have some facts provided, the student having to find the rest: these problems encourage what we called BIG learning, beyond the information given (see p. 95). Open or 'ill-defined' problems present no data, it being entirely up to the student to research the case, which leads to WIG learning, without the information given.

2 *The extent of teacher direction.* The most conservative case, arguably not PBL, is where the teacher controls the amount and flow of information, problems being discussed by the teacher in a lecture. In the case of ill-defined problems, teacher direction is minimal, the students going off on their own to solve the problem. Variations in between depend on how much the teacher provides clues and on information handling support.

What is the best form of PBL to introduce? Practically, it has to be manageable with available resources, consistent at least initially with the educational philosophy of the teachers and tutors participating, and what freedom the students can initially handle (Ryan 1997). In a study at the Polytechnic University of Hong Kong, modifications were introduced to fit the aims of six departments, and the different expectations of full- and part-time students (Tang *et al.* 1997). The full-time students found most difficulty with assessment, not surprisingly given their exam-dominated school background. As one student put it, 'it is difficult to guess what is the marking scheme of the lecturer' (p. 586). Part-time students, on the other hand, took to PBL straight away because it mimicked the workplace: 'when I encounter a problem, I will have a solution, like that in my workplace' (p. 586).

### The nature and construction of the problems

In degree programmes run throughout with PBL, the problems must be directly related to the profession in question, and carefully selected and sequenced through the years. But whether in a complete programme or at unit level, the following are the characteristics of a good problem (Johnston, private communication):

1 It calls on different disciplines and integrates them in solving the problem.
2 It raises options that promote discussion.
3 It activates and incorporates previous knowledge.
4 It requires new knowledge the students don't yet have.
5 It simulates participants to elaborate.
6 It requires self-directed learning.
7 And, of course, it meets the course objectives.

Such problems are open-ended and 'ill-structured', that is they do not present the students with enough information.

Here's a problem for you: You plan to use PBL in teaching your unit. What are you going to do? Ill-structured, definitely. You see straight away that you don't have enough information, and seeking a solution involves higher order WIG thinking, such as hypothesizing, evaluation, reflection (see p. 95). It also involves divergent thinking, as there is likely to be more than one way of reaching a solution. A sensible first step, then, might be to read the rest of this chapter, then some of the readings. Are there any colleagues in your institution using PBL? If so, talk to them.

You now might begin to have a clearer idea of what a problem should look like, so the next step is to construct one and give it a trial.

What luck! David Johnston, Director of the Hong Kong Centre for PBL, is in town and is putting on a workshop 'Designing Problems for PBL'. He has agreed that I can give you a taste of what you might be doing by reproducing some of his material (Box 11.1).

You can now handle Task 11.2.

---

**Box 11.1: Designing a problem**

1 Map all the **concepts** likely to be involved from different disciplines, including the **knowledge** and **skills** required to solve the situation. Maybe a knowledge tree would help.

2 Write the **learning objectives**. What do you expect the students to do with the new knowledge and skills?

3 Identify a **real problem** from a real-life situation that is important to students, such as one they are likely to meet in their future employment. Authenticity is highly motivating.

4 Repeat step 3 until all your objectives are addressed.

5 When **writing** problems make sure to:
   (a) use the present tense, otherwise problems look like another textbook exercise;
   (b) provide a context and specific role of practititioner – what, when, where;
   (c) provide specific rather than vague data;
   (d) require the students to deliver something: a decision or report.

6 Many situations or problems **evolve over time**. It might be appropriate to provide an extended problem (called roll-out problem or case). Such a problem is in parts, covering a sequence of events, or the problem is addressed in stages as more data become available, and may last over more than one semester.

7 Write a **facilitator guide** for others involved in the PBL, including:
   (a) the problem;
   (b) the learning objectives;
   (c) the learning issues, including all the new knowledge you expect particip-ants to learn and discuss;
   (d) content background information for the facilitators;
   (e) suggested resources for students.

*Source*: David Johnston, Director, Hong Kong Centre for PBL, c/o University of Hong Kong.

---

**Task 11.2: Getting going with PBL**

Take a topic you are teaching, and turn it into PBL. Be guided by Box 11.1.

### Assessment in PBL

The full-time student's complaint about guessing the marking scheme signals that assessment is a particularly sensitive issue in PBL. The sensitivity is due to the fact that PBL is an essentially divergent or open-end mode of teaching that is not aligned to the more common convergent formats of assessment.

Implementing successful assessment in PBL is no different in principle from any other teaching system. The questions at the beginning of Chapter 9 can be used, and the answers are clear: CRA, qualitative, holistic, divergent (some convergent), contextualized, and much peer and self-assessment (Tang *et al.* 1997; Wetherell and Mullins 1997). The essential feature of a teaching system designed to emulate professional practice is that the crucial assessments should be performance-based, holistic, allowing plenty of scope for students to input their own decisions and solutions (Kingsland 1995). Some version of the portfolio, as open-ended, may be useful in many programmes, but the assessment has to be suitable for the profession concerned.

Medical PBL developed the Triple Jump (Feletti 1997), where the student is evaluated at each step of the process. The structure however applies to any area:

1 *Dealing with the initial problem or case* – diagnosing, hypothesizing, checking with the clinical database, use made of information, reformulating.
2 *Review of independent study* – knowledge gained, level of understanding, evaluating information gained.
3 *Final problem formulation* – synthesis of key concepts, application to patient's problem, self-monitoring, response to feedback.

While these steps emulate real life, Felletti sees some problems. Do all steps have to be passed or can you average? Is there an underlying 'problem solving ability'? Should performance at the various steps correlate together or not? The answers are no, no and no. All these questions are hangovers from the measurement model.

### Does PBL work?

The goals of PBL were listed above as: structuring knowledge for professional use, developing effective reasoning processes, developing self-directed learning skills, increased motivation for learning, and effective teamwork. How effectively does PBL attain these goals?

If you attend the PBL sections of higher education conferences, or PBL conferences (e.g. *Problarc* in Australia, see end of chapter), you will get a strong impression of enthusiasm and commitment. Yes, say people who use it, PBL works extremely well, and student response is highly positive.

That is nice to know, but harder evidence would be nicer. Several evaluations have gone beyond single case anecdote.

Albanese and Mitchell (1993) conducted a major meta-analysis of all studies published between 1972 and 1992. The results are complex, because PBL was not utilized the same way in all studies, but the following conclusions emerge:

1 Both staff and students rate PBL higher in their evaluations, and enjoy PBL more than traditional teaching.
2 PBL graduates perform as well and sometimes better on clinical performance. More PBL medical graduates go into family practice.
3 PBL students use higher-level strategies for understanding and for self-directed study.
4 PBL students do worse on examinations of basic science declarative knowledge.

Newble and Clarke (1986) compared the approaches to learning, as measured in the Study Process Questionnaire, of students from first to final years in a PBL and in a traditional medical school, and the results were clear. PBL students scored progressively lower on surface and higher on deep approaches from first to final years, whereas traditional students scored progressively higher on surface and lower on deep from year to year. McKay and Kember (1997) describe the introduction of PBL to a paramedical course in Hong Kong: performance significantly improved, as did approaches to learning, the students changed from fairly extreme alienation to high enthusiasm. In other words, PBL beats the system.

Hmelo et al. (1997) argue that PBL by its nature requires a *different way* of using knowledge to solve problems. Their argument takes over from our distinction between acquiring functioning knowledge, and acquiring declarative knowledge which has then to be integrated and converted to be applied. They distinguish two strategies in clinical decision-making:

1 *Data driven* – 'This patient has elevated blood sugar, therefore he has diabetes.'
2 *Hypothesis-driven* – 'This patient has diabetes, therefore blood sugar should be up, and rapid respiration, "fruity" breath odour etc.'

Experienced and expert doctors use the data-driven strategy, except for unfamiliar or complex problems. Novice doctors, such as students in training, lack that experience and should therefore work top-down from first principles, with longer reasoning chains: 'If this, then because of that, it would follow that we should find symptoms X, Y, and Z.' The traditionally taught students tried to follow the experts – and couldn't, they didn't have the background. PBL taught students increasingly used hypothesis-driven reasoning, with longer and clearer reasoning chains. PBL students also used a wider variety of knowledge resources whereas traditionally taught stuck with the textbook. Anyone familiar with PBL would not be at all surprised by these findings because they are completely in line with what PBL is trying to do.

An important aspect of evaluating PBL is its implementation, particularly financial benefits. The economies of large lectures are offset by the economies of self-directed learning, and on the size and number of tutorial groups complementing the lectures. Albanese and Mitchell (1993) estimate that for fewer than 40, and up to around 100 students, PBL once set up can be equivalent in cost to traditional teaching. Savin-Baden (2000) is more optimistic still, saying that because of the move to mass education, fee-paying students from diverse backgrounds are more likely to be attracted to interesting ways of learning like PBL than to mass lectures:

> Students will see kinds of learning such as this as efficient, low cost and fun. Thus, universities who utilize problem-based learning 'infotainment style' will expect to attract more students while at the same time reducing costs.
>
> (p. 24)

Interesting. It is to be hoped that administrations take this long-term view when they consider quality assurance, as we discuss in the next chapter.

**Problem-based problems**

PBL is particularly sensitive to context and climate. Remember the disastrous effect a know-it-all tutor had on the questioning strategy needed for the problem-solving process ('That's for me to know and you to find out') (pp. 77–8). An equally devastating effect was achieved in another case when the course coordinator decided to retain the traditional final-year examination, leaving the students unsure whether their conclusions drawn from case study work would be relevant to the final exam. They were not. Not surprisingly, performance was low and the course evaluation of PBL was unfavourable (Lai *et al.* 1997). We have poor alignment in both cases. The bloody-minded tutor created affective misalignment in that the climate created was incompatible with the spirit of PBL, while the bloody-minded course coordinator created instructional non-alignment in that the assessment matched neither the objectives nor the TLAs used.

Albanese and Mitchell (1993) say that PBL students cover only 80 per cent of the traditional syllabus, and then do not perform as well in standard examinations. That worries traditional critics more than it does PBL teachers, who would prefer the PBL graduate to know less declaratively but put what is known to work more readily; and where that knowledge is insufficient, they have the self-directed skills to know where to go and how to acquire what is required.

The reasons why PBL is not used more widely are not educational but organizational. PBL requires teachers to adopt a different philosophy of professional education, one that states that it is something more than the acquisition of separate bodies of knowledge in one of which the teacher is professed expert. It also requires considerable institutional flexibility. It is much easier for experts to give lectures on their speciality, leaving integration and application as the students' problem to solve – and they probably will, but years down the track. It is more effective and more responsible if integration and application are seen as targets to be achieved *before* the professional has begun to practise rather than after.

### Conclusions

PBL is undoubtedly an effective approach to teaching. It exemplifies a high degree of alignment, which is evident when we unpack Figure 11.1.

To practise as a particular professional requires solving problems that belong to that profession. Thus, professional skill is the goal; professional practice comprises the TLAs, professional skill is what is assessed (amongst other things). It is distinguished from apprenticeship in that it is theory-based: it is not just a matter of performing the skills in an uninformed manner. If you look at the Feletti's Triple Jump for example, the student is required to base decisions in knowledge, to hypothesize, to justify, to evaluate and to reformulate, all of which are the kinds of cognitive activity that are required in professional practice.

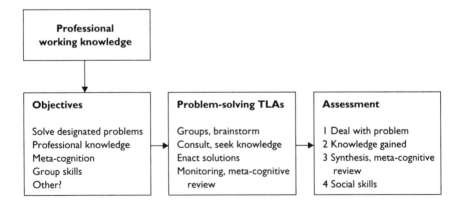

**Figure 11.1:** Alignment in problem-based learning

## The learning portfolio

My last example of aligned teaching is the use of the learning portfolio. This started simply as portfolio assessment in a unit in a professional programme, but the backwash took over and in effect dictated the TLAs. In this case, alignment was created bottom-up.

'The nature of teaching and learning' was a compulsory semester-long unit in the third year of a four-year part-time evening bachelor of education programme at the University of Hong Kong, which I taught with the help of a teaching assistant. The 82 students (technically a large class) were primary and secondary teachers in government schools, in a conservative educational system. The general aim of the unit was not to teach students about psychology (they had already completed a first-year unit in educational psychology), but to get them to demonstrate that they could drive their classroom decision-making with their psychological knowledge, based on reflective practice. Such an aim would be appropriate to advanced units in most professional programmes.

### Formulating and clarifying curriculum objectives

The objectives were formulated as outlined in Chapter 3. It was necessary to decide on the topics to be addressed, and to define the levels that were to be attained for the grading system.

### Topics

These had been taught as declarative knowledge in a first-year unit: the nature of learning and constructivist learning theory, the growth of learning (SOLO), approaches to learning, expectancy–value theory of motivation, principles of assessment. The aim was to turn all that into functioning knowledge. There was some expository teaching, to revise, update and profile the content, but basically the students were required to put this knowledge to work by using it to reflect on their classroom experiences, and make better professional decisions. (During the day they were all practising teachers, which provided them with plenty of problems to solve and critical incidents to ponder.)

*Levels of understanding*
These topics became the knowledge base upon which students could demonstrate extended abstract and relational levels of functioning knowledge. Deriving the criterion-referenced objectives expressed as grading categories was then quite easy, the level of activity defining the category (these verbs are italicized below). Students are to:

A *Reflect* on their own teaching, *evaluate* their classroom decisions in terms of theory, and thereby *improve* their teaching, *formulate* a theory of teaching that demonstrably drives decision-making and practice, *generate* new approaches to teaching on that basis.
B *Apply* course content, *recognize* good and poor applications of principles. 'Missed A', that is had a good try at reflecting but didn't quite make it.
C *Understand* declarative; *discuss* content meaningfully, *know about* content topics. Also include 'missed B'.
D *Understand* in a minimally acceptable way. In essence, 'missed C' or 'badly missed B'.
F 'Missed D': plagiarized, didn't participate satisfactorily, didn't hand in work.

If students could unequivocally demonstrate in their portfolios the level of performance indicated by the verbs in the category, that category grade would be awarded, given that all the other performance tasks were satisfactory. As an aside, category A is what university teachers should be able to do; it is an educational version of the reflective practitioner (Schon 1983; Cowan 1998). How it applies to readers of this book is described in the Chapter 12.

In this example, we can see that formulating the actual objectives was not at all complicated. The ensuing assessment procedures were also straightforward.

### Designing the learning portfolio

The next step was not in fact to choose the TLAs. I wanted to use learning partnerships and a reflective journal, but was thereafter open to negotiation with the students when they realized what they had to do. The crucial step was the choice of the learning portfolio.

In the first class of the semester, I circulated the above objectives and discussed them, making sure the students knew the standards they would have to meet. They were told that they had to convince me that their learning in the unit met the objectives. They were to decide on the evidence for their learning in the form of items for their portfolio, and to explain where they thought the portfolio as a whole met the objectives. Specifically, the requirements were:

1 Four pieces of evidence selected by the student.
2 A reflective journal, including answers to the main idea questions for each plenary session.
3 A justification for selecting the items, and the overall case they were supposed to make as a learning package. This provided very good evidence of students' meta-cognitive awareness of their learning.

A list of suggested items was provided, but original items were encouraged.

The portfolio was a completely new task to them, to which most initially reacted very negatively. They demanded guidelines, examples of possible items, and complained bitterly about the perceived workload. In the event, I have to admit that their initial complaints about the workload were justified. Four items, apart from the journal and the justifications, were too many. Three would have been better.

They were invited to submit a sample item for feedback. This was successful in bringing them round, particularly as they could include that item in their end-of-semester portfolio if they were satisfied with my comments on it. It was at this stage that negotiations on the TLAs began.

**Choosing the TLAs**

The verbs I wanted students to enact are italicized above in the grading scheme. Below are the TLAs (italicized) that were eventually used to elicit those desired learnings. How they came to be chosen was a matter of negotiation, described below.

1 To understand the psychological concepts mentioned above. These were reiterated in *notes* and *readings* to be read before each class. *Self-addressed questions* were responded to in note form in a *journal*. Before the class: 'What do I most want to find out in the next class?' After the class: 'What is the main point I learned today?', and 'What was the main point left unanswered in today's session?' Class time was used for clarification and elaboration, sometimes by *mass lecture*. Each student chose a *learning partner* to help in clarifying and elaborating, and interacting in whatever ways they thought might be helpful.
2 To see how these concepts might be applied to their own teaching. Partners were helpful, but to extend the range of exposure to different views and professional experiences, *groups* of around ten students, teaching in the same general content area, were arranged. The groups had a question to address, but were basically self-directed, and students had to draw their own conclusions.
3 To reflect on their own teaching, in the light of the psychological content current for that week. Reflection was intended to be encouraged by the *journal*, which contained the self-addressed questions for each day. They were asked to record learning-related incidents, particularly critical incidents, and to reflect upon them.

Occasionally, the class remained in plenary session for a mass lecture, but usually they split, half remaining for discussion with me and with learning partners (more manageable with 40 than with 80), the other half moving to an adjoining room which could accommodate four discussion groups of ten each. The medium for group discussion was invariably

Cantonese, and the teaching assistant rotated amongst groups. Her feedback from group discussions was most important in designing future activities. In practice, the groups were student-led.

Initially, the students expected and wanted straight lecturing, but they quickly saw that lecturing would not be much use in compiling their portfolios. The backwash from the portfolio made it evident that different TLAs were needed. These emerged from negotiation. The following dialogue, condensed from several sessions, illustrates how this happened (S are students, T is teacher):

S: What sort of items do we select?

T: That's up to you. Think hard about the objectives. Here's a list of sample items you might include. (I take a few and explain how they might work.)

S: Can we have a trial run?

T: Yes, and if you're happy with my assessment of it you can submit it as an item.

S: How do we show we can reflect?

T: Use your journal.

S: What do we put in it?

T: What you think are critical incidents in your teaching. Talk it over with your colleagues. Form a learning partnership. Sit next to your partner in class, get their phone number. You can help each other.

S: Wouldn't it be better if we had discussion groups of students teaching the same subjects as we do? Then we can share experiences on similar problems.

T: Certainly. You can form groups in the room next door.

S: We need direct teaching on the topics. Will you lecture us?

T: Only if I really need to. There's a topic for each session. The pre-reading should do, just a few pages, before each session. Then answer the first of these questions [the self-addressed question in (1) above]. I'll then meet half the class at a time, while the others are having discussion groups. We can clarify each topic in the lecture, as necessary.

And so on. In short, the assessment task drove the students' learning activities, which had to address the objectives, and the TLAs evolved around that. Student reactions confirmed that this was so. One student referred to the portfolio as a learning tool. In fact, it was difficult to separate what was a TLA and what an assessment task, as is the case in an aligned system. Likewise, students learned how to reflect by using the journal, and it was used later as evidence of reflection; the self-addressed questions ('What was the most important idea . . .') are both learning activities and evidence for the quality of learning. We noted the same thing with PBL and the Gibbs example. Grappling with the task you want students to learn is automatically both a learning process and a learning outcome. The negotiated teaching activities stimulated the students to respond in the way required:

> What [we are expected] to prepare for the portfolio undoubtedly provide me a chance to reflect on my daily teaching. This would never happen if this module proceeds in the same way as the other modules. I would not be so alert about my own teaching and eager to make changes and improvements.

> Instead of bombing us with lengthy lectures and lecture notes, we have to reflect on our own learning experiences and to respond critically . . . I feel quite excited as this course is gradually leading me to do something positive to my teaching career and to experience real growth.

### The assessment results

Individual excellence of particular portfolio items was not sought so much as how the objectives were addressed overall. For example, a balanced portfolio could include a concept map or a letter to a friend (to show how the unit overall is perceived), a lesson plan or an account of a lesson taught (application), a review (critical analysis of related declarative knowledge); and most important, the reflective journal (reflection, application, analysing critical incidents). All items had to be satisfactory, and the grade was awarded corresponding to the level of activity unequivocally displayed. Thirty-seven per cent of the class achieved an A (able to develop a personal theory and teach in terms of that); 40 per cent a B (able to discuss and/or change various teaching and assessment practices in terms of theory); 22 per cent a C (able only to provide evidence that they comprehended the basic taught content); 1 per cent D; and no failures.

Student reactions (drawn from journals and other portfolio items) were as follows. To the *journal*:

> Doing the reflective journal is tough work. However, I like the reflection part in it because it really helps me to stretch my mind to think about each topic deeply. Moreover, by reflecting on my own teaching and learning, I do make a lot of improvements in my teaching . . . [usually] we are so familiar with the daily routine . . . the same old way every year. So reflection really gives me the time to stop and think about my teaching and how my pupils view it.

> The reflective journal is no longer a threat to me. Every time that I write it, I'm pouring out the ideas that I've got.

> I see the idea of keeping a 'reflective journal' as very helpful because as we know more about the nature of learning, our understanding

will change as we reflect on our own experiences. When we read back the reflective journal, we can see the changes taking place as we move along the course.

To the *portfolio*. Initially highly negative:

> How about the assessment? Aiyaa! ANXIETY! ANXIETY! ANXIETY! I was so puzzled and worried about it when I received the handout on the first meeting.

And a backhander to me:

> This [the portfolio] is going to be a nightmare! At least, if it had been an essay, I would have known what is expected of me . . . Have I ever caused the same kind of fear among my students? *I must bear in mind to be more reasonable and careful when giving my students assignments from now on* . . . only give them assignments that are well designed and really necessary to help them in their learning . . . make sure they understand what is expected of them . . . make sure sufficient time is given for completing . . .

By the end of the unit, however, reactions were more positive:

> You will be willing to do more than what the lecturers want you to do. The circumstance is like a little kid who has learned something new in school and can't wait to tell his/her parents.

> I learn more from the portfolio than in the lesson.

> All [the teacher] said was 'show me the evidence of your learning that has taken place' and we have to ponder, reflect and project the theories we have learned into our own teaching . . . How brilliant! If it had only been an exam or an essay, we would have probably just repeated his ideas to him and continued to teach the same way as we always do.

### Conclusions

I call this case study of using a learning portfolio bottom-up alignment, or alignment that evolved in the course of negotiating with students struggling to cope with a new form of assessment, as opposed to the top-down alignment of formally structured PBL. In both cases, alignment with qualitatively and holistically defined objectives brought about quality learning (see Figure 11.2, and compare with Figure 11.1).

It is arguable that the portfolio is an example of PBL. The central problem for students is to select an item of relevant learning, and demonstrate that it manifests the qualities nominated in the objectives. In the course of this, they have to demonstrate:

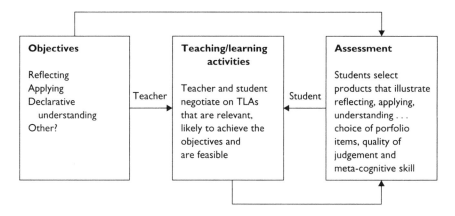

**Figure 11.2:** Alignment in the learning portfolio

1 sufficient mastery of content to show that it can be used in their everyday professional decision-making
2 professional skills relevant to dealing with classroom problems, setting assessments, designing curricula, or whatever came up.
3 meta-cognitive and self-management skills, such as reflection, and independent learning.
4 motivation and involvement with the task.

This is in fact very close to Barrows' (1986) list of goals for PBL (see pp. 233–4).

A portfolio is a neat way of throwing the responsibility of matching the assessment tasks to the objectives onto the student. Alignment is then clinched when the learning activities are themselves the assessment tasks. Had the class been 282 instead of 82, then many of the particular decisions would have been different. We would have had more plenary sessions, but more self-directed tasks involving learning partners outside the classroom; possibly more peer- and self-assessment. Had these students not been part-time, they would not have had the rich database provided every day in their own professional activities. In that case, the tasks would have to have been defined differently. Such decisions are all relative to the context, and cannot be prescribed in advance.

The real point is how you will make those decisions yourself, to fit your context.

## Summary and conclusions

Three examples of effective teaching were discussed in this chapter, all embodying a high degree of alignment.

### Peer assessment as a TLA

Gibbs reports two cases of an otherwise quite traditional lecture, problem session/tutorial and final examination structure, where low-cost adjustments established alignment between objectives, TLAs and assessment tasks. In the first case, peer assessments sharply increased appropriate student learning activity, and in the second, an examination requiring professional decision-making radically changed how students prepared for the exam.

### Problem-based learning

There are many varieties of PBL, depending principally on the amount of teacher-direction. In all forms, though, *problems*, not topics, define the curriculum. In solving these selected problems, the necessary knowledge and skills are acquired, plus skills for acquiring new knowledge, and the meta-cognitive skills for evaluating the knowledge and the effectiveness of problem solutions.

PBL-taught students think differently from traditionally taught students; they have less declarative knowledge, but use what they have more effectively with richer reasoning chains; they have greater self-awareness and self-direction, and manifest more enjoyment, as do teachers. However, PBL is only as good as those who implement it; it is sensitive to insensitive teaching. An institutional problem is that the infrastructure for PBL is not discipline-based, whereas most universities are organized on disciplinary lines. Teachers tend to identify themselves as scholars in their home discipline, and PBL might seem to threaten their academic identity.

### The learning portfolio

The learning portfolio turned out to be a version of PBL. The problem: What shall I put in my portfolio to convince the teacher that I have learned in the way nominated in the objectives? That question dominated the dynamics of teaching and assessing.

The last two examples illustrate the two demands of constructive alignment:

1 A theory of learning that enables the teacher to focus on the high-level cognitive activities determining quality performance in their teaching subjects.
2 An aligned system of teaching and learning, where the objectives are clear and the TLAs and the assessment tasks address those objectives.

Figures 11.1 and 11.2 define two approaches to alignment, one driven by the TLAs flowing directly from the objectives, the other by student reaction to the assessment tasks aligned to the objectives. The first produces alignment by tuning *teaching* to the objectives, the second by tuning the *assessment* tasks to the objectives.

What that means in the teaching of any given subject is entirely dependent on the context and the resources available. The most important resource of all is human: a teacher who teaches from a level 3 perspective.

## Further reading

### On using assessment to improve learning

Gibbs, G. (1999) Using assessment strategically to change the way students learn, in S. Brown and A. Glasner (eds) *Assessment Matters in Higher Education: Choosing and Using Diverse Approaches*. Buckingham: Society for Research into Higher Education/Open University Press.

Gibbs describes in more detail the examples quoted here.

### On problem-based learning

Boud, D. (1985) *Problem-based Learning in Education for the Professions*. Sydney: Higher Education Research and Development Society of Australasia.
Boud, D. and Feletti, G. (eds) (1997) *The Challenge of Problem-based Learning*. London: Kogan Page.
Savin-Baden, M. (2000) *Problem-based Learning in Higher Education: Untold Stories*, Buckingham: Society for Research into Higher Education/Open University Press.
*Research and Development in Problem Based Learning*. The Australian Problem Based Learning Network, c/o Problarc, CALT, University of Newcastle, NSW 2308.

The first describes the principles of PBL from the beginning; Boud and Feletti contains contributions by users in many different areas. Savin-Baden introduces a little-discussed aspect: what happens *inside* when teachers and students experience PBL. All three books are important for anyone seriously interested in PBL. The last is a serial publication of the Australian Problem Based Learning Network, which holds biennial conferences, of which these volumes are the proceedings.

# 12

# The reflective teacher

**So far, this book may simply have provided you with some declarative knowledge about aligned teaching. To achieve its purpose, however, its contents must be put to work as functioning knowledge. The meta-Susans amongst you will have been doing this already, but to be consistent, I should be providing a TLA or two to help everyone do so. The chief TLA in effecting that transformation is reflection, action learning one support structure. This chapter unpacks these ideas in a practical way for the individual teacher. However, teachers work in departments, with colleagues, in an institutional framework. Teaching for quality learning is ultimately an institutional responsibility. That responsibility is addressed in the final chapter.**

## Reflection revisited

Now let us return to the notion of reflective practice. We met Stuart Tyler in Box 10.1, but we haven't yet met Stewart Taylor. Both Stuart and Stewart had problems teaching oedema associated with cardiac failure to nursing students; both thought that the problem needed moving three-dimensional videos to model the process more realistically than lecturing and illustrating with two-dimensional diagrams. Both found little difference in student performance. Stewart concluded that he'd done his best. As a good level 2 teacher, he'd used the most suitable ET – educational technology – according to all the good books, but it turned out not to be worth the extra hassle, so back to lecturing with diagrams. Stuart, on the other hand, reflected: 'It didn't work, and it should have worked. *Why* didn't it?' He had a theory, which when he thought about it, told him that the assessment of the learning episode needed to be aligned to the nature of the learning of the episode. When that was done, the failure rate dropped to near zero (see Box 10.1, p. 215).

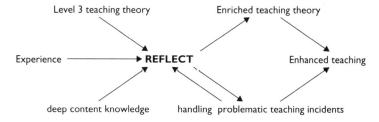

**Figure 12.1:**   Theory and reflective practice in teaching

The reflective process was introduced in Chapter 1. Let us now elaborate (see Figure 12.1).

A reflective teacher starts with three important components:

1 *Experience.* You cannot reflect on a blank slate. When you come across a difficult or challenging situation, the first question is: 'Have I come across anything like this in my past experience? If so, what did I do then? Did it work?' A further set of questions: 'What resources did I need then? What are at my disposal now?'

2 *Deep content knowledge.* You cannot teach effectively if you don't know your subject content very well indeed. So well, for example, that you can see instantly whether an unexpected answer a student confronts you with is original or misconceived (see Billy and the Creamed Wheat, p. 159), and that in your teaching you can see – on the run – powerful but simpler ways of expressing an idea.

3 *A level 3 theory of teaching.* You can reflect with any theory. If you were a level 1 teacher you might say: 'It didn't work because these students are a bit thick. I suppose I could talk more slowly.' As a level 2 teacher you might say (with Stewart): 'Well the video didn't work. I'll do what I know I can do: lecture well.' As a level 3 teacher you say (with Stuart): 'Why aren't they learning? How can I get them to be relevantly active?' *That* is the sort of theory we want here, one that focuses on what the student does. This is a cyclical process; you keep looking at what they do, what they achieve, and link that with what you are doing. You get to know your students as learners very well.

The next stage is to reflect on the teaching incident, using all of the above, plus the specifics of this particular incident. There are several outcomes:

1 *Teaching is enhanced,* eventually. You may need several goes at the problem.

2 *Experience is enriched.* Each go at the problem adds to your store of experiences.

3 *The teaching theory is enriched.* Using the theory in action makes you realize which aspects of the theory work and which do not.

This, then, is the general way in which the reflective teacher operates on a day-to-day basis. It may sound complicated but it is not really. It is a frame of mind, almost an attitude, which says: 'If things are going wrong, I will see if it is within my power to do something about it.' Figure 12.1 unpacks the process of how you would go about that. In sum, there are three questions that the teacher, to be reflective, needs to ask:

1 What is my espoused theory of teaching?
2 Is my current practice in keeping with my theory? How can my theory help me teach more effectively?
3 What, within myself or in my context, is preventing me from teaching the way I should be teaching?

We are back at the two faces of good teaching (see Chapter 4):

1 *Promoting* those factors that support the deep approach, which we now know to be about getting students to be relevantly active, and constructive alignment is a good way of doing that.
2 *Eliminating* those factors that support the surface approach, which were discussed in Chapter 4. See Task 4.2 in particular, which asked you to construct a questionnaire or interview schedule for your students so that they can tell you those things you *should* know about your teaching, but possibly would rather not know.

Now let us look at the more formal sense of systematically exploring your own teaching.

## Researching your teaching

Turn back to where we started: Task 1.1, where you were asked to nominate the three most worrying problems in your teaching. Are you any further down the track towards solving any of them? Decide now which one you would most like to follow up for the present; you can go back to the others later. Or you might like to take a problem nominated by the students in Task 4.2.

I will now suggest some further steps. Keep a note of your thinking as you proceed. We will use an action learning structure to define and then attack your problem.

### Defining the problem

The first step is to define the problem in a way that tells you how you might go about finding a possible solution. However, the search should not be just for a technique that will fix things: that is the level 2 cookbook approach, focusing on what *you* do. The issue is what the *students* are doing: are they doing what you don't want them to do, or not doing what you do want them to do?

The source of the problem – student behaviour – could lie in the object-ives, the climate, your rapport with them, inappropriate TLAs, poor large-class management skills, unaligned assessment tasks, other factors, or any combination of any of them. You need that working theory of teaching to guide you through the possibilities. Finding a solution is a matter of conceptualizing the problem, which is where I hope this book might be most useful.

So the first step is to reflect on the problem, using the constructive alignment theory in Chapter 2, which addresses both students' learning behaviour, and the design of your teaching. Examine your problem in these terms, hypothesize as to the possible reasons for it, and possible solutions. The process can be made much easier with the help of a 'critical friend' (see below).

### Implementing a change

The next step is to find out more about the problem, and possible solutions, from what chapters might be appropriate. If there is not enough relevant material there, you might find it in the further reading in each chapter, or in the particular references in the text. Possible ways of handling the problem then need to be translated into specific action in your context.

### Monitoring the change

Before putting the change into effect, you need to decide how you are going to make sure that what you are proposing to do will be effective. It is necessary to observe systematically what is going on, to know where you and/or the student behaviour started from, and where it ends up after the change has been implemented.

The next step therefore is to obtain a baseline, recording where you are before the problem is addressed. This could involve pre- and post-measures of the troubling student behaviour, such as measures of poor learning outcomes, observations of repetitious material in exams or assign-ments, keeping track of complaints about time-stress, whatever is the focus behaviour you are addressing. Pre- and post-instruments could include ques-tionnaires, student ratings, performance tests, your own controlled observa-tions, your diary entries of what is happening and your own reflections on progress. This diary should be kept whatever other data are collected.

There are instruments available for monitoring such changes. One is the Approaches and Study Skills Inventory for Students (ASSIST) (Tait *et al.* 1998). This instrument is very comprehensive, with four major scales

– deep approach (in four subscales), strategic approach (in five subscales), surface apathetic approach (in four subscales) and preferences for teaching. A shorter version, may be downloaded with full instructions from www.ed.ac.uk/etl/publications. However, this still comprises 68 items and a rating scale, which makes it a useful research instrument, for which it was designed. For present purposes, however, we are probably only interested in the extent to which our classes resort to surface and deep approaches, to see if our students increase deep, and decrease surface, approaches to learning. The two-factor version of the Study Process Questionnaire (SPQ) (Biggs *et al.* 2001) is designed for this purpose: this has only 20 items, and may be copied from the source reference. This instrument is designed to reflect students' reactions to teaching, not to assess the typical approaches of individual students; we are not interested in whether Susan is deeper than Robert. We want to be able to say, 'Before I intervened, the students in the class were on average higher on the surface scale and lower on the deep than they are now. Looks like I'm on the right track.' The class means are the issue, not individual scores.

### Fine-tuning

Action learning recycles: you try something, see if it works, then try again with a slight variation. You will be unlikely to get something as complex as teaching right first time, so it is a matter of looking back over your observations, after you have implemented the change you had decided to make, and see how things are going. Did matters improve? If not, or if not enough, what might have been the problem? This requires reflecting again, back to the first step – defining the problem – but with the extra knowledge of what has happened meantime.

### The role of critical friend

Reflection is often not best carried out alone. You have been living with the problem possibly for some time and may be the last person to find out about it. It is helpful to have a critical friend. This is a complex role, part partner, part consultant, but most of all a mirror to facilitate reflection (Stenhouse 1975). Your own reflections are sharpened if shared with someone with a different perspective – and with some technical expertise. On the other hand, you as action researcher need to retain ownership over the definition and control of the problem; it is *your* own teaching we are talking about. The critical friend should not tell you what to do, because that shuts down the reflection process, and makes your teaching their problem rather than yours.

Different people can take the role of critical friend: a colleague in the same department (but not the head of department, even if he or she is a friend), a teaching developer, or someone else. It is particularly convenient if a colleague in the same department acts as critical friend, because they know the context and at the right time can gently feed in suggestions to be reflected upon. If they have educational expertise, so much the better. Indeed, quality assurance procedures encourage peer review, but it needs to be seen as a formative process, not a judgemental one (see Chapter 13). Teaching developers are ideal, but the teaching development unit may not have the resources to deal with many action learning projects in the one institution.

In one action learning project, comprising 50 independent projects over six separate tertiary institutions, five critical friends, with both content and educational qualifications, were employed at assistant lecturer level, each handling about ten projects in similar content areas (Kember *et al.* 1997; Kember 2001). Interacting with that number of projects meant that their role varied. In some cases, personal facilitator was more important, in others expert consultant; but in whatever role, these critical friends played a vital part in bringing about successful outcomes. Another collection of action research projects is described in Gibbs (1992) (see the case studies referenced in further reading at the end of this chapter).

## The focus for individual change

Let us return to an issue raised in Chapter 2. Does enduring change in a teacher's approach to teaching come about by *thinking* differently about teaching, that is moving from levels 1 or 2 to level 3, or by *acting* differently, for instance by trying portfolio assessment for the first time?

Kember (1998) places teachers' conceptions – 'teacher-centred' (basically levels 1 or 2) or 'student-centred' (level 3) – as presage factors that determine their approach to teaching. This implies that teaching development should not be carried out in the way it usually is, that is by teachers attending workshops in order to change their teaching behaviour. Kember argues that if teachers do not really believe in the new way of teaching, they will simply revert to what they were doing before, as the post-workshop enthusiasm wears off.

The first step in his view is therefore to change teachers' views of teaching. They will be then be more likely to be receptive to adopting techniques that will be attuned to the new view. Changing the way people think is not easy, but Kember cites evidence that such 'perspective transformation' takes place as a result of the plan–reflect–change–reflect cycles of action learning.

Guskey (1986), on the other hand, sees improving teaching as like getting people to quit smoking. Education campaigns, which are aimed at what people think, are not as effective as 'No Smoking' signs, or raising the tobacco tax. Then, when their behaviour is forced to change, people begin to think it might be a good idea to stop smoking anyway. Accordingly, Guskey suggests that teaching development should aim at changing teachers' behaviour first, then their beliefs will follow, and the change will be maintained.

It works both ways. Ho (2001) demonstrated that teaching development workshops, not necessarily in the action learning mould, could produce conceptual change in teachers' thinking. She used a 'confrontation' technique, where teachers were made aware of their own conceptions of teaching, and then confronted with inconsistencies between their thinking and their practice. They were then more willing to explore alternative conceptions, and to look at alternative teaching practices, and so made a commitment to change. In evaluating her procedure, she built in a stringent criterion: not only did the teachers' conceptions and practices have to change, but their students' approaches to learning had to move, from less surface to more deep. Of the nine teachers 'confronted', six changed both conceptions and practices, and the approaches to learning in four classes of those six. A control group went through the same procedures of recording their conceptions and practices but were not 'confronted': none of these teachers changed. In only four workshop sessions, this is remarkable.

Ho created an explicit link between changing conceptions and appropriate teaching behaviour. This link is present in action learning too but is less explicit. Thinking and doing reinforce each other, as in any reflective practice. Let us say you are not really convinced that portfolio assessment is a good idea but you are willing to give it a try, just once. But you find it does work. No longer sceptical, you ask: 'Why does it work?' You see that students were learning things you never anticipated. A chain reaction takes place.

Prosser and Trigwell (1998) also emphasize that ways of teaching are interlinked with what teachers think teaching is. Teachers need to:

1 become aware of the way they conceive of learning and teaching, within the subjects they teach;
2 examine carefully the context in which they are teaching, so that they are aware of how that context affects the way they teach;
3 seek to understand the way their students perceive the learning and teaching situation;
4 continually revise, adjust and develop their teaching in light of this developing awareness.

To help teachers achieve this self-awareness, Prosser and Trigwell have developed the Approaches to Teaching Inventory (ATI), which addresses what they think and what they do. Levels 1 and 2 are combined in an information transmission/teacher-focused approach, which is contrasted with a conceptual change/student-focused approach (level 3). This is a useful instrument in teaching development, making teachers really think about the nature of teaching and learning.

The strategy in teaching development, then, is to address both teacher thinking and teacher behaviour. Teachers always have some sort of theory of teaching, as we saw in connection with Figure 12.1, but it is usually implicit and as such is unexamined. The possibility that there are different ways of looking at teaching does not occur to many teachers. Entwistle (1997: 129) points out that the systemic (level 3) view

> offers a powerful insight to many staff in higher education who have not thought about teaching and learning in this way before . . . Indeed, that insight can bring about a totally new conception of teaching.

And with that insight, will follow the recognition that practice will need to change.

At the end of this chapter, Tasks 12.1–12.6 provide six case studies that I have found useful for discussion in staff workshops for bringing out teachers' *real* conceptions of teaching, as opposed to the conceptions they espouse, and the implications for policy and practice. Unsurprisingly, these case studies use the incredibly sensitive area of assessment to involve teachers' thinking. The cases outline a situation (all real within my experience), and require teachers to endorse an action. On one occasion I introduced some of these at a staff retreat; the head of department was astonished at what certain members of staff *really* thought. It was a very fruitful way of hammering out principle, practice and future departmental policy. I suggest heads of department or teaching developers throw what they think might be particularly salient cases at the next staff retreat. Better still, construct your own cases, arising from real incidents within your own institution.

## Beyond the classroom

### You and your department

Let us move a step further into the system. Teaching is normally the responsibility of departments, or it might be faculty or school. This unit resources teaching, constructs the programmes to which the units you teach contribute, gives its blessing on the curriculum that you are teaching, and often requires that your teaching of the unit is exposed to student evaluations. After that, it is up to you.

You may translate the curriculum into objectives, and the TLAs and specific assessment tasks are yours to decide within resource limitations. The climate you create, once the classroom door is shut, is assuredly yours. My concern here is with helping you deal with those aspects of departmental life that impinge on your own personal teaching. The department's responsibility, as opposed to your responsibilities within the department, are dealt with in the final chapter.

Changes to your own teaching are more likely to be sustained and effective the more those changes are supported by departmental/institutional policy. Say you decide to go completely criterion-referenced in your assessing. In the first year that you try this, you get unusually high numbers of high distinctions and distinctions, say 37 and 40 per cent, respectively, whereas your colleagues usually turn in about 10 and 15 per cent. At the examiners meeting your results are queried, you explain, your results are passed.

The same happens next semester, but mutterings about 'slack standards of assessment' are louder. Your unit is becoming known amongst your colleagues as a soft option – although when the students see what they have to do to get the high distinction, and at what standard, they may not see it as a soft option at all. Perhaps the next step is that the student evaluations rate your unit very highly. You eventually win your colleagues over. Perhaps.

It would have been psychologically (and politically) easier if you and a colleague were critical friends for each other. There would be a replication, as it were, and remaining colleagues at the examiners meeting might be more easily convinced. It is a short step from there for teachers within the department to act as critical friend for each other. The whole department is becoming involved, not just in improving the skills of individuals, but also in subjecting the offerings and working of the department itself to collective reflection. Systems being what they are, that greatly increases the effectiveness of what individuals are doing.

## You and teaching developers

I should say something specifically about teaching developers and their relationship to individual teachers. In the next chapter, I discuss teaching development in the life of the whole institution, but teaching developers frequently interact with individuals, one-to-one, as counsellor or adviser, possibly as critical friend in an action learning project.

Because of this role, teaching developers should not be required to advise on personnel decisions. They may advise on a purely general level – how to assess teaching competency, advice on assembling teaching portfolios and how to assess them – but teaching developers should *not* be involved in assessing individuals and reporting the result to human resources, because that compromises their formative role. The argument is exactly the same as that in Chapter 8 on formative and summative assessment. If they are to help individuals teach better, teachers must feel free to admit their uncertainties, weaknesses and failures. If those admissions go into a personnel file for advice to the committee that is renewing contracts, their role is compromised. The relationship between teaching developer and teacher is exactly the same as that between doctor and patient, psychologist and client, and must be respected accordingly. It is deplorable that in some universities the directors of teaching development units are required to gather such information on individuals for use in personnel decisions.

I have been dealing here with issues about which the individual teacher can do something. There are many other aspects about improving teaching about which the individual can do little except as member of a team or a department and as a staff member having to work within the rules of the whole institution. Thinking beyond the individual brings us to the currently topical issue of quality assurance and quality enhancement at the institutional level. In the last chapter, then, we deal with the reflective institution.

## Summary and conclusions

### Reflection revisited

Effective teaching means becoming a reflective practitioner, and for that you need a theory of teaching. Using that theory, and your experience and knowledge of the content you are teaching, you can ponder how you are handling it and wonder at how you might handle it more effectively. This is a cyclical process; reflective practice is ongoing, and adds cumulatively to our store of knowledge of ourselves as teachers, and of our students, while our theory of teaching becomes progressively enriched. A final word about reflection: if we are educating our students to be reflective practitioners, as doctors, nurses, architects, engineers, or whatever, how can we not be reflective teachers ourselves?

### Researching your teaching

Systematic reflective practice is what action research is about. Action research requires us to define the problem, implement and monitor change, and fine-tune. An important resource is the critical friend, who can see things about your teaching that you cannot.

### The focus for individual change

How do you get people to stop smoking? Do you try to persuade them that smoking is not a good idea? Or do you hang 'No Smoking' signs everywhere? So, how do you get teachers to teach better? By convincing them that level 3 theories are better than level 2 theories of teaching? Or by making them members of a PBL team, thus requiring them to teach in a different way? You do both.

### Beyond the classroom

You can only do so much as an individual. You can seek teaching development on an individual basis, learn new tricks and discover things about your teaching with professional help. Teachers need to teach in a way that they can personally sustain and justify, but teaching also takes place in an interactive system, in an institution with a particular mission statement, with colleagues, in a department that has a particular climate and philosophy.

We have focused so far on changing the individual, it is time we began looking beyond the individual to the whole system of which that teacher is a part.

Quality enhancement of teaching is a collective responsibility that goes beyond the individual. Both believing and practising a level 3 approach to teaching is easier where colleagues also believe and teach in that way, and where the university environment supports level 3 teaching and rewards good teachers for being innovative and reflective. Everybody is in this together, as we discuss in the final chapter.

## Further reading

### On reflective practice

Brockbank, A. and McGill, I. (1998) *Facilitating Reflective Learning in Higher Education*. Buckingham: Society for Research into Higher Education/ Open University Press.

Cowan, J. (1998) *On Becoming an Innovative University Teacher*. Buckingham: Society for Research into Higher Education/Open University Press.

Ho, A. (2001) A conceptual change approach to university staff development, in D.A. Watkins and J.B. Biggs (eds) *Teaching the Chinese Learner: Psychological and Pedagogical Perspectives*. Hong Kong: University of Hong Kong Comparative Education Research Centre/Camberwell, Vic.: Australian Council for Educational Research, pp. 239–54.

Schon, D.A. (1983) *The Reflective Practitioner: How Professionals Think in Action*. London: Temple Smith.

Schon's book deals with the whole question of improving professional practice by reflection, using examples from several professions. The other two books refer specifically to university teaching. After lengthy preambles, Brockbank and McGill provide detailed help in setting up situations (based mainly on the Schon model) to promote reflection with colleagues, and on one's own teaching, with respect to promoting student learning (including higher degree supervision) and formal action learning projects.

Cowan's book is the extended abstract to Brockbank and McGill's relational. It is a delightful and unusual reflective journey by an engineering teacher, now teaching developer, who wanted to 'write something practical on the topic of adult learning' for his fellow teachers, and who 'yearned to avoid the use of jargon and of specialised vocabulary' (p. 18). Cowan distinguishes several kinds of reflection, how teachers can best use reflection, how teachers can encourage their students to reflect, and how to structure groups and reflective learning journals in ways that best promote the appropriate kind of reflection. The book is driven by a cycle of questions, examples, strategies and generalizations from the examples; the clearest example of practising-what-you-preach that I have seen.

Ho's article shows convincingly that reflection and practice go hand in hand.

## On action learning

Elliott, J. (1991) *Action Research for Educational Change.* Buckingham: Open University Press.

Gibbs, G. (1992) *Improving the Quality of Student Learning.* Bristol: Technical and Educational Services.

Kember, D. (2000) *Action Learning and Action Research: Improving the Quality of Teaching and Learning.* London: Kogan Page.

Kember, D. (2001) Transforming teaching through action research, in D.A. Watkins and J.B. Biggs (eds) *Teaching the Chinese Learner: Psychological and Pedagogical Perspectives.* Hong Kong: University of Hong Kong Comparative Education Research Centre/Camberwell, Vic.: Australian Council for Educational Research.

Kember, D. and Kelly, M. (1993) *Improving Teaching through Action Research,* Green Guide No. 14. Campbelltown, NSW: Higher Education Research and Development Society of Australasia.

Kember, D., Lam, B-h., Yan, L., Yum, J.C.K. and Liu, S.B. (eds) (1997) *Case Studies of Improving Teaching and Learning from the Action Learning Project.* Hong Kong: Hong Kong Polytechnic Institute, Action Learning Project.

Kemmis, S. (1994) Action research, in T. Husen and N. Postlethwaite (eds) *International Encyclopedia of Education: Research and Studies.* London: Pergamon Press.

All of these titles address general principles of implementing action research, with many examples of successful implementation, some of which may well address similar problems to your own. For readings on specific stages or aspects of teaching, refer to the further reading for previous chapters: defining objectives (Chapter 3), 'motivation' and diminishing surface approaches (Chapter 4), choosing effective TLAs (Chapter 6), assessment (Chapter 9).

Elliott addresses action learning in schools. As one of the important developers of action research, his book is worth reading as background, while Kemmis deals with principles of different kinds of action research. Action learning has been applied more to the school than to the university sector, but the remaining readings all refer to the tertiary sector. Gibbs's book describes several strategies for deep learning, and ten action research case studies in British tertiary institutions in which one or more of these strategies were used. Kember (2001) or Kember and Kelly (1993) describe how action research may be implemented, and Kember (2001) or Kember *et al.* (1997) describe a number of particular action learning projects conducted in Hong Kong tertiary institutions.

---

### Task 12.1:  Misunderstanding the question

You are marking assignments and find that one student has clearly misunderstood the question, the only one to have done so. It is now past the due date for handing in. If you mark it as it is, she will fail. What do you do?

(a) Fail her.
(b) Hand it back, explain that she has misunderstood, and give her an extension.
(c) As in (b), but mark it pass/fail only, or deduct a grade.
(d) Set her another assignment, to be marked later. Meantime record 'Result withheld'.
(e) Other. What?


What are the reasons for your decision? _____

_____

_____

_____


Would you have decided differently if she would otherwise graduate with distinction?

_____

_____

---

### Task 12.2:   Grading on the curve

The guidelines for awarding a grade of A are outlined in a validated B.Ed. Programme document:

> Outstanding. Demonstrates thorough understanding and interpretation of topics and underlying theories being discussed, and shows a high level of critical thinking and synthesis. Presents an original and thorough discussion. Well organized and structured, fluently written and correctly documented. There is evidence of substantial studies of the literature.

You use these guidelines in grading the assessment tasks of your class of 100 students, and find to your delight that 35 (35 per cent) meet these criteria, so you award A to all of them. Your departmental head, however, is unhappy about this because you are 'not showing enough discrimination between students, and we don't want this department to get a reputation for easy marking.' The results have not been announced yet, so he suggests that you regrade so that only 15 per cent of your students are given an A. What do you do? Why?

(a) You agree you must have been too lenient, so you do as he says, giving A to the top 15 only, the remaining of the original As being given B.
(b) You compromise, splitting the difference: you give As to 25 students.
(c) You say something like: 'Sorry, but the guidelines are clear. I must in all conscience stick with the original. The conclusion to be drawn is that this was an exceptionally good group of students, and that they were taught well.'
(d) 'I must stick with the guidelines. However, I am prepared to entertain a second opinion. If I can be persuaded that I have been too lenient, I will change my grades.'
(e) Other. What?

_____

_____

_____

_____

_____

### Task 12.3:   A matter of length

It is policy that the maximum word length of assignments is 1000 per credit point. You are teaching a 2 credit point module. One of your better students has handed in an assignment of 2800 words. What do you do and why?

(a) Count up to 2000 words, draw a line and mark up to that point only.
(b) Hand it back to the student with the instructions to rewrite, within the limit, with no penalty.
(c) As for (b) but with a penalty (what would you suggest?).
(d) Hand it back unmarked and record a failure.
(e) Mark it, and deduct so many marks according to the excess.
(f) Other. What?

Would your decision have been any different if it was a poor student?

---

### Task 12.4:  Exam strategy

You are discussing the forthcoming final exam with your first-year class. You explain that, as usual, there will be five sections in the paper, each section covering an aspect of the course, and there are two questions per section. They are to choose one of the two, making a total of five questions, to be completed in three hours. You alone will be doing the marking. A student asks: 'If I think I will run out of time, is it better to answer four questions as best as I can, or to attempt all five, knowing I won't finish most questions?'
What do you say in reply and why?

---

### Task 12.5:  Interfering with internal affairs?

You are the head of a department which has decided to use problem-based learning in the senior-level subjects. In PBL, the emphasis is on students applying knowledge to problems, rather than carrying out detailed analyses of the research literature, as has been the tradition in the past. Faculty regulations require you to set a final examination for the major assessment of the course, despite your own judgement and that of your staff that this format is unsuitable for PBL. It is therefore decided that the final exam will contain questions that address application to problem-solving rather than questions that require students to demonstrate their familiarity with the literature. On seeing the paper, however, the external examiner insists that the questions be reworded to address the research literature. You argue, but he insists that 'academic standards' must be upheld. If they are not reworded, you know that he will submit an adverse report to the academic board, where there are vocal critics of your foray into PBL. What do you do?

---

---

---

---

---

### Task 12.6:  What is the true estimate of student learning?

A department is trying to arrive at a policy on the proportion of final examination to coursework assignments. In discussing the issue, the head collates data over the past few years and it becomes clear that coursework assessments are consistently higher than examination results. In discussing this phenomenon, the following opinions are voiced. Which argument would you support?

(a) Such results show that coursework assessments may be too lenient, and because the conditions under which they are undertaken are not standardized, and are unsupervised, the results may well be inflated by collaboration and outright plagiarism. Examination conditions control for these factors. Therefore final exams must be a higher proportion of the final grade than coursework assessments.

(b) The conditions under which final examinations are conducted are artificial: working under time pressure, little (often no) access to tools or data sources, and mode of assessment limited to written expression or MC test, means that exam performances are sampling only a narrow range of students' learning. Therefore coursework assessments must be a higher proportion of final grade than exams.

(c) Other. What?

---

---

---

# 13

## The reflective institution: quality assurance through quality enhancement

**Businesses have long been talking about assuring the quality of their products. Now universities are using the same rhetoric: 'quality assurance' is a term much bandied around university circles today. This book too is about quality: teaching for quality learning. Are we all talking about the same thing? Two kinds of quality assurance (QA) may be distinguished: retrospective QA, which assures quality by requiring conformity to externally imposed standards; and prospective QA, which assures quality by continually striving to improve teaching and learning in the institution. The last meaning is also called quality enhancement (QE), which is the focus here, and the argument is exactly the same for the institution as it is for the reflective teacher.**

### Assuring quality: in retrospect and in prospect

Assuring and enhancing the quality of teaching and learning in universities is currently of major concern amongst providers, politicians and stakeholders. Teaching quality is also the focus of this book. Thus far, I have been discussing how individual teachers might reflect on what they are doing, with some ideas about how they might do it better. We now move to the institution, which provides the infrastructure for all teaching. We may ask the same question. Can institutions reflect on what they are doing, and can this book provide some ideas on how they might do it better? I believe so, which brings us to the concepts of quality assurance and quality enhancement.

Quality assurance (QA) is concerned with maintaining the quality of the work that institutions do. I am restricting discussion here to QA as it applies to teaching and learning only, not to research, managerial efficiency, community service or other aspects of institutional functioning that typically fall within the QA remit. QA is therefore a conservative, bottom-line notion. Unfortunately, it is sometimes confused with, and used interchangeably with, quality enhancement, which is precisely the question asked above about the reflective institution.

But first, what do we mean by quality in this context? Harvey and Green (1993) distinguish three definitions of quality: as value for money, as fit for the espoused purpose, and as transforming.

1 *Quality as value for money.* A 'quality' institution in this view is one that satisfies the demands of public accountability. It produces, for example, more graduates for less public money, more peer-reviewed publications per capita of academic staff, has a high ratio of PhDs on its staff, and a strategic plan that signals high levels of self-funded activities. This view of quality has nothing to say about the quality of teaching and learning, but is all about accountability.

2 *Quality as fit for the purpose.* The 'purpose' is that of the institution. Universities have several purposes, with teaching and research as the most important. The basic question for us is: are our teaching programmes producing the results we say we want in terms of student learning? A related question that has been raised by the Quality Assurance Agency in the UK is 'fitness *of* purpose': that is, the purposes and aims of the institution must themselves be ones that have some kind of public sanction. Without this, an institution could have low-level aims that are met effectively, and so be judged a 'quality' institution.

3 *Quality as transforming.* Quality teaching transforms students' perceptions of their world and the way they go about applying their knowledge to real world problems, as we saw in Chapter 2. Transforming teachers' conceptions of their role as teacher to a level 3 conception, and transforming the culture of the institution itself, are also examples of the notion of quality as transforming.

QA may be retrospective or prospective, depending on the kind of quality to be assured.

*Retrospective QA* looks back to what has already been done, and makes a summative judgement against external standards. The agenda is managerial rather than academic, with accountability a high priority. The procedures are top-down and bureaucratic, and the climate adversarial rather than collegial. Retrospective QA derives from the Thatcher government's demands in the UK for accountability, the framework for which was provided by the Jarratt Committee (Jarratt 1985). This framework became the prototype for many subsequent quality assurance exercises. For example, the Australian Department of Education, Science and Training requires each university to supply annual statistics, including certain compulsory performance indicators, as part of QA procedures. This exercise has little to do with the quality of teaching and learning as such; rather, it quantifies some of the presumed indicators of a particular view of teaching and of management so that governments may come to some cost–benefit decisions. Retrospective QA is about quality as value for money.

*Prospective QA* is concerned with assuring that teaching and learning fits the purpose of the institution now, with commitments to upgrade and improve teaching in the future by requiring that procedures are in place that lead to quality enhancement (QE). So to avoid the confusion when one meaning of QA really means QE, let us drop the term 'prospective QA' and call it simply QE. QE, then, is concerned not with quantifying aspects of the system, but with reviewing how well the whole institution works in achieving its mission, and how it may be improved, which is not to say that there may not be external imperatives to meet. This is analogous to what the reflective teacher does, as discussed in the previous chapter. Like the individual teacher, the institution must operate from an espoused theory of teaching, and try to match practice to the theory.

In the previous chapter, it was suggested that the individual teacher might ask:

1 What is my espoused theory of teaching?
2 Is my current practice in keeping with my theory? How can my theory help me teach more effectively?
3 What within myself or in my context is preventing me from teaching the way I should be?

An institution, or a system, should be asking the same questions of itself. These questions define three important ideas:

1 *The quality model.* The institution, like the individual, needs to make explicit the espoused theory that should be driving teaching-related decisions. This book presents one such model, a level 3 view of teaching based on constructive alignment.
2 *Quality enhancement.* The institution needs not only to design its teaching delivery system in accordance with its espoused theory, but also to establish built-in mechanisms that allow it, like the individual reflective teacher, to continually review and improve current practice. New content knowledge, educational innovations, a changing student population, and changing conditions in the institution and in society, all make such a reflective review necessary.
3 *Quality feasibility.* What can be done to remove the *impediments* to quality teaching? This is a question that institutions have rarely asked, although individual expert teachers continually do, because, as we see below, there is often a conflict between the requirements of trouble-free administration and those of good teaching. It is one thing to have a

model for good teaching, but if there are institutional policies or structures that prevent the model from operating effectively, then, in the interests of good teaching, those policies or structures need to be modified or removed.

In sum, quality is seen here as based on quality as fit for the purpose. A quality institution is one that has high-level aims that it intends to meet, that teaches accordingly, and that continually upgrades its practice while adapting to changing conditions, within resource limitations.

## The quality model: a generic theory of teaching

The quality model (QM) is the theory driving institutional-level decisions about teaching. This book provides a level 3 QM. For example:

1  We have to specify what the 'desired outcomes' are, so that it is clear from the outset what students have to learn, and at what level of skill or understanding. We need to state not only what topics students are to learn, but also what level of understanding is required of them. Unless we stipulate the latter, teaching and assessment are left dangling.
2  We need to arrange teaching/learning activities (TLAs) that encourage students to act in ways most likely to achieve those desired outcomes.
3  We need to assess to see how well the outcomes have been attained at varying levels of acceptability, as reflected in the grading system.

Level 3 thinking takes on board the full implications of the obvious: that it is the students who do the learning. The teacher's job is that of broker: to create a learning environment from which the student cannot easily escape without learning. This is an environment where teaching methods, assessment tasks and classroom climate are aligned to the learning activities most likely to produce the desired outcomes. To do this effectively requires a theory of learning that enables us to operationalize teaching aims and objectives, using SOLO or a similar framework (see Chapter 3), and for making decisions about rich learning activities (Chapters 5, 6, 10) and assessment tasks (Chapters 8, 9, 10).

The QM provides the framework for doing this. It is a generic framework that not only can be used institution-wide, but can also generate specific decisions appropriate to the particular content topics to be taught.

In an aligned system, the quality of learning is there to see. The grades state how effective student learning has been from subject to subject, and monitoring from year to year informs as to the maintenance of standards. Quality is thereby assured – and rather more directly and visibly than filling in forms, convening committees, and holding audits and retrospective accountability exercises.

The next step is to ensure that quality is continually being reviewed under changing conditions, with mechanisms for quality enhancement.

## Quality enhancement: improving learning and teaching

Quality enhancement is about the continuing improvement of teaching in the institution. This goes beyond the teaching of individual teachers. Teaching is a departmental and institutional responsibility, so we are really talking about the whole delivery system, involving individual teachers, departmental and course teams, and the institutional infrastructure underwriting good teaching, including regulatory procedures that encourage better teaching, and supports for teaching development.

Provision for teaching development in the institution is the heart of the matter as far as QE is concerned, so that the whole delivery system is geared to improve student learning. One institution that does take this holistic approach is Alverno College, Milwaukee, where all policies and procedures are dedicated to optimal teaching and learning (for details, see Alverno College Faculty 1994; Mentowski 2000).

Typically, however, teaching development is undertaken in workshops run by the teaching development centre (these have various names; here I use the generic TDC), and it is usually left to individual teachers to decide whether or not to attend. The ones who decide to do so are most frequently the already good teachers; the ones who decide to stay away are frequently those who most need to attend. The effect is to widen the gap between good and poor teachers. This is not the fault of the TDCs, rather it is a structural problem, in that TDCs are rarely involved in the decision-making on policies and processes about teaching, yet it seems self-evident that all central decisions that bear upon teaching and learning *should* involve the experts in teaching and learning.

Too often TDCs are perceived through level 2 lenses, as places for providing tips for teachers, or as remedial clinics for poor or beginning teachers. We saw in Chapter 10 that many TDCs are being subordinated to educational technology (ET) units, apparently in the belief that training in ET is all the teaching development needed these days.

A worse situation is when TDC staff are used as 'teaching police', required by administration to supply information about individuals on their teaching competency for personnel decisions, such as contract renewal. This utterly compromises the TDC. The argument is the same as that about revealing error in summative as opposed to formative assessment (see p. 192). The TDC's role is formative, not summative, and teachers must feel free to expose their weaknesses in teaching and express their doubts. Additionally, there is the issue of professional ethics, that the relationship between any professional person and client is based on confidentiality and acting in the client's interests.

### The role of the department

Because operational decisions on programmes, courses and content are made in departments, TDCs should have a formal relationship with each teaching department. In this way, decisions relating to the setting up, design and administration of courses and programmes can draw on the knowledge base of teaching within the chosen QM framework. Operating at the departmental level, with the delivery of the course or unit as target, means that the problem of the reluctant, underperforming teacher is drastically redefined. Teaching is now the focus, not the problems that individual teachers might have.

Following are some QE structures and procedures at departmental level:

1 *Strong ties with the TDC,* which in turn would provide regular semesters and workshops tuned to the department's particular needs. Some faculties and schools have their own TDC, particularly in medicine and law.
2 *A teaching quality committee* which would monitor teaching, define problems and benchmark with similar departments locally and overseas. A member of the TDC should be on this committee, and a student.
3 *A well thought out criterion-referenced assessment system,* making clear what students are to learn if they are to meet course and programme objectives. Outcome statements are expressed in various categories of acceptability (A, B, C, D, F), which become the framework for the grading system. The As that one teacher awards should be as equivalent as can be in the sought-for qualities, allowing for year level and subject differences, as those another teacher awards.
4 *A review system,* so that once the grading categories are fixed, deviations from expectations can be spotted and remedies proposed. Out of this too can come ideas for action research at a departmental level. It is important to keep track with data that reflect change, such as student feedback, samples of student learning outcomes, staff reports, performance statistics and so on, which are kept in departmental archives.
5 *A peer review or buddy system,* where colleagues (sharing the same QM) sit in on each other's classes as critical friend. This not only helps teachers become aware of problems in their teaching they had been unaware of, it also helps them to be self-critical. The teacher

and critical friend between them may then work out an action research programme (see Chapter 12). The head of department, however trusted, should not be a critical friend because there is a conflict between that role and the head's role in making summative personnel decisions.

6 *Action research* across the whole department. Smith *et al.* (1997) report such a departmental action project on assessment and found that not only did they clear up many assessment-related issues, such as what standards to assess to and spreading assessment workloads, but the staff workshops raised curriculum and teaching issues as well. Smith *et al.* emphasize that collaboration works well only as long as there is a common purpose and philosophy (QM).

7 *Regular 'sharing sessions'* where staff can tell each other what is working for them and what is not working. Alternatives that achieve better alignment may be explored, by pooling colleagues' ideas and by consulting the TDC. A genuine sharing of problems and solutions through the lenses of the QM can lift the game of the whole department.

8 *A staff–student consultative committee*, meeting sufficiently early in the semester to allow inputs into current teaching.

9 *Student feedback on teaching*, organized through the department, not the faculty or central administration (see below). Beyond the use of questionnaires, students could be interviewed about the quality of their learning experiences, and be asked to submit what they think are their best performances, to be placed in departmental archives as exemplars of good learning.

10 *Strong encouragement to research and publish in teaching* the content area, as well as research in the content itself.

11 *An annual departmental retreat* where teaching-related matters are top of the agenda.

These are just some examples. Other possible enhancement mechanisms are two-edged, such as validation panels, external examiners and outstanding teacher awards. These, and their two edges, are discussed in the section on QF.

The departmental role is summed up in Box 13.1, which gives a simplified version of the Education Quality Work (EQW) Maturity Scale (Massy, forthcoming). You are invited to rate your own department.

The EQW Maturity Scale mentions several ways in which departments can improve teaching, but overriding particular QE mechanisms is the emphasis on teaching as a *collective responsibility*, where all staff members subscribe to the same QM, and all curricular, and teaching- and assessment-related decisions are made within that framework. The EQW Maturity Scale makes the distinction between improving teachers and improving teaching quite clear.

---

**Box 13.1:   How mature is your department?**

Following are five levels of Education Quality Work Maturity (not to be confused with levels 1, 2 and 3 in this book, although there are parallels). At which level is your current department? Does this help you to see where the responsibility for good teaching lies: with you as an individual, or with your department collectively?

- **Level 1.** Little discussion of educational quality, little regard to any mechanisms that might assist it. Traditional teaching methods, no consideration of alternatives.
  *Comment.* Level 1 indeed: transmission model. Our teaching is fine; if there is any problem it is the students we are forced to take on board these days.

- **Level 2.** Individual staff begin experimenting; students benefit from attention to curriculum reform, new teaching or assessment methods, but progress is ad hoc, firefighting problems when they occur, and reactive to institutional initiatives.
  *Comment.* Reflection by some teachers, but focus is on what they might be doing, not specifically on student learning.

- **Level 3.** The department more reflective as a whole, dealing more systematically with teaching issues, in-built mechanisms to track and plan teaching initiatives, can justify what it does. Procedures accepted by all or most staff.
  *Comment.* The department is beginning to build a sense of collegial responsibility for teaching and is becoming aware of how the quality model applies to the department.

- **Level 4.** Departments routinely discuss and modify teaching, curriculum and assessment as normal departmental procedure. More sophisticated methods of tracking teaching and learning quality than those of the institution itself; occasional in depth debates (e.g. in retreats) on educational quality. Changes based on principles all staff accept.
  *Comment.* The department is orchestrated to deliver quality teaching, with QE mechanisms established.

- **Level 5.** The department is wholeheartedly focused on educational quality, QE central to its culture. Members freely share information about the successes and failure of their innovations, and across and outside the institution.
  *Comment.* Such a department would be entirely dedicated to teaching quality; an example at the institutional level would be Alverno College, Milwaukee.

*Source:* Adapted from Massy, W. (forthcoming) *Quality and Cost Containment: Rebuilding the University's Core Competency.* Boston, MA: Anker.

### At the institutional level

Beyond the department, there are other levels of decision-making that can encourage or discourage the enhancement of teaching. We deal with some of the factors that actually discourage good teaching in the next section on quality feasibility.

Probably the most important message that encourages good teaching is to be found in the climate created at faculty and institutional level, which says, in essence, that teaching is *valued*, and resources and rewards will flow to those individuals and departments that continually strive to improve their teaching. Most institutions pay lip service to good teaching in contract renewal and promotion, but, particularly in the old redbrick universities, everyone knows that research productivity is what brings prestige and frequently money to the university. This must change, and it undoubtedly is beginning to, but more quickly in some universities than in others.

Even rewards for good teaching are focused on what individuals do, and retrospectively at that. It is even more important for the institution to show that it values teaching by spending time, trouble and money in building up a self-enhancing teaching system: to become a reflective institution no less. This can be done not only by financing group and departmental teaching development projects, but perhaps most importantly, by establishing a strong, high-profile TDC with integral links to the loci where significant teaching-related decisions are made, and by reflecting on what structures and policies might be impeding good practice. We turn to that last issue now.

## Quality feasibility: what impedes quality teaching?

Quality enhancement will not be feasible if the institution is not purged of those factors that inhibit quality learning. This is the issue of quality feasibility (QF).

### Assuring or diminishing quality? Some marginal procedures

Several common QA procedures are two-edged. They are discussed below.

*External examiners*
The traditional role of external examiner in the British system is a time-honoured means of ensuring that similar standards operate across institutions. It is important to bring outside perspectives and contacts to bear, and to feel confident that one's own standards are comparable to those elsewhere.

Frequently, however, the external examiner is asked to focus on the final assessments more than other formative aspects, and the role is often restricted to examining the setting and marking of final papers. The person doing this needs to be completely aware of, and in sympathy with, the aims of teaching and the approach to assessment. There have been cases where the examiner has required the examination questions to be changed well into the teaching of the course concerned. To accede to such a request can easily destroy alignment, yet the pressure to do so is considerable in institutions where the external examiner's comments are seen and discussed outside the department concerned – ironically, often as part of QA procedures. The use of external examiners, who are usually selected for their content rather than for their educational expertise, may too readily discourage innovative assessment practices. The pressure is to restrict assessment tasks to those that can easily be understood out of context.

The positive values of external examiners can be achieved in other ways. Replace the word 'examiner' with 'consultant', and the activity as 'benchmarking', and there you have it: an outside adviser who can visit the department and give all the advice and help that an external examiner can give, without the distortions created when examiners perceive their brief as simply adjudicating the summative assessment of student products.

### Validation panels

Accrediting and approving courses by external validation panels is a common QA procedure that has obvious value, particularly where staff are required to deliver new courses in directions in which they have had little experience. In such cases, course accreditation provides useful scaffolding to ensure minimal standards. A similar argument applies to programmes that have to be approved by external professional committees. Both procedures, however, discourage innovative teaching.

One danger is that external panels exert strong pressure to include more and more content. Each panel member thinks his or her own special interest must be given 'adequate' (= intensive) treatment. As committees tend to resolve matters in ways that do not offend members, the result almost inevitably is an overloaded curriculum. The same effect is achieved when the course director anticipates such pressures – departments or course teams design courses that they think are likely to be approved – and so the curriculum is overloaded from the start. Teaching subsequently becomes a frantic scramble to 'cover' all the listed topics – yet we know that coverage is 'the greatest enemy of understanding' (Gardner 1993: 24).

Another danger is that panels encourage conservatism in teaching. While lip service is paid to innovation, being innovative may be perceived as too risky, particularly when the panel has key figures from the profession concerned, whose knowledge of education is what they went through years ago in their own professional training. So, the erring is on the side of caution: 'Let's get the validation over first, then we will innovate as much as we like!'

That, however, is unlikely. Once the course has been approved, it tends to be set in stone. It may easily turn out that the curriculum is too broad, or is otherwise unsuitable; that the student intake has changed; that very recent research, post-validation, suggests strongly that the curriculum should be changed. It may be possible to make minor modifications immediately, but any major changes are either not allowed, because they were not in the validated documents, or they have to go through yet another round of committees. Changing an already validated course can be difficult, and administrators usually discourage any attempt to do so. In one institution a move to problem-based learning was vetoed by a senior administrator: 'The course may have to be revalidated. What if it doesn't succeed? What then?'

In sum, the QA mechanisms of external examiners and course validation may too easily discourage innovation and changed practice after reflection, the very qualities that public agencies for QE are trying to foster (see below).

### Distinguished teacher awards

One of the commonest calls in QA procedures is to require that good teaching be recognized, not only in personnel decision-making as discussed, but in distinguished teacher awards (DTAs). It is good to reward people for doing an outstanding job, but it has to be done carefully.

All too easily, the message to the great majority of teachers – by definition the undistinguished ones – is that distinguished teachers are born, not made. The very names 'distinguished teacher' or 'outstanding teacher' suggest that here we have a bird of a rare species, whose exotic plumage ordinary teachers cannot hope to match. They therefore cannot be blamed if they follow what nature intended, and teach on in their own undistinguished way.

DTAs encourage the perception that an outstanding teacher is one who does teacherly things better than other teachers do. Therefore, while distinguished teachers themselves tend to operate from level 3, as reflective practitioners (Dunkin and Precians 1992), DTAs promulgate a level 2 view of teacher-as-performer. Reward the excellent teachers by all means, but if we want quality teaching at an institutional level, the focus should be not on what the individual teacher does, but on the teaching *system* in the university.

For one thing, teaching is increasingly a team affair, particularly in large undergraduate courses. So DTAs miss all that crucial developmental teamwork – curriculum development, tutor mentoring, decisions as to delivery and assessment – that makes it possible for the star teacher to perform. A revealing slant on this comes from an international comparison of mathematics teaching carried out by Stigler and Hiebert (1999). They analysed videotapes of classroom teaching in three different countries, and found that each culture developed its own 'script' for teaching. Japan had a much more effective script (it was a level 3 conception) than the US script (which was learning routines at level 1); not surprisingly, Japanese students achieved better results than did American students. What determined high-level learning outcomes was the script, not the particular actor delivering it. Awarding Oscars to the actors is not likely to improve their scripts. Just so in QE, we should be focusing on the script, not on the actor.

Another problem is that a generous DTA system may absolve management from further support for teaching development. The Australian federal government has set up a generous system, the Australian Awards for University Teaching, with wonderful prizes to individuals, and an expensive annual ceremony in Canberra for the presentations. All this costs roughly A$650,000 (£234,000), the largest slice from its A$1 million budget for teaching development. Money spent on DTAs is spent retrospectively, it does not make teaching across the board better in future. It is not QE, although it masquerades as that. By contrast, let us look briefly at DTAs in the Chinese school system:

> Good teachers may be honoured with titles (and salary bonuses). Such titles are awarded after they have been observed and have given demonstration lessons in a competitive situation, at one to three days' notice, in front of tens or hundreds of their peers ... The teachers ... act as mentors to younger teachers and their mentoring role includes giving further demonstration lessons.
>
> (Cortazzi and Jin 2001: 121)

In other words, good teaching is seen here as a collective responsibility that works *prospectively* to enhance future teaching in the institution or district. There are lessons here for us in the West to learn.

*Student feedback questionnaires*

Many institutions have mandatory student feedback questionnaires (SFQs) as summative evaluations at the end of each course, using standard questions across all courses. Often the questionnaire items are worded so that they can be used across all departments, so lecture and tutorials are assumed to be the norm. A teacher using problem-based learning (PBL) would score low on a standard question such as: 'The lecturer is organized in presenting to the class ...'. When low ratings have a high cost, in terms of promotion or contract renewal, teachers are obviously discouraged from innovating (Lai and Tang 1999). Further, students rate according to their own conceptions of teaching, and penalize teachers using methods deriving from other conceptions (Kember and Wong 2000).

SFQs, like DTAs, typically focus on the actor, not on the script. They tend to measure charisma, the 'Dr Fox effect', not teaching effectiveness in terms of improved student learning (Ware and Williams 1975; see above p. 99). Used formatively, however, SFQs make eminent sense where questions are tailored to specific courses on aspects on which feedback is required. Some universities use forms specific to PBL or to web-based teaching, focusing on the course or context, not the teacher. But even these used summatively for personnel decisions can be damaging. It is unlikely that one would get an innovation right on its first use, and if as a result of that trial the students' responses carry weight in deciding renewal of contract, say, then teachers are severely discouraged from innovating.

In short, some common QA procedures have the opposite effect to that intended, conceived as they are within a retrospective QA framework. While these procedures may be well-meant, if two-edged, other institutional aspects are unequivocally negative, as we see below.

### Factors that inhibit good teaching

*A quantitative mind-set*
Quantitative assumptions reduce complex issues to units that can be handled independently, rather than as part of the larger interactive system to which they belong. Thus, the curriculum becomes a collection of independent competencies, basic skills, facts, procedures and so on; passing becomes a matter of accruing sufficient independent correct answers.

A particular problem, already discussed in Chapter 8, is the misapplication of the measurement model of assessment. Table 13.1 summarizes.

**Table 13.1:** The demands of the measurement model and those of good teaching

| Measurement model | Good teaching |
| --- | --- |
| Performances need to be quantified, so they are reduced to correct/ incorrect units of equivalent value that can be added | Students need to learn holistic structures that cannot meaningfully be reduced to units of equal importance |
| A good test creates 'a good spread' between students, preferably normally distributed | Good teaching produces reduced variance |
| The characteristic being measured is stable over time | Good teaching produces change: it is called 'learning' |
| Students need to be tested under standardized conditions | Students need to be tested under conditions that best reveal an individual's learning |

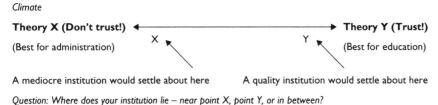

*Climate*

**Theory X (Don't trust!)** ◄─────────────────────────────► **Theory Y (Trust!)**

(Best for administration)           X           Y           (Best for education)

A mediocre institution would settle about here     A quality institution would settle about here

*Question: Where does your institution lie – near point X, point Y, or in between?*

**Figure 13.1:**  Quality feasibility – striking the right balance

The demands of the measurement model are simply incompatible with those of good teaching (see pp. 147–53 for further elaboration).

*Distorted priorities*
Distorted priorities are a major source of mis- or non-alignment. Probably all institutions would put educational considerations as their top priority in their mission statements. However, there is an institution to run, which generates a set of administrative priorities. Administrators want things to run on schedule; they want to ensure that plagiarism cannot occur, that public criticism about standards or fairness should be avoided, that awkward cases are anticipated and legislated for before they arise and cause trouble, that research is promoted over teaching because the university's prestige is based on research output, and on and on.

For all this to happen (or not to happen), the safest working assumption is that students, and more recently teachers, are not to be trusted; the answer is to establish a theory X climate. Unfortunately, as we saw in Chapter 4, good learning thrives in a theory Y climate. However, as a completely theory X climate would be unbearable, and a completely theory Y climate unmanageable, we compromise (see Figure 13.1).

How the two sets of priorities are balanced is what separates a quality from a mediocre institution. A quality institution is biased towards establishing the optimal conditions for learning (point Y), a mediocre one towards administrative convenience (point X). Where does your institution lie?

What sorts of things distort priorities? Examples are easy to find:

• Norm-referenced assessment (see pp. 190–1, 203–4), in particular grading on the curve. We can decree that the top 15 per cent of graduates will achieve first class honours, and then boast: 'See here, all our departments are teaching to the same high standard.' Fifteen per cent is about right for those who think this way; 25 per cent might invite snorts of 'Slack standards', and 5 per cent, 'Poor teaching'.
• Invigilated examinations (see pp. 174–6) are hard to justify educationally, but are useful logistically, and for assuring the public that plagiarism is under control.

- Assigning the most junior teachers, who can't argue back, to teach those enormous first-year classes that the senior teachers don't want to teach.
- Emphasize research at the expense of teaching. Excellence in teaching and excellence in research do not usually occur in the same institutions: a university may be excellent in one or the other, but not both (Ramsden 1998b). Although many universities officially place equal emphasis on teaching and research, research is almost invariably perceived as the activity of greater prestige, and in promotions is rewarded more than teaching. Some department heads do not even recognize as 'real' research those publications on research into teaching the very subject the department is charged to teach.
- The corporatization of universities, which illustrates misalignment at its starkest. Here commercial priorities and administrative structures have been imposed on institutions whose previous function was to create and to disseminate knowledge. The result in some institutions has been a dramatic deterioration in the quality both of teaching and of research (Coady 2000; Biggs and Davis 2001; Senate Employment, Workplace Relations, Small Business and Education Committee 2001).

In sum, impediments to quality teaching and learning result from poor alignment to the fundamental purpose of the institution. Where quality is defined as fitness for purpose – and fitness *of* purpose – quality teaching means trying to enact the aims of the institution by setting up a delivery system that is aligned to those aims. In practice, however, many institutions in their policies, practices and reward systems actually downgrade teaching. Some of this is externally imposed, ironically by some aspects of retrospective QA itself. Other practices fall into the category of institutional habits; it has always been that way, and it does not occur to question them. Whatever the reasons for their existence, any adverse effects such practices might have on teaching and learning need to be identified and minimized.

How does this apply to your own department?

## QA and QE in three countries

How do current QA/QE systems appear in the light of this chapter? We look briefly at three countries, the UK, Australia and Hong Kong, bearing in mind that the systems are currently in a state of rapid change in all three.

In the UK, Australia and to an extent in Hong Kong, there are two levels of what is in effect QA:

---

**Task 13.1:   Quality feasibility – an item for your next staff meeting**

For your next staff meeting, place an item on the agenda: 'Quality Feasibility'.

When it comes up, you will be looked at questioningly. Explain what it means, and use as an example some procedure or policy in your own department that impedes good practice in teaching or assessment or classroom climate. Hopefully, you will take an example that has been bugging you personally, and here is your chance to get it out in the open. Alternatively, take one or more of the six cases in Tasks 12.1–12.6 and use as an exercise at the meeting. It is certain that the discussion will throw up matters pertinent to QF.

Discussion would then be directed towards whether you and your colleagues think you have a QF problem in your department. If you have, you will then need to do something about it.

---

1 Reporting to government in terms of graduation and attrition rates, performance indicators, and all the other retrospective statistics and information that are deemed to assure quality.
2 Institutional evaluations by separate bodies that increasingly are about QE rather than QA. In the UK, this body is the Quality Assurance Agency, and in Australia, the Australian University Quality Agency. In Hong Kong, the University Grants Committee itself conducts its QE exercise, the Teaching and Learning Quality Process Review.

I am interested here only in the second level, and I'll take each country separately.

**The UK**

In the UK, the thinking about QA got off to a bad start under the Jarratt Committee recommendations (Jarratt 1985). This was retrospective QA with a vengeance, a highly quantitative accountability system being the top priority. Most indicators of performance concentrated on administrative procedures rather than on 'the stuff of the academic enterprise . . . It is not clear how these procedures . . . can have any bearing whatsoever on the quality of what universities are' (Goodlad 1995: 9). While Jarratt provided the initial conceptual framework, however, QA procedures were modified out of recognition over the years.

In 1992, a two-tier UK-wide audit system focusing on institutional QA systems and subjects was introduced. Following the Dearing Report (Dearing 1997), the Quality Assurance Agency (QAA) was established, and the focus at subject level shifted from the process of learning to the outcomes of learning. Another review was undertaken in 2001, and the revised processes, varying in different parts of the UK, took effect from September 2002. The new processes virtually eliminate the subject-level audits, which are subsumed under the institutional review as the amazingly entitled 'disciplinary audit trails', in the hope that institutions will be encouraged to set up their own QE procedures. In Scotland, institutions are already required to develop and implement a strategy for continuous quality improvement of learning and teaching. This will probably become a requirement elsewhere in the UK.

The areas of institutional review of interest here are the appropriateness of intended learning outcomes, referencing to subject benchmarks, the appropriateness of the teaching, learning and assessment methods used to achieve the intended outcomes, and the actual achievement of students. These make a template close to constructive alignment.

Those designing programmes and creating standards need to be explicit about what it is that students are to learn and how they are to learn it. Institutions are also required to relate what they are doing to external standards, to demonstrate the basis for academic standards has validity beyond an individual teaching team (Jackson 2002a: 2).

After on-site visits, the QAA panel judges if and how well the guidelines for good teaching have been met. Corrective action is suggested, if need be. Previously, points were awarded over these and other areas, and institutions ranked on their score, but that is no longer the case.

In all this activity, the concept of brokering emerged (Jackson 2002b), whereby higher education institutions can seek help from separate agencies, such as the following:

- The Learning and Teaching Support Network (LTSN), a network of 24 subject centres funded by the four higher education centres in England, Scotland, Wales and Northern Ireland. LTSN offers support to 'anyone and any organisation that has an interest in promoting student learning in HE . . . to develop a culture of continuous improvement, rather than one driven by standards and compliance.'
- The Institute for Learning and Teaching in Higher Education (ILT), which is the professional body for all who teach and support learning in higher education.
- The Higher Education Staff Development Agency (HESDA), the national training organization for higher education.
- The National Coordination Team (NCT), a coordinating unit of the Higher Education Funding Council, which supports the development of institutional teaching and learning strategies.

In addition, a large tranche was taken from general university funding, dedicated to the improvement of teaching: £89 million annually in England, alone. This money is spent on establishing new and strengthening existing teaching development centres, and funding research into teaching, notably through the Teaching and Learning Research Programme. One such project, conducted out of Edinburgh by Entwistle and Hounsell, involves a study of 25 subject departments in thinking about ways of encouraging high-quality learning using constructive alignment as the theoretical framework.

### Australia

The Australian arrangements for QA were signalled in 1999 by the then minister for education, training and youth affairs, David Kemp, when he announced the formation of the Australian University Quality Agency (AUQA):

> The Australian approach is one that values the autonomy of our universities while insisting on accountability and 'value for money'. It entails the development of a national framework which safeguards the integrity of our system and allows Australia to market a quality product internationally.
>
> (Kemp 1999)

And:

> The Commonwealth reports on quality and QA processes while recognising that universities themselves have ultimate responsibility for the quality of what they do, and individual students are responsible for carefully selecting the institution and course which suits their particular needs. The focus is on the student as customer and client, and pressure is on institutions to provide value for money through quality teaching and learning.
>
> (Kemp 1999)

This is straight from Jarratt, emphasizing accountability and *laissez-faire* economic theory. If institutions want the students' fees, they had better attract the students.

Fortunately, once AUQA was established, the minister's vision of quality being determined by market forces was replaced with a rather more enlightened one, emphasizing QE, albeit in the language of auditing. There is now no stipulation of performance indicators (although the government audit still requires them), and with maximal institutional autonomy:

> AUQA's anchor point for drawing conclusions on quality is always the objectives of the auditee, together with any implicit or explicit external objectives, and the effectiveness of the auditee's system in achieving those objectives.
>
> (Australian Universities Quality Agency 2002)

The audit covers 'not merely what the auditee is doing (processes) but also the consequences of what it is doing (the outcomes) ... [and] to identify the need for and consequences of doing things differently' (Australian Universities Quality Agency 2002). The effect, unlike in the UK and Hong Kong, is a 'value-free' approach to quality, or to put it another way, there is no common QM, a model defining good teaching – that is up to each institution to decide.

AUQA asks universities to submit a portfolio which outlines goals and the strategies adopted to achieve them, and a self-evaluation of how well they are being achieved and how achievement might be improved. A few months after the portfolio has been submitted, the five-member audit team visits the campus. The first audits are yet to start at the time of writing, and no doubt there will be changes as AUQA itself does some reflective practice.

Brokering in Australia is much less developed than in the UK. The major public body that is involved is the Australian Universities Teaching Committee, which was established in 2000 for three years to promote quality and excellence in university teaching and learning (Borden *et al.* 2002). The annual budget is about A$1 million, nearly two-thirds of which is spent on individual teaching awards (DTAs), as mentioned above. The remainder is spent on projects the AUTC identifies, and calls for expressions of interest, the successful ones often comprising joint project teams from several institutions. Other brokering occurs on the initiative of institutions themselves, and several projects are in progress on teaching/learning-related matters.

## Hong Kong

Hong Kong's University Grants Committee (UGC) conducts a Teaching and Learning Quality Process Review (TLQPR) on all UGC-funded institutions. The UGC has established four goals for the TLQPR:

1  To maintain the focus on teaching and learning as the primary mission of Hong Kong's tertiary institutions.
2  To assist institutions in their efforts to continuously improve the quality of teaching and learning.
3  To enable the UGC and the institutions to discharge their obligation to maintain accountability for the quality of teaching and learning.
4  To inform, in respect of UGC-funded institutions, the UGC's consideration of the triennial funding, on the basis of the review outcomes.

The design is based generally on the early UK model, but whereas the present UK model is moving away from subject review, the UGC is interested in reviewing the teaching carried out in departments, and establishing that departments themselves have processes in place that show a concern for continuing improvement in teaching. The TLQPR panel nominates a few departments they wish to visit, and the institution nominates some.

The TLQPR lists five domains as foci:

1 Design of curricula.
2 Design of teaching and learning processes.
3 Design of student assessment, and use of assessment results.
4 The quality of implementation and of student experience.
5 Commitment of resources to education quality work (EQW).

These five domains are evaluated against the following criteria where appropriate: the processes and outcomes of learning, the degree to which quality processes are coherent (aligned to intended and actual outcomes), and mechanisms for continuous improvement. An important point is that delivery is seen as a collaborative responsibility of all staff in the department.

Departments are asked to state any exemplary practice they think they might have in these domains, to self-assess against the relevant criteria how they stand with each domain, and then to rate themselves on their education quality work (see Box 13.1, p. 273). They then have to justify their evaluations to the TLQPR review panel.

Brokering exists between institutions, often through UGC-funded teaching development grants: HK$ 115 million (£9.5 million) is available for the 2002–04 triennium. Two major projects on action learning have been completed; ongoing projects include the Hong Kong Centre for PBL, which brokers PBL development across institutions; many projects in educational provisions, including online staff development; curriculum design and teaching in particular disciplines; the student experience, and many others.

## Summary

In this chapter, I have emphasized prospective QA rather than retrospective, and there can be little doubt, now that QA has in large part been taken away from politicians and civil servants, that that distinction is much more clearly understood. The agencies that have been set up, albeit under the name of QA, are more and more interested in QE. That can only be good.

The emerging processes in the UK and Hong Kong seem to adhere well to the first two of our three components, QM and QE. The quality model in both cases emphasizes the need for active learning and alignment between curriculum, teaching and assessment, which then becomes the conceptual framework for self-evaluation. The reflective component is particularly strong in Hong Kong, which targets individual departments as well as the institution itself, whereas in the UK, the subject (departmental) review is being left to the institution. It remains to be seen how this works out. It is to be hoped that those doing the reflecting in the reflective institution will include those doing the teaching.

In Australia, there is strong emphasis on institutions thinking hard about their goals, how well they might be achieving them, and how they might improve themselves. However, leaving the conceptualization entirely to institutions might make genuine reflective practice, focusing on my third factor, QF, a hard call. There are some general principles of good teaching and learning that could be helpful.

The feasibility of enhancing quality (QF) is where theory is particularly important because it creates the tension between what is currently the case and what changes are needed to do it better. Many policies currently in place evolved because they were useful. Let's use my favourite example of grading on the curve. There is no doubt it makes grading easy and it looks good administratively. The only reason why one might question it is from the standpoint of educational theory. If you didn't have a theory, you wouldn't question it.

It depends on how deeply *teaching* staff are involved in the audits. If it is left to heads, deans and higher, they will in the nature of the case be thinking as administrators, not necessarily as educators. The reflective practice for teaching is best done by teachers thinking as teachers, *then* they might drive, bottom-up, any changes that need to be made on educational grounds. The UK expects a strong internal departmental review processes, and the LTSN brokering agency provides resources to support self-review at subject level. In Australia, such departmental or subject review seems up to the institution.

Table 13.2 compares the three systems.

There are, then, strong similarities between the systems in general outline, but differences exist. The most amazing is the first line (the UK figure is for England only). England and Hong Kong *pro rata* spend, respectively, 80 and 26 *times* more on teaching development than does Australia. And you can multiply that by another 2.5 times if you remove the amount spent on DTAs. Here is one reason why more brokering agencies exist in the UK, while the future of the only agency in Australia is problematic.

Another difference is the focus on departmental teaching, which used to be automatically included in the UK as a subject review but is now carried out by the institution rather than by the QAA. Only in Hong Kong is departmental teaching looked at from outside the institution. The danger in Australia is that the individuals doing the reflecting in the reflective institution may not be those doing the teaching, which could be a source of some misalignment.

**Table 13.2:** Similarities and differences in QA/QE processes in the UK, Australia and Hong Kong

| Item | UK | Australia | Hong Kong |
| --- | --- | --- | --- |
| Money spent on teaching development per annum (A$ pro-rated to Australian population) | £89 million (England only) (A$80 million) | A$1 million (A$0.35m without DTAs) | HK$38.3 million (A$26 million) |
| QM to define good teaching | Yes, alignment | No, up to institution | Yes, alignment, collective responsibility |
| QE processes required | Yes, in Scotland, increasingly elsewhere | Yes | Yes |
| Teaching of subjects audited | Included in institutional review | Unclear. Up to institution | Selected departments |
| Brokering | LTSN, ILT, NTC, HESDA, funded projects | AUTC until 2003, then? Funded projects | Funded projects |
| Reflective institutions? | Self-review is required, more QE when the Scottish model is followed. The impact of teacher involvement unclear as yet | Yes, with the self audit, but theory-free reflection could be problematic. Make sure teachers are involved | Yes, at both departmental and institutional levels |

## Summary and conclusions

### Assuring quality: in retrospect and in prospect

The term quality assurance has come to mean two widely disparate things: retrospective QA based on accountability, and prospective QA based on maintaining and improving teaching. Table 13.3 contrasts the attributes of retrospective and prospective QA.

Retrospective QA is an accountability exercise that is conducted according to managerial priorities. Despite the rhetoric, retrospective QA actually damages teaching because the conceptions and actions are not driven by a level 3 model of teaching and learning. Prospective QA is so driven, and if

**Table 13.3:** Some contrasting attributes of retrospective and prospective QA

|  | *Retrospective QA* | *Prospective QA* |
|---|---|---|
| Quality as . . . | Value for money, meeting external standards | Fitness for purpose, transforming |
| Function | Audit, status quo mechanisms | QM, QE, QF |
| Aim | Meet externally imposed standards | Meet own standards developed internally |
| Priority | Managerial, entrepreneurial | Educational |
| Focus | On the past | On present and future |
| Nature | Top-down | Bottom-up |
| Climate | Theory X, adversarial | Theory Y, collegial |
| Model | Deficit | Systemic |
| Style | Judgemental | Supportive |
| Framework | Quantitative, closed | Qualitative, open |
| Use of data | Summative | Formative |

it operates within budget, it renders retrospective QA, with its expensive audits and huge time demands, gratifyingly redundant.

### The quality model: a generic theory of teaching

Prospective QA refers to a delivery system of teaching that fits what we know about best practice. Such a system is achieved by designing a quality model, based on a level 3 theory of teaching, to suit the particular institution's circumstances. Where teaching is tuned to the objectives as well as to the assessment tasks, and where the institutional infrastructure is prioritized towards best practice in teaching, a quality assured-system is in place.

### Quality enhancement: improving learning and teaching

QE is designed to improve the ongoing system of teaching and learning. The teaching development centre, as the place where expertise in teaching and learning is located, should be closely involved with departments and the institution generally where decisions about teaching and its enhancement are made. Really effective QE can only take place when the whole support system of teaching is targeted, rather than individual teachers.

### Quality feasibility: what impedes quality teaching?

QF, the removal of factors in the institutional climate or structures that are deleterious to learning and good teaching, seems to have received scant attention. Such factors mostly result from confused or distorted priorities. However, it is rather difficult for administrations to admit that their policies and procedures are actually undermining their own mission statement. Nevertheless, if they want to be seen as quality institutions, they, like individual professionals, will have to engage in some reflective QF, painful though that might be.

### QA/QE in three countries

The present model of QA/QE was used to evaluate the systems currently operating in the UK, Australia and Hong Kong. Each has an evolving system in place, with many points in common. The system in the UK is moving away from subject or departmental reviews, and locating them at the institutional level of review, and is becoming more oriented to QE, for which a complex support or brokering structure exists to help institutions. The Australian system has only just got off the ground, and takes a postmodern line: institutions can themselves decide what good teaching is, and then convince the AUQA audit team that it is living up to that notion. Hong Kong's system is based on an earlier British model, with strong emphasis on external departmental-level reviews as well as institutional review.

The UK and Hong Kong models seem closest to that developed in this chapter, with more room for genuine reflective practice by those doing the teaching. The most staggering difference between systems, however, lies in the amounts of money dedicated to teaching development. I hope that by the third edition of this book, these figures will have equalized: upwards.

## Further reading

Brennan, J. and Shah, T. (2000) *Managing Quality in Higher Education.* Buckingham: Society for Research into Higher Education / Open University Press.

Goodlad, S. (1995) *The Quest for Quality: 16 Forms of Heresy in Higher Education.* Buckingham: Society for Research into Higher Education / Open University Press.

Liston, C. (1999) *Managing Quality and Standards.* Buckingham: Open University Press.

The area of QA/QE is changing rapidly, as thinking changes. Goodlad is one of a few seminal books discussing general principles. Quite a different perspective is provided by Liston who discusses mainly from a retrospective QA framework. Brennan and Shah discuss QA processes in 14 countries.

The following websites are useful for information on QA/QE:

The Australian Universities Quality Agency: www.auqa.edu.au.
The Hong Kong Universities Grants Committee (yet to be updated to give full details of the current procedure): www.ugc.edu.hk.
The Institute for Learning and Teaching in Higher Education: www.ilt.ac.uk.
The Learning and Teaching Support Network: www.ltsn.ac.uk.
The Quality Assurance Agency for Higher Education (QAA): www.qaa.ac.uk.

# References

Abercrombie, M.L.J. (1969) *The Anatomy of Judgment*. Harmondsworth: Penguin.

Abercrombie, M.L.J. (1980) *Aims and Techniques of Group Teaching*. London: Society for Research into Higher Education.

Albanese, M. and Mitchell, S. (1993) Problem-based learning: a review of literature on its outcomes and implementation issues, *Academic Medicine*, 68: 52–81.

Alverno College Faculty (1994) *Student Assessment-as-learning at Alverno College*. Milwaukee: Alverno College Institute.

Anderson, C. (1997) Enabling and shaping understanding through tutorials, in F. Marton, D. Hounsell and N. Entwistle (eds) *The Experience of Learning*. Edinburgh: Scottish Universities Press.

Andreson, L.W. (1994) *Lecturing to Large Groups: A Guide to Doing it Less . . . But Better*. Birmingham: Staff and Educational Development Association.

Ashworth, P., Bannister, P. and Thorne, P. (1997) Guilty in whose eyes? University students' perceptions of cheating and plagiarism, *Studies in Higher Education*, 22: 187–203.

Australian Universities Quality Agency (2002) *Audit Manual*. Available at www.auqa.edu.au/qualityaudit/auditmanual (accessed 16 March 2002).

Ausubel, D.P. (1968) *Educational Psychology: A Cognitive View*. New York: Holt, Rinehart & Winston.

Baillie, C. and Toohey, S. (1997) The 'power test': its impact on student learning in a materials science course for engineering students, *Assessment and Evaluation in Higher Education*, 22: 33–48.

Ballard, B. and Clanchy, J. (1997) *Teaching International Students*. Deakin, ACT: IDP Education Australia.

Barrows, H.S. (1986) A taxonomy of problem-based learning methods, *Medical Education, 1986*, 20: 481–6.

Battacharya, B. (2002) Collaboration: a new model for off-campus distance education. Paper presented to the International Distance Education and Open Learning Conference, 5 March.

Baumgart, N. and Halse, C. (1999) Globalisation v. cultural diversity, *Assessment in Education*, 6: 321–39.

Bereiter, C. and Scardamalia, M. (1987) *The Psychology of Written Composition*. Hillsdale, NJ: Lawrence Erlbaum.

Berliner, D. (1986) In pursuit of the expert pedagogue, *Educational Researcher*, 15(7): 5–13.

Biggs, J.B. (1973) Study behaviour and performance in objective and essay formats, *Australian Journal of Education*, 17: 157–67.

Biggs, J.B. (1979) Individual differences in study processes and the quality of learning outcomes, *Higher Education*, 8: 381–94.

Biggs, J.B. (1987a) *Student Approaches to Learning and Studying*. Hawthorn, Vic.: Australian Council for Educational Research.

Biggs, J.B. (1987b) Process and outcome in essay writing, *Research and Development in Higher Education*, 9: 114–25.

Biggs, J.B. (1989a) Approaches to the enhancement of tertiary teaching, *Higher Education Research and Development*, 8: 7–25.

Biggs, J.B. (1989b) Some reflections on teaching at HKU. Hong Kong University Staff Newsletter.

Biggs, J. (1991) Approaches to learning in secondary and tertiary students in Hong Kong: some comparative studies, *Educational Research Journal*, 6: 27–39.

Biggs, J.B. (1992a) A qualitative approach to grading students, *HERDSA News*, 14(3): 3–6.

Biggs, J.B. (1992b) *Why and How do Hong Kong Students Learn? Using the Learning and Study Process Questionnaires*, Education Papers 14. Hong Kong: University of Hong Kong.

Biggs, J.B. (1993a) What do inventories of students' learning processes really measure? A theoretical review and clarification, *British Journal of Educational Psychology*, 63: 1–17.

Biggs, J.B. (1993b) From theory to practice: a cognitive systems approach, *Higher Education Research and Development*, 12: 73–86.

Biggs, J.B. (1994) What are effective schools? Lessons from East and West, *The Australian Educational Researcher*, 12: 9–39.

Biggs, J.B. (1996a) Enhancing teaching through constructive alignment, *Higher Education*, 32: 1–18.

Biggs, J.B. (1996b) Assessing learning quality: reconciling institutional, staff, and educational demands, *Assessment and Evaluation in Higher Education*, 21: 5–15.

Biggs, J.B. (1996c) Stages of expatriate involvement in educational development: colonialism, irrelevance, or what? *Education Research Journal*, 12: 157–64.

Biggs, J.B. and Collis, K.F. (1982) *Evaluating the Quality of Learning: The SOLO Taxonomy*. New York: Academic Press.

Biggs, J. and Davis, R. (eds) (2001) *The Subversion of Australian Universities*. Available at www.uow.edu.au/arts/sts/bmartin/dissent/documents/sau/ (accessed 28 March 2002).

Biggs, J.B. and Moore, P.J. (1993) *The Process of Learning*. Sydney: Prentice Hall.

Biggs, J.B., Kember, D. and Leung, D.Y.P. (2001) The Revised Two Factor Study Process Questionnaire: R-SPQ-2F, *British Journal of Educational Psychology*, 71: 133–49.

Bligh, D.A. (1972) *What's the Use of Lectures?* Harmondsworth: Penguin.

Bloom, B.S., Hastings, J.T. and Madaus, G.F. (1971) *Handbook of Formative and Summative Education of Student Learning*. New York: McGraw-Hill.

Borden, V., Chalmers, D., Olsen, M. and Scott, I. (2002) An international perspective on brokerage, in N. Jackson (ed.) *Changing Higher Education through Brokerage.* Aldershot: Ashgate.

Boud, D. (1985) *Problem-based Learning in Education for the Professions.* Sydney: Higher Education Research and Development Society of Australasia.

Boud, D. (1986) *Implementing student self-assessment,* Green Guide No. 5. Sydney: Higher Education Research and Development Society of Australasia.

Boud, D. (1995) *Enhancing Learning through Self-assessment.* London: Kogan Page.

Boulton-Lewis, G.M. (1998) Applying the SOLO taxonomy to learning in higher education, in B. Dart and G. Boulton-Lewis (eds) *Teaching and Learning in Higher Education.* Camberwell, Vic.: Australian Council for Educational Research.

Bourner, T. and Flowers, S. (1997) Teaching and learning methods in higher education: a glimpse of the future, *Reflections on Higher Education,* 9: 77–102.

Boyer, E.L. (1990) *Scholarship Reconsidered: Priorities for the Professoriate.* Princeton, NJ: Carnegie Foundation for the Advancement of Teaching.

Brew, A. (1999) Towards autonomous assessment: using self-assessment and peer-assessment, in S. Brown and A. Glasner (eds) *Assessment Matters in Higher Education.* Buckingham: Society for Research into Higher Education/Open University Press.

Brockbank, A. and McGill, I. (1998) *Facilitating Reflective Learning in Higher Education.* Buckingham: Society for Research into Higher Education/Open University Press.

Brown, G. and Atkins, M. (1988) *Effective Teaching in Higher Education.* London: Methuen.

Brown, S. and Glasner, A. (eds) (1999) *Assessment Matters in Higher Education.* Buckingham: Society for Research into Higher Education/Open University Press.

Brown, S. and Knight, P. (1994) *Assessing Learners in Higher Education.* London: Kogan Page.

Burns, R.B. (1991) Study, stress, and culture shock among first year overseas students in an Australian university, *Higher Education Research and Development,* 10: 61–78.

Candy, P.C. (1991) *Self-direction for Lifelong Learning: A Comprehensive Guide to Theory and Practice.* San Francisco: Jossey-Bass.

Chalmers, D. and Fuller, R. (1996) *Teaching for Learning at University.* London: Kogan Page.

Chalmers, D. and Kelly, B. (1997) *Peer Assisted Study Sessions (PASS).* University of Queensland, Teaching and Educational Development Institute.

Chalmers, D. and Volet, S. (1997) Common misconceptions about students from South-East Asia studying in Australia, *Higher Education Research and Development,* 16: 87–100.

Chan, C.K.K. (2001) Promoting learning and understanding through constructivist approaches for Chinese learners, in D.A. Watkins and J. Biggs (eds) *Teaching the Chinese Learner: Psychological and Pedagogical Perspectives.* Hong Kong: Comparative Education Research Centre, University of Hong Kong/Camberwell, Vic.: Australian Council for Educational Research.

Chan, C.K.K., Lee, E.Y.C. and van Aalst, J. (2001) Assessing and fostering knowledge building inquiry and discourse. Paper presented at the 9th European Conference for Research on Learning and Instruction, Fribourg, Switzerland.

Coady, T. (ed.) (2000) *Why Universities Matter.* Sydney: Allen & Unwin.

Cohen, S.A. (1987) Instructional alignment: searching for a magic bullet, *Educational Researcher*, 16(8): 16–20.

Cole, N.S. (1990) Conceptions of educational achievement, *Educational Researcher*, 18(3): 2–7.

Collier, K.G. (1983) *The Management of Peer-group Learning: Syndicate Methods in Higher Education.* Guildford: Society for Research in Higher Education.

Collis, K.F. and Biggs, J.B. (1983) Matriculation, degree requirements, and cognitive demands in universities and CAEs, *Australian Journal of Education*, 27: 41–51.

Cortazzi, M. and Jin, L. (2001) Large classes in China: 'Good' teachers and interaction, in D. Watkins and J. Biggs (eds) *Teaching the Chinese Learner: Psychological and Pedagogical Perspectives.* Hong Kong: Comparative Education Research Centre, University of Hong Kong/Camberwell, Vic.: Australian Council for Educational Research.

Cowan, J. (1998) *On Becoming an Innovative Teacher.* Buckingham: Open University Press.

Cowan, J. (2001) *Plus/Minus Marking – A Method of Assessment Worth Considering?* York: Institute for Learning and Teaching in Higher Education. ILT Members Resource Area [Internet], 27 April. Available to ILT members at www.ilt.ac.uk/redirectportal.asp?article=JCowan01a

Crooks, T.J. (1988a) The impact of classroom evaluation practices on students, *Review of Educational Research*, 58: 438–81.

Crooks, T.J. (1988b) *Assessing Student Performance*, Green Guide No. 8. Sydney: Higher Education Research and Development Society of Australasia.

Davis, B.G. (1993) *Tools for Teaching.* San Francisco: Jossey-Bass.

Davis, G. and McLeod, N. (1996a) Teaching large classes: the silver lining, *HERDSA News*, 18(1): 3–5, 20.

Davis, G. and McLeod, N. (1996b) Teaching large classes: the final challenge – assessment and feedback, *HERDSA News*, 18(2): 5–7, 12.

Dearing, R. (1997) *Higher Education in the Learning Society*, Report of the National Committee of Inquiry into Higher Education (Dearing Report). Norwich: HMSO.

Department of Employment, Education, Training, and Youth Affairs (1998) *Annual Statistics.* Canberra, ACT: Government Printing Office.

Diederich, P.B. (1974) *Measuring Growth in English.* Urbana, Ill: National Council of Teachers of English.

Dienes, Z. (1997) *Student-led Tutorials: A Discussion Paper.* Falmer: School of Experimental Psychology, University of Sussex.

Dunkin, M. and Biddle, B. (1974) *The Study of Teaching.* New York: Holt, Rinehart & Winston.

Dunkin, M. and Precians, R. (1992) Award-winning university teachers' concepts of teaching, *Higher Education*, 24: 483–502.

Eley, M.G. (1992) Differential adoption of study approaches within individual students, *Higher Education*, 23: 231–54.

Elliott, J. (1991) *Action Research for Educational Change.* Buckingham: Open University Press.

Ellsworth, R., Duell, O.K. and Velotta, C. (1991) Length of wait-times used by college students given unlimited wait-time intervals, *Contemporary Educational Psychology*, 16: 265–71.

Entwistle, N. (1997) Introduction: phenomenography in higher education, *Higher Education Research and Development*, 16: 127–34.

Entwistle, N. and Entwistle, A. (1997) Revision and the experience of understanding, in F. Marton, D. Hounsell and N. Entwistle (eds) *The Experience of Learning*. Edinburgh: Scottish Universities Press.

Entwistle, N. and Ramsden, P. (1983) *Understanding Student Learning*. London: Croom Helm.

Entwistle, N., Kozeki, B. and Tait, H. (1989) Pupils' perceptions of school and teachers. II: Relationships with motivation and approaches to learning, *British Journal of Educational Psychology*, 59: 340–50.

Falchikov, N. and Boud, D. (1989) Student self-assessment in higher education: a meta-analysis, *Review of Educational Research*, 59: 395–400.

Feather, N. (ed.) (1982) *Expectations and Actions*. Hillsdale, NJ: Erlbaum.

Feletti, G. (1997) The Triple Jump exercise: a case study in assessing problem solving, in G. Ryan (ed.) *Learner Assessment and Program Evaluation in Problem Based Learning*. Newcastle: Australian Problem Based Learning Network.

Fleming, N. (1993) What works and what doesn't in staff development, *HERDSA News*, 15(2): 12–13.

Fox, D. (1989) Peer assessment of an essay assignment, *HERDSA News*, 11(2): 6–7.

Frederiksen, J.R. and Collins, A. (1989) A systems approach to educational testing, *Educational Researcher*, 18(9): 27–32.

Fullan, M. (1993) *Change Forces: Probing the Depth of Educational Reform*. London: Falmer Press.

Gabrenya, W.K., Wang, Y.E. and Latane, B. (1985) Cross-cultural differences in social loafing on an optimizing task: Chinese and Americans, *Journal of Cross-cultural Psychology*, 16: 223–64.

Galton, F. (1889) *Natural Inheritance*. New York: Macmillan.

Gardner, H.W. (1989) *To Open Minds: Chinese Clues to the Dilemma of Contemporary Education*. New York: Basic Books.

Gardner, H.W. (1993) Educating for understanding, *The American School Board Journal*, July: 20–4.

Getzels, J. and Jackson, P. (1962) *Creativity and Intelligence*. New York: Wiley.

Gibbs, G. (1992) *Improving the Quality of Student Learning*. Bristol: Technical and Educational Services.

Gibbs, G. (1999) Using assessment strategically to change the way students learn, in S. Brown and A. Glasner (eds) *Assessment Matters in Higher Education: Choosing and Using Diverse Approaches*. Buckingham: Society for Research into Higher Education/Open University Press.

Gibbs, G. and Jenkins, A. (eds) (1992) *Teaching Large Classes in Higher Education*. London: Kogan Page.

Gibbs, G., Habeshaw, S. and Habeshaw, T. (1984) *53 Interesting Ways to Teach Large Classes*. Bristol: Technical and Educational Services.

Gibbs, G., Jenkins, A. and Wisker, G. (1992) *Assessing More Students*. Oxford: PCFC/Rewley Press.

Ginsburg, H. and Opper, S. (1987) *Piaget's Theory of Intellectual Development*. Englewood Cliffs, NJ: Prentice Hall.

Goodlad, S. (1995) *The Quest for Quality: 16 Forms of Heresy in Higher Education*. Buckingham: Society for Research into Higher Education/Open University Press.

Goodlad, S. and Hirst, B. (eds) (1990) *Explorations in Peer Tutoring.* Oxford: Basil Blackwell.

Goodnow, J.J. (1991) Cognitive values and educational practice, in J. Biggs (ed.) *Teaching for Learning: The View from Cognitive Psychology.* Hawthorn, Vic.: Australian Council for Educational Research.

Gow, L. and Kember, D. (1990) Does higher education promote independent learning? *Higher Education,* 19: 307–22.

Gow, L. and Kember, D. (1993) Conceptions of teaching and their relation to student learning, *British Journal of Educational Psychology,* 63: 20–33.

Guilford, J.P. (1967) *The Nature of Human Intelligence.* New York: McGraw-Hill.

Gunstone, R. and White, R. (1981) Understanding of gravity, *Science Education,* 65: 291–9.

Guskey, T. (1986) Staff development and the process of teacher change, *Educational Researcher,* 15(5): 5–12.

Guttman, L. (1941) The quantification of a class of attributes: a theory and a method of scale construction, in P. Horst (ed.) *The Prediction of Personal Adjustment.* New York: Social Science Research Council.

Hales, L.W. and Tokar, E. (1975) The effects of quality of preceding responses on the grades assigned to subsequent responses to an essay question, *Journal of Educational Measurement,* 12: 115–17.

Harris, D. and Bell, C. (1986) *Evaluating and Assessing for Learning.* London: Kogan Page.

Harris, R. (1997) Overseas students in the United Kingdom university system, *Higher Education,* 29: 77–92.

Harvey, L. and Green, D. (1993) Defining quality, *Assessment and Evaluation in Higher Education,* 18: 8–35.

Hattie, J. and Purdie, N. (1998) The SOLO model: addressing fundamental measurement issues, in B. Dart and G. Boulton-Lewis (eds) *Teaching and Learning in Higher Education.* Camberwell, Vic.: Australian Council for Educational Research.

Hattie, J. and Watkins, D. (1988) Preferred classroom environment and approach to learning, *British Journal of Educational Psychology,* 58: 345–9.

Hattie, J., Biggs, J. and Purdie, N. (1996) Effects of learning skills interventions on student learning: a meta-analysis, *Review of Educational Research,* 66: 99–136.

Hess, R.D. and Azuma, M. (1991) Cultural support for schooling: contrasts between Japan and the United States, *Educational Researcher,* 20(9): 2–8.

Hmelo, C.E., Gotterer, G.S. and Bransford, J.D. (1997) A theory driven approach to assessing the cognitive effects of PBL, *Instructional Science,* 25: 387–408.

Ho, A. (2001) A conceptual change approach to university staff development, in D.A. Watkins and J.B. Biggs (eds) *Teaching the Chinese Learner Psychological and Pedagogical Perspectives.* Hong Kong: University of Hong Kong Comparative Education Research Centre/Camberwell, Vic.: Australian Council for Educational Research.

Hore, T. (1971) Assessment of teaching practice: an 'attractive' hypothesis, *British Journal of Educational Psychology,* 41: 327–8.

Hudson, L. (1966) *Contrary Imaginations.* London: Methuen.

International Association for the Evaluation of Educational Achievement (1996) *The Third International Maths and Science Study.* Paris: OECD.

Jackson, N. (ed.) (2002a) *The QAA Policy Framework*, briefing paper no. 1. York: Learning and Teaching Support Network.

Jackson, N. (ed.) (2002b) *Changing Higher Education through Brokerage*. Aldershot: Ashgate.

Jarratt (1985) *Report of the Steering Committee for Efficiency Studies in Universities*. London: Committee of Vice-Chancellors and Principals.

Johnson, D.W. and Johnson, R.T. (1990) *Learning Together and Alone: Co-operation, Competition and Individualisation*. Englewood Cliffs, NJ: Prentice Hall.

Jones, J., Jones, A. and Ker, P. (1994) Peer tutoring for academic credit, *HERDSA News*, 16(3): 3–5.

Jones, R.M. (1968) *Fantasy and Feeling in Education*. New York: New York University Press.

Keller, F. (1968) 'Goodbye Teacher . . .', *Journal of Applied Behavior Analysis*, 1: 79–89.

Kember, D. (1998) Teaching beliefs and their impact on students' approach to learning, in B. Dart and G. Boulton-Lewis (eds) *Teaching and Learning in Higher Education*. Camberwell: Australian Council for Educational Research.

Kember, D. (2000) *Action Learning and Action Research: Improving the Quality of Teaching and Learning*. London: Kogan Page.

Kember, D. (2001) Transforming teaching through action research, in D.A. Watkins and J.B. Biggs (eds) *Teaching the Chinese Learner Psychological and Pedagogical Perspectives*. Hong Kong: University of Hong Kong Comparative Education Research Centre/Camberwell, Vic.: Australian Council for Educational Research.

Kember, D. and Gow, L. (1991) A challenge to the anecdotal stereotype of the Asian student, *Studies in Higher Education*, 16: 117–28.

Kember, D. and Kelly, M. (1993) *Improving Teaching through Action Research*, Green Guide No. 14. Campbelltown, NSW: Higher Education Research and Development Society of Australasia.

Kember, D. and McKay, J. (1966) Action research into the quality of student learning: a paradigm for faculty development, *Journal of Higher Education*, 67: 528–54.

Kember, D. and Wong, A. (2000) Implications for evaluation from a study of students' perceptions of good and poor teaching, *Higher Education*, 39: 69–97.

Kember, D., Lam, B-h., Yan, L., Yum, J.C.K. and Liu, S.B. (eds) (1997) *Case Studies of Improving Teaching and Learning from the Action Learning Project*. Hong Kong: Hong Kong Polytechnic University, Action Learning Project.

Kember, D., Charlesworth, M., Davies, H., McKay, J. and Stott, V. (1998) Evaluating the effectiveness of educational innovations: using the Study Process Questionnaire to show that meaningful learning occurs, *Studies in Educational Evaluation*, 23: 141–57.

Kemp, D. (1999) Quoted on the website for the Department of Education, Science and Training at www.dest.gov.au/archgive/highered/pubs/quality/overview.htm (accessed 14 March 2002).

King, A. (1990) Enhancing peer interaction and learning in the classroom through reciprocal questioning, *American Educational Research Journal*, 27: 664–87.

Kingsland, A. (1995) Integrated assessment: the rhetoric and the students' view, in P. Little, M. Ostwald and G. Ryan (eds) *Research and Development in Problem*

*Based Learning. Volume 3: Assessment and Evaluation.* Newcastle: Australian Problem Based Learning Network.

Lai, P. and Biggs, J.B. (1994) Who benefits from mastery learning? *Contemporary Educational Psychology,* 19: 13–23.

Lai, P. and Tang, C. (1999) Constraints affecting the implementation of a problem-based learning strategy in university courses. Implementing problem-based learning, *Proceedings from the 1st Asia-Pacific Conference on Problem-Based Learning.* The Problem-based Learning Project, pp. 49–54.

Lai, P., Tang, C. and Taylor, G. (1997) Traditional assessment approaches: saints or devils to learning fostered by PBL?, in J. Conway, R. Fisher, L. Sheridan-Burns and G. Ryan (eds) *Research and Development in Problem Based Learning. Volume 4: Integrity, Innovation, Integration.* Newcastle: Australian Problem Based Learning Network.

Lake, D. (1999) Helping students to go SOLO: teaching critical numeracy in the biological sciences, *Journal of Biological Education,* 33: 191–8.

Laurillard, D. and Margetson, D. (1997) *Introducing a flexible Learning Methodology: Discussion Paper,* occasional paper no. 7. Nathan, Queensland: Griffith Institute for Higher Education, Griffith University.

Leach, L., Neutze, G. and Zepke, N. (2001) Assessment and empowerment: some critical questions, *Assessment and Evaluation in Higher Education,* 26: 293–305.

Lee, W.O. (1996) The cultural context for Chinese learners: conceptions of learning in the Confucian tradition, in D. Watkins and J. Biggs (eds) *The Chinese Learner: Cultural, Psychological and Contextual Influences.* Hong Kong: Centre for Comparative Research in Education/Camberwell, Vic.: Australian Council for Educational Research.

Leinhardt, G., McCarthy Young, K. and Merriman, J. (1995) Integrating professional knowledge: the theory of practice and the practice of theory, *Learning and Instruction,* 5: 401–8.

Lejk, M. and Wyvill, M. (2001a) Peer assessment of contributions to a group project: a comparison of holistic and category based approaches, *Assessment and Evaluation in Higher Education,* 26: 61–72.

Lejk, M. and Wyvill, M. (2001b) The effect of inclusion of self-assessment with peer assessment of contributions to a group project: a quantitative study of secret and agreed assessments, *Assessment and Evaluation in Higher Education,* 26: 551–62.

Lohman, D.F. (1993) Teaching and testing to develop fluid abilities, *Educational Researcher,* 22(7): 12–23.

MacDonald-Ross, R.M. (1973) Behavioural objectives: a critical review. *Instructional Science,* 2: 1–51.

McGregor, D. (1960) *The Human Side of Enterprise.* New York: McGraw-Hill.

McKay, J. and Kember, D. (1997) Spoon feeding leads to regurgitation: a better diet can result in more digestible learning outcomes, *Higher Education Research and Development,* 16: 55–68.

McKeachie, W., Pintrich, P., Lin, Y-G. and Smith, D. (1986) *Teaching and Learning in the College Classroom.* University of Michigan: Office of Educational Research and Improvement.

MacKenzie, A. and White, R. (1982) Fieldwork in geography and long-term memory structures, *American Educational Research Journal,* 19(4): 623–32.

McLeish, J. (1976) The lecture method, in N. Gage (ed.) *The Psychology of Teaching Methods*, 75th Yearbook of the National Society for the Study of Education. Chicago: University of Chicago Press.

Magin, D. (2001) A novel technique for comparing the reliability of multiple peer assessments with that of single teacher assessments of group process work, *Assessment and Evaluation in Higher Education*, 26: 139–52.

Maier, P. and Warren, A. (2000) *Integrating Technology in Learning and Teaching*. London: Kogan Page.

Maier, P., Barnett, L., Warren, A. and Brunner, D. (1998) *Using Technology in Teaching and Learning*. London: Kogan Page.

Marginson, S. (1997) Competition and contestability in Australian higher education, *Australian Universities Review*, 40(1): 5–14.

Marland, P. (1997) *Towards More Effective Open and Distance Teaching*. London: Kogan Page.

Marton, F. (1981) Phenomenography – describing conceptions of the world around us. *Instructional Science*, 10: 177–200.

Marton, F. and Booth, S.A. (1997) *Learning and Awareness*. Hillsdale, NJ: Lawrence Erlbaum.

Marton, F. and Säljö, R. (1976a) On qualitative differences in learning. I: Outcome and process, *British Journal of Educational Psychology*, 46: 4–11.

Marton, F. and Säljö, R. (1976b) On qualitative differences in learning. II: Outcome as a function of the learner's conception of the task, *British Journal of Educational Psychology*, 46: 115–27.

Marton, F., Dall'Alba, G. and Beaty, E. (1993) Conceptions of learning, *International Journal of Educational Research*, 19: 277–300.

Massy, W.F. (forthcoming) *Quality and Cost Containment: Rebuilding the University's Core Competency*. Boston, MA: Anker.

Masters, G. (1987) *New Views of Student Learning: Implications for Educational Measurement*, research working paper 87.11. Melbourne: Centre for the Study of Higher Education, University of Melbourne.

Masters, G.N. (1988) Partial credit model, in J.P. Keeves (ed.) *Handbook of Educational Research Methodology, Measurement and Evaluation*. London: Pergamon Press.

Mazur, E. (1998) *Peer Instruction: A User's Manual*. Englewood Cliffs, NJ: Prentice Hall.

Mentowski, M. (2000) *Learning that Lasts*. San Francisco: Jossey-Bass.

Messick, S.J. (1989) Meaning and values in test validation: the science and ethics of assessment, *Educational Researcher*, 18(2): 5–11.

Meyer, J.H.F. (1991) Study orchestration: the manifestation, interpretation and consequences of contextualised approaches to learning, *Higher Education*, 22: 297–316.

Moodie, G. (2001) Virtual learning gets the reboot, *The Australian*, 17 October.

Morris, S. (2001) Too many minds miss the mark, *The Australian*, 5 September.

Moss, P.A. (1992) Shifting conceptions of validity in educational measurement: implications for performance assessment, *Review of Educational Research*, 62: 229–58.

Moss, P.A. (1994) Can there be validity without reliability? *Educational Researcher*, 23(2): 5–12.

Mullins, G., Quintrell, N. and Hancock, L. (1995) The experiences of international and local students at three Australian universities, *Higher Education Research and Development*, 14: 201–32.

National Center for Supplemental Instruction (1994) *Review of Research Concerning the Effectiveness of SI*. Kansas City, MO: University of Missouri.

Newble, D. and Clarke, R. (1986) The approaches to learning of students in a traditional and in an innovative problem-based medical school, *Medical Education*, 20: 267–73.

Nicholls, P.D. (1994) A framework for developing cognitively diagnostic assessments, *Review of Educational Research*, 64: 575–603.

Nightingale, P., Te Wiata, I., Toohey, S., Ryan, G., Hughes, C. and Magin, D. (eds) (1996) *Assessing Learning in Universities*. Kensington, NSW: Committee for the Advancement of University Teaching/Professional Development Centre, UNSW.

Niland, J. (2000) Interview in *Campus Post, South China Morning Post*, 26 October.

Novak, J.D. (1979) Applying psychology and philosophy to the improvement of laboratory teaching, *The American Biology Teacher*, 41: 466–70.

Pearson, C. and Beasley, C. (1996) Reducing learning barriers amongst international students: a longitudinal development study, *The Australian Educational Researcher*, 23: 79–96.

Perkins, D. (1991) Technology meets constructivism: do they make a marriage? *Educational Technology*, May: 18–23.

Perraton, H. (1997) The virtual wandering scholar: policy issues for international higher education, in R. Murray-Harvey and H.C. Sims (eds) *Learning and Teaching in Higher Education: Advancing International Perspectives*. Adelaide: Flinders Press.

Poliquin, L. and Maufette, Y. (1997) PBL vs. integrity of discipline content: the experience of integrated PBL in a BSc. in Biology, in J. Conway, R. Fisher, L. Sheridan-Burns and G. Ryan (eds) *Research and Development in Problem Based Learning. Volume 4: Integrity, Innovation, Integration*. Newcastle: Australian Problem Based Learning Network.

Pope, N. (2001) An examination of the use of peer rating for formative assessment in the context of the theory of consumption values, *Assessment and Evaluation in Higher Education*, 26: 235–46.

Popham, W.J. and Husek, T.R. (1969) Implications of criterion-referenced measurement, *Journal of Educational Measurement*, 6: 1–9.

Prosser, M. and Trigwell, K. (1998) *Teaching for Learning in Higher Education*. Buckingham: Open University Press.

Purdie, N. and Hattie, J. (1996) Cultural differences in the use of strategies for self-regulated learning, *American Educational Research Journal*, 33: 845–74.

Ramsden, P. (1992) *Learning to Teach in Higher Education*. London: Routledge.

Ramsden, P. (1984) The context of learning, in F. Marton, D. Hounsell and N. Entwistle (eds) *The Experience of Learning*. Edinburgh: Scottish Academic Press.

Ramsden, P. (1998a) *Learning to Lead in Higher Education*. London: Routledge.

Ramsden, P. (1998b) For good measure, *The Australian Higher Education*, 28 January.

Ramsden, P., Beswick, D. and Bowden, J. (1986) Effects of learning skills interventions on first year university students' learning, *Human Learning*, 5: 151–64.

Romizowski, A.J. (1981) *Designing Instructional Systems*. London: Kogan Page.

Ryan, G. (1997) Promoting educational integrity in PBL programs – choosing carefully and implementing wisely, in J. Conway, R. Fisher, L. Sheridan-Burns and G. Ryan (eds) *Research and Development in Problem Based Learning. Volume 4: Integrity, Innovation, Integration.* Newcastle: Australian Problem Based Learning Network.

Saberton, S. (1985) Learning partnerships, *HERDSA News*, 7(1): 3–5.

Santhanam, E., Leach, C. and Dawson, C. (1998) Concept mapping: how should it be introduced, and is there a long term benefit? *Higher Education*, 35: 317–28.

Samuelowicz, K. (1987) Learning problems of overseas students: two sides of a story, *Higher Education Research and Development*, 6: 121–34.

Savin-Baden, M. (2000) *Problem-based Learning in Higher Education: Untold Stories.* Buckingham: Society for Research into Higher Education/Open University Press.

Scardamalia, M., Bereiter, C. and Lamon, M. (1994) The CSILE project: trying to bring the classroom into World 3, in K. McGilley (ed.) *Classroom Lessons: Integrating Cognitive Theory and Classroom Practice.* Cambridge, MA: MIT Press, pp. 201–28.

Scardamalia, M. and Bereiter, C. (1999) Schools as knowledge-building organizations, in D. Keating and C. Hertzman (eds) *Today's Children, Tomorrow's Society: The Developmental Health and Wealth of Nations.* New York: Guilford.

Schon, D.A. (1983) *The Reflective Practitioner: How Professionals Think in Action.* London: Temple Smith.

Schmidt, W. with 14 others (1996) *A Summary of Characterizing Pedagogical Flow: An Investigation of Mathematics and Science Teaching in Six Countries.* London: Kluwer.

Schmeck, R. (ed.) (1988) *Learning Strategies and Learning Styles.* New York: Plenum.

Scollon, R. and Wong Scollon, S. (1994) *The Post-Confucian Confusion*, Department of English research report no. 37. Hong Kong: Hong Kong City Polytechnic University.

Scouller, K.M. (1996) Influence of assessment methods on students' learning approaches, perceptions, and preferences: assignment essay versus short answer questions, *Research and Development in Higher Education*, 19(3): 776–81.

Scouller, K. (1997) Students' perceptions of three assessment methods: assignment essay, multiple choice question examination, short answer examination. Paper presented to Higher Education Research and Development Society of Australasia, Adelaide, 9–12 July.

Scouller, K. (1998) The influence of assessment method on students' learning approaches: multiple choice question examination vs. essay assignment, *Higher Education*, 35: 453–72.

Senate Employment, Workplace Relations, Small Business and Education Committee (2001) *Universities in Crisis.* Available at www.aph.gov.au/senate/committee/EET_CTTE/public%20uni/report/index.htm (accessed 14 March 2002).

Shepard, L.A. (1993) Evaluating test validity, *Review of Research in Education*, 19: 405–50.

Shuell, T.J. (1986) Cognitive conceptions of learning, *Review of Educational Research*, 56: 411–36.

Shulman, L.S. (1987) Knowledge and teaching: foundations of the new reform, *Harvard Educational Review*, 57: 1–22.

Smith, B., Scholten, I., Russell, A. and McCormack, P. (1997) Integrating student assessment practices: the significance of collaborative partnerships for curriculum and professional development in a university department, *Higher Education Research and Development*, 16: 69–85.

Starch, D. (1913a) Reliability of grading work in mathematics, *School Review*, 21: 254–9.

Starch, D. (1913b) Reliability of grading work in history, *School Review*, 21: 676–81.

Starch, D. and Elliott, E.C. (1912) Reliability of the grading of high school work in English, *School Review*, 20: 442–57.

Stedman, L.C. (1997) International achievement differences: an assessment of a new perspective, *Educational Researcher*, 26(3): 4–15.

Steffe, L. and Gale, J. (eds) (1995) *Constructivism in Education*. Hillsdale, NJ: Lawrence Erlbaum.

Stenhouse, L. (1975) *Introduction to Curriculum Research and Development*. London: Heinemann Educational.

Stephenson, J. and Laycock, M. (1993) *Using Contracts in Higher Education*. London: Kogan Page.

Sternberg, R.J. and Zhang, L.F. (eds) (2001) *Perspectives on Thinking, Learning, and Cognitive Styles*. Mahwah: Lawrence Erlbaum.

Stevenson, H.W. and Stigler, J. (1992) *The Learning Gap: Why Our Schools are Failing and What We Can Learn from Japanese and Chinese Education*. New York: Summit Books.

Stigler, J. and Hiebert, J. (1999) *The Teaching Gap*. New York: Free Press.

Tait, H., Entwistle, N.J. and McCune, V. (1998) ASSIST: a reconceptualisation of the *Approaches to Study Inventory*, in C. Rust (ed.) *Improving Students as Learners*. Oxford: Oxford Centre for Staff and Learning Development, Oxford Brookes University.

Tang, C. (1991) Effects of two different assessment procedures on tertiary students' approaches to learning. Unpublished doctoral dissertation, University of Hong Kong.

Tang, C. (1993) Spontaneous collaborative learning: a new dimension in student learning experience? *Higher Education Research and Development*, 12: 115–30.

Tang, C. (1996) Collaborative learning: the latent dimension in Chinese students' learning, in D. Watkins and J. Biggs (eds) *The Chinese Learner: Cultural, Psychological and Contextual Influences*. Hong Kong: Centre for Comparative Research in Education/Camberwell, Vic.: Australian Council for Educational Research.

Tang, C. (1998) Effects of collaborative learning on the quality of assessments, in B. Dart and G. Boulton-Lewis (eds) *Teaching and Learning in Higher Education*. Camberwell, Vic.: Australian Council for Educational Research.

Tang, C., Lai, P., Tang, W. and 10 others (1997) Developing a context based PBL model, in J. Conway, R. Fisher, L. Sheridan-Burns and G. Ryan (eds) *Research and Development in Problem Based Learning. Volume 4: Integrity, Innovation, Integration*. Newcastle: Australian Problem Based Learning Network.

Taylor, C. (1994) Assessment for measurement or standards: the peril and promise of large scale assessment reform, *American Educational Research Journal*, 31: 231–62.

Taylor, J.C. (1995) Distance education technologies: the fourth generation, *Australian Journal of Educational Technology*, 11(2): 1–7.

Thomas, E.L. and Robinson, H.A. (1982) *Improving Reading in Every Class: A Source Book for Teachers.* Boston: Allyn & Bacon.

Tomporowski, P.D. and Ellis, N.R. (1986) Effects of exercise on cognitive processes: a review, *Psychological Bulletin,* 99: 338–46.

Topping, K.J. (1996) The effectiveness of peer tutoring in further and higher education: a typology and review of the literature, *Higher Education,* 32: 321–45.

Torrance, H. (ed.) (1994) *Evaluating Authentic Assessment: Problems and Possibilities in New Approaches to Assessment.* Buckingham: Open University Press.

Trigwell, K. and Prosser, M. (1990) Using student learning outcome measures in the evaluation of teaching, *Research and Development in Higher Education,* 13: 390–7.

Trigwell, K. and Prosser, M. (1991) Changing approaches to teaching: a relational perspective, *Studies in Higher Education,* 22: 251–66.

Trigwell, K. and Prosser, M. (1996) Congruence between intention and strategy in science teachers' approach to teaching, *Higher Education,* 32: 77–87.

Trigwell, K. and Prosser, M. (1997) Towards an understanding of individual acts of teaching and learning, *Higher Education Research and Development,* 16: 241–52.

Trueman, M. and Hartley, J. (1996) A comparison between the time-management skills and academic performance of mature and traditional-entry university students, *Higher Education,* 32: 199–215.

Tulving, E. (1985) How many memory systems are there? *American Psychologist,* 40: 385–98.

Tyler, R.W. (1949) *Basic Principles of Curriculum and Instruction.* Chicago: University of Chicago Press.

Tyler, S. (2001) The perfect teaching tool? Paper given to the Learning Matters Symposium 2001, Victoria University, Melbourne, 6–7 December.

Tynjala, P. (1998) Writing as a tool for constructive learning: students' learning experiences during an experiment, *Higher Education,* 36: 209–30.

Volet, S. and Kee, J.P.P. (1993) *Studying in Singapore – Studying in Australia: A Student Perspective,* occasional paper no. 1. Murdoch, WA: Murdoch University Teaching Excellence Committee.

Volet, S. and Ang, G. (1998) Culturally mixed groups on international campuses: an opportunity for inter-cultural learning, *Higher Education Research and Development,* 17: 5–24.

Volet, S. and Renshaw, P. (1996) Chinese students at an Australian university: continuity and adaptability, in D. Watkins and J. Biggs (eds) *The Chinese Learner: Cultural, Psychological and Contextual Influences.* Hong Kong: Centre for Comparative Research in Education/Camberwell, Vic.: Australian Council for Educational Research.

Walker, J. (1998) Student plagiarism in universities: what are we doing about it? *Higher Education Research and Development,* 17: 89–106.

Ware, J. and Williams, R.G. (1975) The Dr Fox Effect: a study of lecturer effectiveness and ratings of instruction, *Journal of Medical Education,* 50: 149–56.

Watkins, D. and Biggs, J. (eds) (1996) *The Chinese Learner: Cultural, Psychological and Contextual Influences.* Hong Kong: Centre for Comparative Research in Education/Camberwell, Vic.: Australian Council for Educational Research.

Watkins, D. and Hattie, J. (1985) A longitudinal study of the approach to learning of Australian tertiary students, *Human Learning,* 4: 127–42.

Watkins, D., Regmi, M. and Astilla, E. (1991) The Asian-as-rote-learner stereotype: myth or reality? *Educational Psychology*, 17: 89–100.

Watson, J. (1996) Peer assisted learning in economics at the University of NSW. Paper given to Fourth Annual Teaching Economics Conference, Northern Territory University, Darwin, 28 June.

Watson, J. (1997) A peer support scheme in quantitative methods. Paper given to Biennial Conference, Professional Development Centre, University of NSW, 20 November.

Webb, G. (1997) Deconstructing deep and surface: towards a critique of phenomenography, *Higher Education*, 33: 195–212.

Weller, M. (2002) Assessment issues in a web-based course, *Assessment and Evaluation in Higher Education*, 27: 109–16.

Wetherell, J. and Mullins, G. (1997) Self-assessment in dentistry, in G. Ryan (ed.) *Learner Assessment and Program Evaluation in Problem Based Learning*. Newcastle: Australian Problem Based Learning Network.

Whitehill, T., Stokes, S.F. and MacKinnon, M. (1997) Problem based learning and the Chinese learner, in R. Murray-Harvey and H.C. Sims (eds) *Learning and Teaching in Higher Education: Advancing International Perspectives*. Adelaide: Flinders Press.

Wiggins, G. (1989) Teaching to the (authentic) test, *Educational Leadership*, 46: 41–7.

Wilson, K. (1997) Wording it up: plagiarism and the interdiscourse of international students. Paper given to Annual Conference, Higher Education Research and Development Society of Australasia, Adelaide, 8–11 July.

Wittrock, M.C. (1977) The generative processes of memory, in M.C. Wittrock (ed.) *The Human Brain*. Englewood Cliffs, NJ: Prentice Hall.

Wiske, M.S. (ed.) (1998) *Teaching for Understanding: Linking Research and Practice*. San Francisco: Jossey-Bass.

Woodley, C. (2001) Activity focused: a constructivist approach to online curriculum. Paper given to the Learning Matters Symposium 2001, Victoria University, Melbourne, 6–7 December.

Wong, C.S. (1994) Using a cognitive approach to assess achievement in secondary school mathematics. Unpublished M.Ed. dissertation, University of Hong Kong.

Zeng, K. (1999) *Dragon Gate: Competitive Examinations and their Consequences*. London: Cassell.

# Index

Note: Only the first author of multi-authored work is listed. Authors are not listed when only a passing reference is made to their work.

# The Society for Research into Higher Education

The Society for Research into Higher Education (SRHE), an international body, exists to stimulate and co-ordinate research into all aspects of higher education. It aims to improve the quality of higher education through the encouragement of debate and publication on issues of policy, on the organization and management of higher education institutions, and on the curriculum, teaching and learning methods.

The Society is entirely independent and receives no subsidies, although individual events often receive sponsorship from business or industry. The Society is financed through corporate and individual subscriptions and has members from many parts of the world. It is an NGO of UNESCO.

Under the imprint *SRHE & Open University Press*, the Society is a specialist publisher of research, having over 80 titles in print. In addition to *SRHE News*, the Society's newsletter, the Society publishes three journals: *Studies in Higher Education* (three issues a year), *Higher Education Quarterly* and *Research into Higher Education Abstracts* (three issues a year).

The Society runs frequent conferences, consultations, seminars and other events. The annual conference in December is organized at and with a higher education institution. There are a growing number of networks which focus on particular areas of interest, including:

| | |
|---|---|
| Access | Learning Environment |
| Assessment | Legal Education |
| Consultants | Managing Innovation |
| Curriculum Development | New Technology for Learning |
| Eastern European | Postgraduate Issues |
| Educational Development Research | Quantitative Studies |
| FE/HE | Student Development |
| Funding | Vocational Qualifications |
| Graduate Employment | |

## Benefits to members

### Individual

- The opportunity to participate in the Society's networks
- Reduced rates for the annual conferences
- Free copies of *Research into Higher Education Abstracts*
- Reduced rates for *Studies in Higher Education*
- Reduced rates for *Higher Education Quarterly*

- Free copy of *Register of Members' Research Interests* – includes valuable reference material on research being pursued by the Society's members
- Free copy of occasional in-house publications, e.g. *The Thirtieth Anniversary Seminars Presented by the Vice-Presidents*
- Free copies of *SRHE News* which informs members of the Society's activities and provides a calendar of events, with additional material provided in regular mailings
- A 35 per cent discount on all SRHE/Open University Press books
- The opportunity for you to apply for the annual research grants
- Inclusion of your research in the *Register of Members' Research Interests*

## *Corporate*

- Reduced rates for the annual conferences
- The opportunity for members of the Institution to attend SRHE's network events at reduced rates
- Free copies of *Research into Higher Education Abstracts*
- Free copies of *Studies in Higher Education*
- Free copies of *Register of Members' Research Interests* – includes valuable reference material on research being pursued by the Society's members
- Free copy of occasional in-house publications
- Free copies of *SRHE News*
- A 35 per cent discount on all SRHE/Open University Press books
- The opportunity for members of the Institution to submit applications for the Society's research grants
- The opportunity to work with the Society and co-host conferences
- The opportunity to include in the *Register of Members' Research Interests* your Institution's research into aspects of higher education

*Membership details*: SRHE, 76 Portland Place, London
W1B 1NT, UK Tel: 020 7637 2766. Fax: 020 7637 2781.
email: srhe@mailbox.ulcc.ac.uk
world wide web: http://www.srhe.ac.uk./srhe/
*Catalogue*: SRHE & Open University Press, Celtic Court,
22 Ballmoor, Buckingham MK18 1XW. Tel: 01280 823388.
Fax: 01280 823233. email: enquiries@openup.co.uk

**BEING A TEACHER IN HIGHER EDUCATION**

**Peter T. Knight**

*Being a teacher in Higher Eduction* draws extensively on research literatures to give detailed advice about the core business of teaching: instruction, learning activities, assessment, planning *and* getting good evaluations. It offers hundreds of practical suggestions in a collegial rather than didactic style.

This is not, however, another book of tips or heroic success stories. For one thing Peter Knight appreciates the different circumstances that new, part-time and established teachers are in. For another, he insists that teaching well (and enjoying it) is as much about how teachers feel about themselves as it is about how many slick teaching techniques they can string together. He argues that it is important to develop a sense of oneself as a good teacher (particularly in increasingly difficult working conditions); and it is for this reason that the final part of this work is about career management and handling change.

This is a book about doing teaching and being a teacher: about reducing the likelihood of burn-out and improving the chances of getting the psychic rewards that make teaching fulfilling. It is an optimistic book for teachers in universities, many of whom feel that opportunities for professional fulfilment are becoming frozen.

**Contents**

256pp    0 335 20930 0 (Paperback)    0 335 20931 9 (Hardback)

## PROBLEM-BASED LEARNING IN HIGHER EDUCATION: UNTOLD STORIES

**Maggi Savin-Baden**

Problem-based learning is contested and murky ground in higher education. In her study, Maggi Savin-Baden clears the thickets, offering a bold ambitious framework and, in the process, gives us a compelling argument for placing problem-based learning in the centre of higher education as an educational project. It is a story not to be missed.

Professor Ronald Barnett

This is a challenging and very worthwhile read for anyone concerned with the future of higher education, and issues of teaching and learning. The metaphor of 'untold stories' is powerfully explored at the level of staff and student experience of problem-based learning.

Professor Susan Weil

Problem-based learning is becoming increasingly popular in higher education because it is seen to take account of pedagogical and societal trends (such as flexibility, adaptability, problem-solving and critique) in ways which many traditional methods of learning do not. There is little known about what actually occurs *inside* problem-based curricula in terms of staff and student 'lived experience'. This book discloses ways in which learners and teachers manage complex and diverse learning in the context of their lives in a fragile and often incoherent world. These are the untold stories. The central argument of the book is that the potential and influence of problem-based learning is yet to be realized personally, pedagogically and professionally in the context of higher education. It explores both the theory and the practice of problem-based learning and considers the implications of implementing problem-based learning organizationally.

### Contents

*Part 1: A web of belief? – Part 2: Problem-based learning: an unarticulated subtext? – Part 3: Learning at the borders – Part 4: Problem-based learning reconsidered – Epilogue – Glossary – References – Index.*

176pp      0 335 20337 X (Paperback)      0 335 20338 8 (Hardback)

## DESIGNING COURSES FOR HIGHER EDUCATION

### Susan Toohey

- What issues need to be considered in designing a course or unit of study in higher education?
- Who should be involved in designing a course, and how can they best work together?
- What should students get out of a course?

Susan Toohey focuses not on teaching techniques but on the strategic decisions which must be made before a course begins. She provides realistic advice for university and college teachers on how to design more effective courses without underestimating the complexity of the task facing course developers. In particular, she examines fully the challenges involved in leading course design teams, getting agreement among teaching staff and managing organizational politics. She also explores the key role played by academics' own values and beliefs (often unexamined) in shaping course design and student experience. In doing so, she offers course designers both an understanding and a framework within which to clarify their own teaching purposes.

*Designing Courses for Higher Education* is an accessible, jargon free text, providing practical assistance and enlivened by many examples of innovative practice and interviews with academics involved in course design. It is a key resource for college and university teachers.

### Contents

*Introduction – Pressure for change – The course design process – Beliefs, values and ideologies in course design – Thinking about goals and content – The structure of the course – Making learning opportunities more flexible – Deciding on goals and objectives for units of study – Choosing teaching strategies – Assessment – Implementing the new course – References – Index – The Society for Research into Higher Education.*

224pp     0 335 20049 4 (Paperback)     0 335 20050 8 (Hardback)

# openup

ideas and understanding
in social science

## www.**openup**.co.uk

 **Browse, search and
order online**

 **Download detailed
title information and
sample chapters***

*for selected titles

www.**openup**.co.uk